P9-CBX-396

A Story of Glory

JOHN DEVANEY

QUINLAN PRESS
BOSTON

Copyright © 1987
by John Devaney
All rights reserved,
including the right of reproduction
in whole or in part in any form.
Published by Quinlan Press
131 Beverly Street
Boston, MA 02114

Library of Congress Cataloging-in-Publication Data

Devaney, John.
  A story of glory.

  1. New York Giants (Football team)—History.
2. Football players—United States—Biography.
I. Title.
GV956.N4D45   1987   796.332'64'097471   87-42761
ISBN 0-933341-42-3 (soft)

Cover design by Lawrence Curcio

Cover photograph by David Austin

Printed in the United States of America
August 1987

For Domenico and Teenie

My thanks to Ed Croke of the New York Giants and his staff for their help, and to Barry Gottehrer's landmark book *The Giants of New York.*

John Devaney watched the Giants play for the first time when the team played in the Polo Grounds. He remembers watching the likes of Al Blozis, Ward Cuff and Bill Paschal. Mr. Devaney grew up in New York City. He has written on sport for *Reader's Digest* and other magazines. Among his most recent books is *Right From the Horse's Mouth*. His wife, Barbara, is a magazine art director. They have two children, John and Luke.

CONTENTS

It's Up to You, New York...

Like a long, writhing blue snake, the Giants ran in single file out of the mouth of the tunnel and into the sunshine of the Rose Bowl. More than 100,000 spectators let out a loud roar. The first half of this game had been among the most exciting — if not the most exciting — in Super Bowl history. The Broncos had jumped ahead with a field goal. The Giants pushed to the front with a touchdown. The Broncos forged ahead with a touchdown. At the half the Broncos led, 10-9. As the filled Rose Bowl awaited the second half, uneasiness stirred in the minds of Giant fans. Many had given 9 points and more in bets with the fans of a Bronco team that now led by 1.

The Giants were still coming onto the field when the Rose Bowl loudspeakers boomed out the rhythmic growl of Frank Sinatra. As his lilting words blared out above the crowd's roar, thousands of blue-clad New Yorkers stood and swayed to the lyrics:

It's up to you, New York, New York...

Indeed, the Giants knew it was up to them to do what no Giants team had done in more than a quarter of a century: win a National Football League championship. Many of these 1986 Giants — Phil Simms, L.T., Mark Bavaro, Phil McConkey — sat in kindergarten or the first grade in 1963, the year the Giants last appeared in an NFL championship game. The Giant quarterback in that game, Y.A. Tittle, now watched from a Rose Bowl seat. He could have been the grandfather of any of these Giants streaming onto the field below him.

Seventy-year-old Wellington Mara sat near Y.A. The Duke, as his friends call him, was the son of the man who bought this team in 1925 for five hundred dollars. As a nine-year-old, he had been the ballboy of the first Giants team, which included one of the greatest players of the game and a co-founder of the NFL — Jim Thorpe. From the Giants' bench or the stands Wellington Mara had watched Mel Hein, Tuffy Leemans, Ed Danowski, Ken Strong, Frank Gifford, Tom Landry, Kyle Rote, Pat Summerall, Charlie Conerly, Y.A., Sam Huff — names now high in the pantheon of Giant legends. He had been with the team for the NFL's first forty years, when the Giants had ranked almost every year among the league's powers, winning fifteen division titles and four world championships.

For the last twenty-two years they had stumbled through sixteen seasons during which their record was .500 or worse. Season tickets were set afire in the parking lot of Giants Stadium. In the 1978 season a Giant quarterback, with the game won and the last seconds ticking away, botched a handoff when he should have knelt to run out the clock; an Eagle picked up the ball and ran it into the end zone for the winning touchdown.

It's up to you, New York, New York...

As Sinatra's voice crackled around them, these 1986 Giants knew that the ghastly memories of twenty-two years could be buried during the next thirty minutes of Super Bowl action.

It's up to you, New York, New York...

So far, the game had proved something to the millions watching around the world—the Giants defense was human. It had given up only three points in the eight previous quarters of the playoffs. True, the Bronco runners had been bounced backward by the Giant forward wall. But Denver quarterback John Elway had put frowns on the faces of the Giant coaches by tossing 13 of 20 passes for 186 yards, more than the Giants often gave up in a whole game. And the Giants had not done what they had planned to do—bottle up Elway when he scrambled. He had scrambled for one touchdown, and his first dash, for 10 yards, had been the opening shot in the Broncos' drive for their field goal.

In the Giant dressing room during the halftime break, the team's captain and spiritual leader, the bearded Harry Carson, stood and told the Giants that this was the game of their lives. You have got to make the most of it, he told them. Later he said to a friend, "I just felt like we were a better ball club than what we showed in the first half. There were 130 million people watching, and we didn't really play Giant football in the first half. I think everybody was playing kind of tentatively. Everybody was somewhat nervous."

The Giants' backup quarterback, Jeff Rutledge, sat with Phil Simms as coaches went over the plays for the second half with their two quarterbacks. Unless the unthinkable happened—Phil getting hurt and not being able to play—Jeff, an eight-year NFL veteran, would watch the game from the bench, coming in only to hold the ball for a field goal or extra point. During the season he had run the offense only during trick plays, like faking a field-goal try and throwing a pass.

Jeff would not throw a pass in this game, but he would again assume one of his mystery roles. What he did, as a member of a punting team that didn't punt, would prove to be the turning point of Super Bowl XXI.

The game began in brilliant California sunshine. A dirigible floated above like a big balloon at a birthday party. The Giants' Raul Allegre kicked off. Denver's Gene Lang caught the ball at the 2 and ran it back to the 24. Elway and his offense trotted into the game. Right from go, he would be passing.

The Giants had expected that. During the two weeks of preparing for this game, the motto of the Giant defensive backs had been Get Back! They expected Elway to scramble. Said defensive coordinator Bill Belichick: "We didn't want our guys to relax when Elway started scrambling and let their receivers get behind us."

But when Elway stepped back to pass, the Giant defense fell so far back that there was room for an eight-lane superhighway beyond the line of scrimmage. Elway sprinted through the hole to the 34 for a first down. The Giants piled up two rushes around the line of scrimmage. On third and eight, Elway completed his first pass — he would hit on six of six in this period — as he connected with Mark Jackson for a 24-yarder to the Giant 39.

The Broncos pushed against a stiffening Giant defense to near the 30. On third down Sammy Winder slammed into the line, but outside linebacker Carl Banks stopped him in his tracks.

In came Rich Karlis to try for a field goal from the 48. His kick rode straight and true between the uprights — tying the record for the longest field goal in Super Bowl history. Soon he would own another record he would not like nearly as much.

Down 3-0, Simms came back firing. After Lee Rouson returned the kickoff to the 21, Simms looped a 17-yard strike to wideout Lionel Manuel that put the ball on the 38. Another pass moved the Giants to midfield. Joe Morris bolted to the Bronco 41. Another Morris dash, to the Bronco 28, was wasted by a holding penalty. But Morris then galloped for 8. On third and long, Simms threw to wideout Stacy Robinson for an 18-yard gain to the 23.

"I was surprised they changed their whole offensive attack," Bronco linebacker Karl Mecklenburg said later. "Pass first, run second. It surprised us. We thought they would try to establish the running game, but they went against their tendencies, and they did a good job of it."

From the 23 Simms completed his fourth in a row, thread-needling a 17-yarder to Mark Bavaro, and the Giants stood within 6 yards of their first-ever Super Bowl touchdown.

Again on first down — he would pass on 9 of 11 first-down plays in the half — Simms threw to tight end Zeke Mowatt, who was cutting on a post pattern across the middle of the end zone, safety Denis Smith in his wake. Mowatt clutched the ball, and after Allegre's extra point, the Giants had jumped ahead, 7-3.

"Conditions were just perfect for passing," Simms said. "I could see that the ball was carrying better. The weather was great. I was used to throwing in the cold. Now I could grip the ball any way I wanted to. I could make it do anything I wanted."

But so, it seemed, could Elway. The Bronco's Ken Bell took a short kick at the 14 and zipped up the field 28 yards to the Bronco 42. His long arm flashing in the sunlight, Elway threw to Sammy Winder for 14, then to tight end Orson Mobley for 11. At the Giant 33 he tossed a short pass to Winder, who was ridden out of bounds by Harry Carson. An official ruled that Harry had ridden too hard and too late. When Harry's fellow linebacker, Lawrence Taylor, expressed his displeasure by tossing an official's flag, the Giants were socked with 19 yards of penalties that moved the ball to their 6.

Elway then sent running back Steve Sewell on a hunt for the touchdown, but the Giants bounced him back 3 yards. About then, as he confided later, Elway began to realize that his running game was not going to get the job done against these Giants.

He went back to doing what had worked—throwing the short pass. He hit Vance Johnson, his fourth straight of the drive, and the ball rested on the Giant 4. Again Elway stepped back. Giant linebackers scurried to cover backs coming at them. Elway saw a huge hole yawn in the middle. He sprinted through, sliding across the goal line like a base stealer toeing his way into second base. He lifted the ball high into the air—a touchdown, the first to be scored against the Giants in the playoffs.

Denver still led, 10-7, as the second period began. Neither passer had missed a man; combined, they had completed 13 of 13. Parcells had told his defense not to become alarmed if Elway threw a hot hand at them. "I told them not to worry about him getting completions early and making plays. Keep wearing them down. Just don't let the receivers turn into runners. After a while we'll make some plays, or they'll run out of room."

The Giant defense, especially Harry Carson, did worry about Elway and his hot hand. But Parcells proved to be right—Elway would run out of room.

On third and twelve at his 18, Elway dashed out of the pocket, pursued by Giants. He saw Vance Johnson break clear of a Giant defender and flung a bomb that Johnson caught and carried to the Giant 29, a 54-yard play. Succeeding on two third-down plays in a row, both passes, Elway steered the Broncos to the 1. First down, a yard to go for the touchdown that would put them ahead, 17-7. (And 26-7 for the by-now-salivating bettor who had taken the underdog Broncos and nine points.)

But the Giants were about to make the greatest goal-line stand in Super Bowl history. They sent in their goal-line offense—an offensive tackle and a tight end.

On first down Elway rolled to his right, but that offensive tackle, Bill Roberts, with L.T. and nose tackle Erik Howard, whacked him for the loss of about a yard. Fullback Gerald Willhite stormed up the middle on a trap play, but Harry Carson came flying forward to fill the hole and stop him for no gain.

Third down. Many spectators thought what had worked best, a pass play, would be Reeves's next choice against the bunched-up Giant defense. Reeves, however, decided on one more run. Later his quarterback defended the choice. "Down there," said Elway, "you've only got 11 yards in front of you. There are too many people in front of you and not enough room."

In a season when he was rarely wrong, Bill Parcells had once more struck the right gong.

Yet the decision was a surprising one considering that the Broncos had made only about a dozen yards rushing. On this, his team's last try for the touchdown, Elway pitched to Sammy Winder cutting toward the left sideline. Outside linebacker Carl Banks had watched films showing the Broncos scoring on that play in their regular-season game against the Giants. "I expected that play again," he said. He stepped in front of Winder and he, Harry Carson and cornerback Perry Williams slashed Winder to the ground for a 4-yard loss.

Now came the really bad news for the Broncos. Rich Karlis tried for the field goal from the 23. The ball shot wide on the right side. The co-holder of the record for the longest field goal now held the record for the shortest miss. The Giants had to breathe a long relieved sigh. "If we hadn't stopped them down there," said George Martin, "we would have been in big trouble."

The Broncos tried to mask their anguish. But self-doubt had to be nagging their minds. "We knew we had blown a great opportunity," said guard Keith Bishop. "That had to be in the back of our minds at halftime, I know it was in my mind."

"The Giants let the air out of our ball when they stopped us on the 1 and we didn't get even three points," receiver Steve Watson said. "We never recovered from that."

A little later the Broncos took the ball at their 14 after a Giant punt. On first down Elway was knocked over by Leonard Marshall for a 2-yard loss. On second down Elway tossed a low line drive to tight end Clarence Kay, who dived for the ball. The officials ruled the ball had hit the ground. Reeves screamed. The referee called a timeout so officials in the press box could study the tapes. The tapes—at least the ones the officials stared at for about a minute—cast no light on whether Kay had caught the ball or trapped it. The incomplete ruling stood. The decision cost the Broncos a first down and, probably, two points.

On the next play Elway went back again to pass. End George Martin lined up against right tackle Ken Lanier. "I gave him an inside move," Martin later said, "and he bit and I went outside. I just went around him and right at Elway." Backpedaling, Elway had no chance to throw the ball away. Martin bowled him over in the end zone for a safety that put the Giants within a point, 10-9.

The Broncos had to punt to the Giants, who went three and nothing, and had to punt back, Denver taking the ball at its 28 for what would be its last drive for the lead. By now Elway knew he was running into a stone wall when he tried a rushing play. On his 35 he sprinted to his left, then threw an across-the-field pass to wideout Steve Watson, who dashed to the Giant 32. There was less than a minute to play in the half.

A short pass to Willhite moved the ball to the 21. But three straight Elway passes went high, wide or low. Karlis came in to try for a 34-yard field goal. In the regular season he had missed only one of twelve from insde the 39 — but this one also went wide.

"Both times I didn't get my hips all the way through the kick," the longhaired Karlis said later in the clubhouse, his eyes moist with emotion. "I was steering the ball and I know better than that. I felt the team unravel after that. I really hurt them. I'm sorry."

Dan Reeves walked to the dressing room for the halftime break talking to himself. As he said later, "We knew we couldn't afford to give away points to the Giants. We should have had 20 points at the half — instead we had only 10."

Sinatra's ringing challenge was still refraining in the minds of many spectators as Bill Parcells, once criticized for being too conservative, showed just how daring he and his 1986 Giants had become.

The Giants took the second-half kickoff to the 37. Three plays moved the ball to the 46. Fourth down, a foot to go for the first down, the Giants trailing by a point. Parcells sent in his punting team. One member of the team was Jeff Rutledge, the backup quarterback and a gridiron actor who wore several faces.

At first glance he looked like just another figure in a punt formation as Sean Landeta stood 15 yards back. Bronco eyes fixed on Landeta, the punter. Then the Giants shifted, Rutledge hurrying forward to hunch over the center, Landeta flanked wide to his left. Now everyone's eyes were on Rutledge.

He began to call out numbers, slowly and deliberately; the Broncos sensed a trick to draw them offside. They stayed stock-still, frozen, seeming to say to Rutledge: We know what you are doing.

Rutledge glanced at the play clock. There were about six seconds left. He looked over to the sideline and stared at Parcells. Parcells nodded, the signal that, unless the quarterback saw trouble, Rutledge should go for the first down.

Rutledge looked once more at the clock. Four seconds left. He stared at the Bronco linebackers. "If they had walked up to the line," he said later, "I would have taken the delay of game penalty and Sean would punt."

But the linebackers did not come forward — and the momentum of this game swung away from Denver.

"Shift!" Rutledge shouted, the signal to Bart Oates to center the ball. Rutledge grabbed the ball, stepped to his right, then charged behind guard Chris Godfrey into the line, leaping over churning bodies. He leaped for 2 yards; the Giants had the first down — and the tide of this Super Bowl had made its turn.

"This was for the world championship," Parcells said later of the gamble. "This was not for fainthearted people."

Phil Simms and his offense ran back into the game. Rutledge and Parcells had given them their chance — now, indeed, New York, it is all up to you.

Simms tossed to Joe Morris for a first down at the Bronco 42. Running back Lee Rouson took a short pitch and weaved 23 yards to the Bronco 18. Two bangs up the middle moved the ball to the 13. Then Simms skipped back into the pocket and drilled a liner that Mark Bavaro caught as he cut across the middle of the end zone. As Bavaro knelt in the end zone, gripping the ball and looking prayerfully to the heavens, the Giants had forged to the front. Raul Allegre kicked the extra point and the Giants, ahead 16-10, were in front for good.

The Giants kicked to the Broncos, but Elway had lost his magic, at least for the third quarter. The Broncos punted. Phil McConkey, perhaps the fastest twenty-nine-year-old extant, sped 25 yards to the Bronco 35. Knocked to the ground, he jumped up, waving his arms to whip up even more roars from the large scarlet and blue patches of Giant fans.

On third and five at the 32, Joe Morris twisted 9 yards for the first down. But the drive stalled inside the 5. Raul Allegre came on to kick the chip shot that Karlis had missed, a 21-yarder. The Giants led, 19-10.

Again the Broncos went three and out, three Elway passes missing. The Broncos trudged off the field looking as though they might be wilting in the seventy-five-degree temperature. Later Karl Mecklenburg was asked how much the two missed field goals had hurt. "The way the Giants moved the ball in the second half," he answered, "six points wouldn't have made a difference."

It was bewitching time again. The Rutledge dive after a fake punt formation had been what the players call "a gotcha." Now, with the old-fashioned flea flicker, the Giants got the Broncos a second time.

The ball sat on the Bronco 45. Simms took the snap and handed off to the stumpy Morris. Joe dashed forward, then stopped, spun and tossed the ball back to Simms. The Broncos jumped at the lure. Their linebackers rushed up to tackle Morris. Phil McConkey snaked behind the linebackers, turned in the open field and caught the ball at the 20. He streaked to the 5, was hit and fell at the 1.

"We've run the flea flicker in practice for I don't know how long," Simms said. "When that play got to the 1, I knew that was the game."

"We've used it in practice," Morris said. "But I often tossed the ball over Phil's head in practice. When we botched it in practice, Bill Parcells, being so superstitious, wouldn't want to use it in the game. But on the Friday before the Super Bowl, he came to me and he said we would use it. Still, I was surprised when he did."

From the 1, Morris rammed across for the touchdown. It was the third score by the Giants in three straight possessions. Allegre kicked the extra point and the Giants led, 26-10.

The next time the Giants got the ball, they scored a fourth straight time. Cornerback Elvis Patterson pulled down an Elway pass, and the Giants had the ball near midfield. On second down Simms arrowed a pass through a crack in the Bronco zone. Wideout Stacy Robinson caught the ball at the 16. Two plays later, the Broncos were penalized for pass interference, and the ball was placed at the 6. Simms danced back into his pocket. He saw Mark Bavaro slant into a gang of defenders. Phil threw a dart. Bavaro reached up a hand and tipped the ball. A blue jersey knifed through the air. Blue-shirted hands grabbed the ball. A blue-shirted body fell in the end zone.

Phil McConkey, the old helicopter pilot, had flown through the air to grab the tipped ball. The five-ten, 170-pound McConkey was hoisted into the air by the six-four, 250-pound Bavaro. After coming within thirty-six inches of a Super Bowl touchdown a few minutes earlier on the flea flicker, Phil had that Super Bowl TD — and a ball he would carry proudly back to New York.

"It's something to dream about, scoring a Super Bowl touchdown," McConkey said later. "When it happens, you think about every pushup you ever did, everybody who ever helped you. You think about the great players who never got to the Super Bowl."

Undaunted, the gallant Elway rallied his team. The Broncos went 84 yards, the big play a 36-yard pass from Elway to Vance Johnson. But the drive bogged down outside the 10. Surprisingly, behind by 23 in the last period, the Broncos opted for a field goal, perhaps to stiffen Karlis's confidence for next season. Karlis put the ball through (now that three points meant nothing, Denver fans had to be thinking). Denver trailed by 20, 33-13, and Giant fans who had given nine points seemed to have little to worry about.

Each team would score once more in what the players call "garbage time," the scoring having no bearing on the outcome. The Giants went 46 yards on five plays, the big play a 22-yard bootleg by Phil Simms, who by now had been selected as the game's most valuable player.

Simms would miss only 3 of 25 passes all afternoon. One pass was a hurried throw to the sideline, one a throw that Bavaro almost caught and the third missed because McConkey fell down. After McConkey caught the pass that Bavaro tipped, Simms told McConkey, "You owed me that one after falling down."

The Broncos — no one could accuse them of quitting — kept right on battling despite the hopelessness of their situation. They charged to midfield, where Elway hit Vance Johnson with a 47-yard touchdown bomb that ended the scoring, Giants 39, Broncos 20. As more than one person said later, "The score was 39 to 20, but the game wasn't even that close."

The game winding down, the "Lunch Pail Gang," as these 1986 Giants called themselves, pulled their usual prank. Harry Carson sneaked up behind Bill Parcells, who knew very well Harry was coming (as did millions who watched TV's John Madden chart the route Harry would take). Harry drenched Parcells with the usual barrel of Gatorade.

Nearby, a much more dramatic scene unfolded. Wellington Mara, whose father had bought these Giants for five hundred dollars, walked to the Giant bench. George Martin saw him coming and stood up.

They embraced—the seventy-year-old owner, the thirty-three-year-old defensive end. "We brought it back," Martin said, "we brought it back."

Martin and his teammates had brought back the championship that New York had first won in 1927 and had last won in 1956.

The years had to walk backward in Wellington Mara's mind, back to a time when he was an eight-year-old parochial school boy in knickers, a time when his father walked into a Manhattan office building intent on buying a part of a fighter named Gene Tunney and left that building owning a football team.

Super Bowl Statistics

		1	2	3	4	OT	Total
VISITOR	Denver Broncos	10	0	0	10		20
HOME	New York Giants	7	2	17	13		39

Team	Period	Elapsed Time	SCORING PLAY	Drive, Time	Score Visitor	Home
DEN	1	4:09	FG Karlis 48	(8-45, 4:09)	3	0
NY	1	9:33	Mowatt 6 pass from Simms (Allegre kick)	(9-78, 5:24)	3	7
DEN	1	12:54	Elway 4 run (Karlis kick)	(6-58, 3:21)	10	7
NY	2	12:14	Safety—Elway sacked by Martin	(3-(-)15, 0:47)	10	9
NY	3	4:52	Bavaro 13 pass from Simms (Allegre kick)	(8-63, 4:52)	10	16
NY	3	11:06	FG Allegre 21	(9-32, 5:07)	10	19
NY	3	14:36	Morris 1 run (Allegre kick)	(5-68, 2:14)	10	26
NY	4	4:04	McConkey 6 pass from Simms (Allegre kick)	(6-52, 3:50)	10	33
DEN	4	8:59	FG Karlis 28	(13-73, 4:55)	13	33
NY	4	10:42	Anderson 2 run (kick wide)	(5-46, 2:43)	13	39
DEN	4	12:54	V. Johnson 47 pass from Elway (Karlis kick)	(5-69, 1:12)	20	39

BRONCOS

Rushing	No	Yds	Avg	Long	TD
Lang	2	2	1.0	4	0
Elway	6	27	4.5	10	1
Winder	4	0	0.0	3	0
Willhite	4	19	4.8	11	0
Sewell	3	4	1.3	12	0
Totals	19	52	2.7	12	1

Passing	No	Cp	Yds	Sk	Yds	Lg	TD	I
Elway	37	22	304	3	26	54	1	1
Kubiak	4	4	48	1	6	23	0	0
Totals	41	26	352	4	32	54	1	1

Receiving	No	Yds	Lg	TD
Lang	1	4	4	0
Winder	4	34	14	0
Willhite	5	39	11	0
M. Jackson	3	51	24	0
Mobley	2	17	11	0
Sewell	2	12	7	0
V. Johnson	5	121	54	1
Watson	2	54	31	0
Sampson	2	20	11	0
Totals	26	352	54	1

Intercepts	No	Yds	Lg	TD
Totals	0	0	0	0

Punting	No	Yds	Avg	Tb	I20	Lg
Horan	2	82	41.0	0	0	42
Totals	2	82	41.0	0	0	42

Punt Returns	No	FC	Yds	Lg	TD
Willhite	1	1	9	9	0
Totals	1	1	9	9	0

Kick Returns	No	Yds	Lg	TD
Lang	2	36	23	0
Bell	3	48	28	0
Totals	5	84	51	0

GIANTS

Rushing	No	Yds	Avg	Long	TD
Rouson	3	22	7.3	18	0
Simms	3	25	8.3	22	0
Morris	20	67	3.3	11	1
Anderson	2	1	0.5	2	1
Carthon	3	4	1.3	2	0
Rutledge	3	0	0.0	2	0
Galbreath	4	17	4.3	7	0
Totals	38	136	3.6	22	2

Passing	No	Cp	Yds	Sk	Yds	Lg	TD	I
Simms	25	22	268	1	5	44	3	0
Totals	25	22	268	1	5	44	3	0

Receiving	No	Yds	Lg	TD
Rouson	1	23	23	0
Manuel	3	43	17	0
Bavaro	4	51	17	1
Morris	4	20	12	0
Robinson	3	62	36	0
Mowatt	1	6	6	1
Carthon	4	13	7	0
McConkey	2	50	44	1
Totals	22	268	44	3

Intercepts	No	Yds	Lg	TD
Patterson	1	-7	0	0
Totals	1	-7	0	0

Punting	No	Yds	Avg	Tb	I20	Lg
Landeta	3	138	46.0	1	1	59
Totals	3	138	46.0	1	1	59

Punt Returns	No	FC	Yds	Lg	TD
McConkey	1	1	25	25	0
Totals	1	1	25	25	0

Kick Returns	No	Yds	Lg	TD
Rouson	3	56	22	0
Flynn	1	-3	0	0
Totals	4	53	22	0

The Giants: 1925-1985
A Family Affair

Tim Mara, a genial and beefy six-footer, strode into Billy Gibson's office. A framed photo of heavyweight boxer Gene Tunney hung on the wall, the photo inscribed to Gibson, Tunney's manager and agent. Tim, a bookmaker, had come to Gibson's office to talk about buying into the ownership of Tunney.

Tim had arrived late for his talk with Gibson on this warm August afternoon in 1925. Seated around a desk were Gibson and two visitors from Ohio, Harry March and Joe Carr. Carr was the president of the National Professional Football League. Now four years old, the league had eighteen teams scattered across the Midwest, mostly in small towns—the Duluth Kelleys, the Pottsville Maroons. One small-town team, the Decatur Staleys, had moved to Chicago and called themselves the Bears.

Gibson turned to Mara as the big man, mopping sweat from his ruddy face, slouched into a chair.

"Say, maybe you'd be interested in this, Tim," Gibson said, pointing to Carr and March.

"What is it?"

"A professional football franchise for New York."

"How much?" Though a familiar figure at Yankee and Giant baseball games, Mara had never seen a football game.

"They want five hundred dollars for the franchise."

"Any franchise in New York has to be worth five hundred dollars," Mara said. He scribbled out a check and handed it over to Carr. "Now that I have a franchise," he asked, "what do I do with it?"

"Just leave that to me," March said.

During the next few weeks March hired a fiery-tempered ex-wrestler, Bob Folwell, as coach.

One of the first players signed was a New York City physician, Joe Alexander, who had starred at end for Syracuse a few years earlier. The team's box office draw, however, would be the husky Jim Thorpe, still thought by most Americans to be the nation's all-time greatest athlete. Now thirty-seven, Thorpe had won the decathlon and pentathlon at the 1912 Olympics but officials stripped him of his medals after he admitted playing minor league pro baseball. But twenty years of crashing into bodies and swilling from bottles had drained Thorpe's body of its once-awesome speed and strength.

Mara ordered scarlet and blue jerseys for his new players. He named them the Giants after Manhattan's darlings—John McGraw's baseball Giants. On Sunday, October 10, 1925, some twenty-five thousand spectators, many of whom had come through the turnstiles with passes given out by Mara's press agents, sat in the double-tiered stands. The first New York Giant football team came down the spike-marked steps of the baseball clubhouse in deep centerfield and trotted onto a football gridiron for its first home game.

— 1925 —			
8-4			
4th			
Bob Folwell			
L	Providence	0-14	A
L	Frankford	3-5	A
L	Frankford	0-14	H
W	Cleveland	19-0	H
W	Buffalo	7-0	H
W	Columbus	19-0	H
W	Rochester	13-0	H
W	Providence	13-12	H
W	Kansas City	9-3	H
W	Dayton	23-0	H
L	Chicago Bears	7-19	H
W	Chicago Bears	9-0	A

The Giants lost that first home game to the Frankford Yellow Jackets, 14-0. Thorpe staggered out of a pileup, wobbled to the bench and collapsed. He never played again for the Maramen, as sportswriters called the team. Earlier, the Giants had lost their first two away games. March and Folwell brought in a batch of younger players and taught them Folwell's single-wing offense and seven-man diamond defense. The line, averaging 206 pounds, was the heaviest in the league.

After the loss to Frankford, the Giants won seven straight games. But crowds as thin as twelve hundred sat through games at the Polo Grounds, and Tim Mara's five-hundred-dollar investment had by now cost him almost fifty grand.

Meanwhile, a wiry, redheaded University of Illinois halfback was packing college stadiums wherever he played. Football fans wanted to see the

Galloping Ghost, Red Grange, flash for touchdowns—as many as a half dozen in a game. Grange left college in November and agreed to play the rest of the 1925 season for the Chicago Bears. Mara juggled his schedule so Grange and the Bears could play in New York on December 6. Crowds came early on a sunny, pleasant afternoon. They knocked over barricades, jammed the stands, spilled out onto wooden bleachers put up along the sidelines and behind the end zones. More than 73,000, then a pro football record, paid $143,000 (Grange took thirty thousand). The Bears won, 19-7, but Mara went home smiling. He had made up his loss and had a profit on his five-hundred-dollar investment of fifteen thousand dollars.

"Grange," Tim Mara said years later, "proved to me that pro football didn't have to be a losing proposition. That, more than anything else, kept me in pro football."

	— 1926 — 8-4-1 7th Joe Alexander		
W	Hartford	21-0	A
W	Providence	7-6	A
L	Chicago Bears	0-7	A
L	Frankford	0-6	A
L	Frankford	0-6	H
W	Kansas City	13-0	H
T	Canton	7-7	H
W	Chicago Cardinals	20-0	H
W	Duluth	14-13	H
L	Los Angeles	0-6	H
W	Providence	21-0	H
W	Brooklyn	17-0	A
W	Brooklyn	27-0	H

Grange came back to Manhattan a year later to haunt Mara and his young Giants. Grange and a partner, C.C. (Cash and Carry) Pyle, organized a new American Professional Football League. Three of its nine teams were plopped into the New York area—Newark, Brooklyn and Yankee Stadium, where Grange's team would play. To keep his Giants from jumping to the new league, Mara had to raise his salaries to an average of fifty dollars a game.

For five-hundred dollars, a large sum for the time, he bought the contract of a 240-pound tackle from the Kansas City Cowboys. The tackle, Steve Owen, son of an Oklahoma farmer, was not impressed. "I had seen a lot of fat hogs go for more than they paid for me," he said years later, "but in those days a fat hog was a lot more valuable than a fat tackle."

Mara feared he would lose this box office duel with Grange and Pyle. He told Harry March: "I guess the only reason I'm staying in the war is Jack and Wellington. You've seen them at the games." His young sons, Jack and Wellington, rooted excitedly from the Giant bench during games. "If the Giants ever amount to anything, it's all theirs. I've still got the bookmaking and they'll have the Giants." Tim lost sixty thousand dollars during that season of bloodletting competition with Pyle, but Pyle lost $100,000 and his league broke up.

The Giants won five of their last six games, but for one game as few as 4,000 were scattered through the towering stands. The night before the final game a snowstorm blanketed the field with two-foot banks. Mara had to call the game as he stared up into rows of seats that held not a single ticket-buyer.

— 1927 —
11-1-1
1st
Earl Potteiger

W	Providence	8-0	A
T	Cleveland	0-0	A
W	Pottsville	19-0	A
L	Cleveland	0-6	H
W	Frankford	13-0	A
W	Frankford	27-0	H
W	Pottsville	16-0	H
W	Duluth	21-0	H
W	Providence	25-0	H
W	Chicago Cardinals	28-7	H
W	Chicago Cardinals	13-7	H
W	New York Yankees	14-0	H
W	New York Yankees	13-0	A

By 1927 Joe Alexander had replaced Bob Folwell as coach, but Dr. Joe decided to go back to the study of the human lung. His assistant, Earl (Potty) Potteiger, replaced him. A new face in the clubhouse sat square over an iceblock of a body. At six-five and 250 pounds, Cal Hubbard (later a big-league umpire) stood as the tallest and heaviest Giant. A tackle, he cemented a barrier that would become the strength of all Giant championship teams — the defense. "We were pretty much a smash-and-shove gang," Steve Owen later said. "We were bonecrushers, not fancy dans."

During the summer, big crowds streamed into Yankee Stadium, across the Harlem River from the Polo Grounds, to watch Babe Ruth and his Yankees, but they stayed away from the Polo Grounds in the fall. Some 35,000 watched the Giants beat the Providence Steamroller, 25-0; most, however, had bought fifty-cent "student" tickets.

The knots of spectators—only 80 at one game—cheered loudest for Indian Joe Guyon, a running back and ferocious blocker. In a game against the Bears, Chicago player-coach George Halas tried to clip Joe from behind. Joe wheeled and snapped both knees into Halas's chest. The Bears carried their employer off the field. Guyon turned to Steve Owen and said, "That fellow ought to know you can't sneak up on an Indian."

The Giants beat the Bears in a match so bruising that players sat, wilted, on the field for five minutes after the game ended before trudging to the clubhouse. The Giants needed to beat Red Grange's Yankees in their last two games. They won, 14-0 at the Polo Grounds, 13-0 at Yankee Stadium, for their first NFL championship. In thirteen games they had scored 197 points, yielded only 20.

"It was the best football team of its time," Red Grange later said. "The line wore you down, the backs would move the ball. But they would have been passed off the field by the top teams of the thirties."

— 1928 —
4-7-2
6th
Earl Potteiger

W	Pottsville	12-6	A
W	Green Bay	6-0	A
L	Chicago Bears	0-13	A
L	Detroit	0-28	A
W	New York Yankees	10-7	A
T	Frankford	0-0	H
W	Pottsville	13-7	H
T	Detroit	19-19	H
L	Green Bay	0-7	H
L	Providence	0-16	A
L	New York Yankees	13-19	H
L	Frankford	0-7	A
L	New York Yankees	6-7	A

In 1928 squabbling among the champions turned to brawling. In one game a rookie runner, Bruce Caldwell, missed a few blocks. Other Giant backs stepped aside when Caldwell carried the ball. Tacklers flattened Caldwell, up to then the Giants' best rusher. The Giants lost the game, 19-13.

Tim Mara and Harry March ranted and roared at team meetings, but the team lost its last five games. In thirteen games the ex-champions scored only 79 points.

Mara stared glumly at a forty-thousand-dollar loss for the season. He let go of eighteen players, plus Potty Potteiger, and told March: "Let's get Friedman!"

	— 1929 —		
	13-1-1		
	2nd		
	LeRoy Anderson		
T	Orange	0-0	A
W	Providence	7-0	A
W	Staten Island	19-9	H
W	Frankford	32-0	H
W	Providence	19-0	H
W	Chicago Bears	26-14	A
W	Buffalo	45-6	A
W	Orange	22-0	H
W	Chicago Bears	34-0	H
L	Green Bay	6-20	H
W	Staten Island	21-7	A
W	Chicago Cardinals	24-21	H
W	Frankford	12-0	A
W	Frankford	31-0	H
W	Chicago Bears	14-9	A

The stock market streaked downward, but the Giants' new coach and the team's new quarterback made men smile on Wall Street. Mara hired Detroit Wolverine coach LeRoy Anderson and Wolverine quarterback Benny Friedman, a one-time University of Michigan All-American.

The shrewd Friedman did not share the conventional wisdom of the time, that the forward pass was an act of desperation when the run had failed. "Why wait to pass on third down when the defense is waiting for it?" he argued. "The time to pass is on first and second down."

He passed often enough on first down to loosen up defenses, their centers dropping back to bat down passes, leaving holes in the middle for runners. "Benny revolutionized football," George Halas once said. "He forced the defenses out of the dark ages."

Benny could toss the beachball-like pigskin of the day with accuracy and velocity. In their first home opening-game victory ever, the Giants beat their across-the-bay rivals, the Staten Island Stapleton Stapes, 19-9. The

Giants won their next six games and ran head-on into another un-beaten team, Green Bay's Packers, for the game that would decide the championship.

Green Bay's huge line, ex-Giant Cal Hubbard towering over it, smacked down Giant runners. But Friedman threw a touchdown pass. As the third period closed, Green Bay led, 7-6. Then Johnny Blood grabbed a 26-yard pass to set up one Packer touchdown, and Green Bay picked off a Friedman pass for another, winning 20-6.

No one else beat the Giants that season, but the Packers also did not lose. The 12-0-1 Packers edged the 13-1-1 Giants for the championship. The gunslinging Friedman and the rest of the 1929 Giants set a record by averaging 25,000 paid attendance at their home games.

Tim Mara lost his fortune in the Wall Street Crash. He had one chip left to try to win a new fortune—his five-hundred-dollar Giants.

```
┌─────────────────────────────────────┐
│         — 1930 —                    │
│            13-4                      │
│            2nd                       │
│        LeRoy Anderson                │
│                                      │
│  W  Newark            32-0   A       │
│  W  Providence        27-7   A       │
│  L  Green Bay          7-14  A       │
│  W  Chicago Bears     12-0   A       │
│  W  Chicago Cardinals 25-12  H       │
│  W  Frankford         53-0   H       │
│  W  Providence        25-0   H       │
│  W  Newark            34-7   H       │
│  W  Staten Island      9-7   H       │
│  W  Portsmouth        19-6   A       │
│  W  Chicago Cardinals 13-7   A       │
│  L  Chicago Bears      0-12  H       │
│  W  Green Bay         13-6   H       │
│  L  Staten Island      6-7   A       │
│  L  Brooklyn           6-7   H       │
│  W  Frankford         14-6   A       │
│  W  Brooklyn          13-0   A       │
└─────────────────────────────────────┘
```

Beset by money problems, Tim Mara turned over some of the operation of the team to his twenty-two-year-old son, Jack, a Fordham Law School student. Fourteen-year-old Wellington served after high school as a general helper. Stout Steve Owen, nearing the end of his playing days, still worked a sixty-minute game, as did most starters of the time, especially as the Depression grew darker. Owners tried to trim rosters to eighteen players.

Joining Benny Friedman in the backfield—and attracting college fans to the game—was the newest Giant, Chris (Red) Cagle, a razzle-dazzle runner who had starred for Army.

As in 1929, the winner of the Packer-Giant battle at the Polo Grounds seemed likely to win the championship. The Giants has already lost to Green Bay earlier in the season. The Giants led, 13-6, with a minute to go, as Arnie Herber pitched the Packers to the Giant 1 yardline. There Stout Steve and his pals threw back the Packers to save the victory.

That battle, however, took so much out of the Giants that they lost to two lowly teams, the Stapes and the Brooklyn Dodgers, both by 7-6 scores. Those losses allowed Green Bay to slip ahead and take the title for the second straight year. The losses also rattled head coach LeRoy Anderson. The coach began to snipe at Owen and Friedman. The two stars growled about Anderson to Tim Mara, who fired the coach.

The season ended on a triumphant note. College football's most glamorous team was Notre Dame; its coach, Knute Rockne. Rockne put together an all-star team of past Irish heroes, including the famous Four Horsemen, to meet the Giants. Box office proceeds would aid New York's jobless. The Giants pasted the Four Horsemen and the Irish, 22-0.

"That was the greatest football machine I ever saw," Rockne said after the game. His salute gave the Giants and pro football a long push toward being accepted by the public as football's best.

	— 1931 —		
	7-6-1		
	5th		
	Steve Owen		
W	Providence	14-6	A
L	Providence	6-14	A
L	Green Bay	7-27	A
L	Chicago Bears	0-6	A
W	Staten Island	7-0	H
W	Brooklyn	27-0	H
W	Portsmouth	14-0	H
W	Frankford	13-0	H
L	Chicago Bears	6-12	H
L	Green Bay	10-14	H
L	Staten Island	6-9	A
T	Providence	0-0	H
W	Brooklyn	19-6	A
W	Chicago Bears	26-6	A

Steve Owen took over as coach of the Giants while continuing to play for two more seasons. Benny Friedman went off to Yale as an assistant coach. Giant scouts had gone all the way to Washington State to bring back a find who would soon outshine both Benny and Stout Steve. His name: Mel Hein, a six-foot-three, 210-pound center with a boyish face that masked a veteran's guile, courage and tenacity. He wore number 7, a number no other Giant would ever wear.

When the Giants lost three of their first four games, Tim Mara talked Benny into returning. The Giants won their next four. Then they lost 12-6 to the Bears and 14-10 to the Packers, the Pack on their way to a third straight title. At season's end, as Friedman played his last game in scarlet and blue, the Giants trounced the Bears, 25-6. "By that last game we were as good," said Benny, "as anybody in the league." But by then, of course, the racers had run the course.

Benny Friedman had an offer to go to the Dodgers as a player-coach. He told Tim Mara he would stay at the Polo Grounds if he were given shares of Giant stock. "Benny, I'm sorry," Tim said, "but this is a family business."

	— 1932 —		
	4-6-2		
	5th		
	Steve Owen		
L	Portsmouth	0-7	A
L	Green Bay	0-13	A
L	Boston	6-14	A
W	Brooklyn	20-12	A
T	Boston	0-0	H
L	Portsmouth	0-6	H
L	Chicago Bears	8-28	H
W	Staten Island	27-7	H
W	Green Bay	6-0	H
T	Staten Island	13-13	A
W	Brooklyn	13-7	A
L	Chicago Bears	0-6	A

The nation skidded along at the bottom of the Depression. There had been eighteen NFL teams when the Giants were born in 1925—now that number had shrunk to eight. (They were the Giants, Bears, Packers, Dodgers, Chicago Cardinals, Stapleton Stapes, Portsmouth Spartans and the Boston Braves—later the Washington Redskins.)

Friedman was gone and Cagle was no longer a breakaway threat. Steve

Owen called on veteran back Jack McBride, whose passing arm had enough left in it to spring the upset of the year.

The Packers, NFL champs for three years running, had won their first nine games when they came to the Polo Grounds. The strong Giant line, led by Mel Hein and Stout Steve, bottled up Packer passer Arnie Herber. It hit Johnny Blood so hard he fumbled near the end of the first half of a scoreless game. A Giant jumped on the loose ball. On fourth down at the Packer 32, McBride angled a crossfield pass to end Ray Flaherty, who snagged the ball on the 5 and scored. That was the game's first and only score, and the Giants won, 6-0.

Flaherty led the league with 21 catches, the first time the league recognized a receiving champion.

— 1933 —
11-3
1st Eastern Division
Steve Owen

W	Pittsburgh	23-2	A
L	Portsmouth	7-17	A
W	Green Bay	10-7	A
L	Boston	20-21	A
W	Philadelphia	56-0	H
W	Brooklyn	21-7	H
L	Chicago Bears	10-14	A
W	Portsmouth	13-10	H
W	Boston	7-0	H
W	Chicago Bears	3-0	H
W	Green Bay	17-6	H
W	Brooklyn	10-0	A
W	Brooklyn	27-3	H
W	Philadelphia	20-14	A

NFL Championship

L	Chicago Bears	21-23	A

The NFL split its ten teams into two five-team divisions, the Eastern and Western. To make scoreboards click faster—and catch the attention of fans who filled college-football stadiums—the league loosened up its passing rules. And it moved the goalposts from the rear of the end zone to the goal line, making field goals ten yards easier to kick.

The Giants found a kicker who could arrow the ball between those closer goalposts, acquiring former NYU star Ken Strong, who could also run, pass and block. Steve Owen and his scouts liked the looks of a stumpy University of Michigan passing whiz, Harry Newman, and he became the team's passer out of the then-fashionable single-wing formation. Teenage Wellington Mara, Duke to the players, became an assistant to the assistant coaches.

The Giants quickly showed their heels to the rest of the Eastern Division — Brooklyn, Boston, Philadelphia and Pittsburgh. They beat Philadelphia, 56-0, at that point the highest score in Giant history. They won the first Eastern title by a wide margin over the Brooklyn Dodgers, then tried to accomplish what their 1933 namesakes had done in baseball — win the world championship.

The Chicago Bears had won the Western Division title. The two teams met at Wrigley Field in the NFL's first playoff game for a championship. Early in the game the Giants sprang a trick play. They shifted so that center Mel Hein stood at the end of the line — and thus became an eligible pass receiver. Hein centered the ball to Newman, who handed the ball back to the burly center. The Bears rushed Newman, who spun and fell, as though protecting the ball. Hein strolled forward some 12 yards, ignored, then bolted for the goal line. The Bears, seeing him run, realized he had the ball. They hauled him down 15 yards away from a touchdown.

But Chicago's mammoth line held and the Giants didn't score. The Bears' Jack Manders kicked a field goal, the Bears drawing first blood to lead, 3-0. The lead changed hands six times in front of more than 30,000 spectators. Late in the fourth period, the Bears ahead, 23-21, the Giants had time for only one more play. In the huddle Newman called for a pass to end Red Badgro, who would be one-on-one against Red Grange. The old Galloping Ghost's legs had given way on him, but he still had a head for the game, playing mostly on defense. Badgro was supposed to catch the pass, then lateral to Dale Burnett, who would speed by the lone Grange for the winning touchdown.

Grange smelled trickery. As Badgro caught the pass, Grange hit him high, gripping his arms as he went down. Badgro couldn't flip the ball to Burnett. The Bears had won the first NFL playoff game for a championship.

L	Detroit	0-9	A
L	Green Bay	6-20	A
W	Pittsburgh	14-12	A
W	Boston	16-13	A
W	Brooklyn	14-0	H
W	Pittsburgh	17-7	H
W	Philadelphia	17-0	H
L	Chicago Bears	7-27	A
W	Green Bay	17-3	H
L	Chicago Bears	9-10	H
W	Boston	3-0	H
W	Brooklyn	27-0	A
L	Philadelphia	0-6	A

NFL Championship

W	Chicago Bears	30-13	H

The Bears still looked awesome to the rest of the league and to the Giants. In the first New York-Chicago meeting of the season, the Bears' Bronko Nagurski, a King Kong of his time at six-two and 230 pounds, rampaged through the Giant line in a 27-7 rout.

The Giants had won thirteen straight home games when the Bears came to the Polo Grounds for their second meeting of the season. The Giants led, 9-7, with two minutes to play. The Bears fell on a Giant fumble at the Giant 33. Jack Manders, so accurate he was dubbed Automatic Jack, kicked a 23-yard field goal to win the game 10-9. The Bears finished 13-0-0, seeming to leave no doubt who owned the NFL for a second straight year.

The 8-5 Giants finished first in the weaker East—they were the only team above .500. The Bears came to New York three-to-one favorites, their players an average of a dozen pounds heavier than the Giants.

Giants passer Harry Newman had been wrecked by the Bears in the two regular season games. Replacing him for the title game was a rookie out of Fordham, Ed Danowski, who often needed a pep talk from Steve Owen to convince him that he could play with the NFL's big boys.

A frigid wind and arctic, near-zero temperatures froze the field so hard that cleats could not dig into the turf. "Why don't we wear sneakers?" Ray Flaherty asked Steve Owen. But the Giants had no sneakers, and sporting-goods stores were closed on this wintry Sunday morning. But a trainer had a key to the Manhattan College locker room. While he went off to find sneakers, the Giants came out with their cleated high-top shoes.

Some 35,000, including Dodger manager Casey Stengel and Mayor Fiorello LaGuardia, huddled in the stands, many drinking coffee laced with whiskey to feel some warmth. A 1932 poll had predicted that one day pro football would be more popular than college football. *Herald Tribune* sportswriter Stanley Woodward gazed with astonishment at the freezing faces in the crowd and later wrote that he had never believed the poll's findings, but "now I am converted."

The Bears and Giants skidded through the first half, the Bears taking the lead, 10-3. As the Giants trooped into the clubhouse at the half, the breathless, red-cheeked trainer arrived carrying a dozen pairs of sneakers. One of the Bears saw the trainer arrive. "They're changing into sneakers," he told coach George Halas.

"Good," snapped Halas. "Step on their toes."

The sneakers didn't seem to help during the third period. Jack Manders's field goal put the Bears ahead, 13-3. Then a freak play—and perhaps the sneakers—turned the game around.

Ed Danowski tossed a long floater. As the ball arched toward Dale Burnett near the goal line, a Bear skidded in front of Burnett and picked off the pass. But the Giants' Mal Frankian ripped the ball from the Bears' numbed hands and stepped into the end zone. The Giants were within three, 13-10.

Then the Giants began to zig and zag, especially those in sneakers, while the Bears seemed helpless to stop their runs and passes. The Giants erupted for 27 points in the last 15 minutes to win, 30-13, their second NFL championship, their first in a playoff. Each winner got $621, each loser $414, the equivalent for many of almost a half-season's wages.

Did the sneakers win what history has called The Sneaker Game? Ken Strong, who scored a championship-game record 17 points, said, "Yes, the sneakers saved us."

Years later, though, Strong told author George Sullivan about a fuel that may have set off the Giant fourth-period explosion. "We put whiskey into our water bucket to keep us warm," he said, "and by the fourth period we didn't feel the cold any more. In the fourth period we scored most of our points because it was then that we began to feel the effects of the whiskey."

```
┌─────────────────────────────────────┐
│          — 1935 —                   │
│            9-3                       │
│      1st Eastern Division            │
│          Steve Owen                  │
│                                      │
│  W  Pittsburgh          42-7   A     │
│  L  Green Bay            7-16   A     │
│  W  Boston             20-12   A     │
│  W  Brooklyn            10-7   H      │
│  W  Boston              17-6   H      │
│  L  Chicago Cardinals  13-14   H     │
│  L  Chicago Bears       3-20   H     │
│  W  Chicago Bears       3-0    A     │
│  W  Philadelphia       10-0    H     │
│  W  Brooklyn           21-0    A     │
│  W  Philadelphia       21-14   A     │
│  W  Pittsburgh         13-0    H     │
│                                      │
│         NFL Championship             │
│  L  Detroit             7-26   A     │
└─────────────────────────────────────┘
```

In 1935 Ed Danowski took over as the number-one Giant passer. In only two seasons, kicking field goals and running for touchdowns, Ken Strong had become the all-time leading Giants scorer. Another Fordham rookie, center Johnny Dell Isola, had so much confidence he once walked onto the field during a game and told All-Pro center Mel Hein he was taking his place. Hein punched him in the eye. Dell Isola growled so loudly about sitting on the bench that Steve Owen made him a starter—at guard.

The Giants opened the season with a 42-7 rout of the Steelers. Later they beat an old nemesis, the Bears, 3-0, and won their last four games, three by shutouts, for a third straight Eastern Division championship.

Ed Danowski, now brimming with confidence, led the league in passing (57 of 113), and cocky Tod Goodwin led in catches (26 for 432 yards). Elvin Richards ranked second in rushing, Danowski sixth. On defense, the team had yielded the league's fewest points.

The Detroit Lions, champions in the West with a 7-3-2 record, seemed a pushover in the championship game. But on a snow-swept field in Detroit, the Lions picked off two Danowski passes, and Detroit runners Buddy Parker and Ace Gutowsky spun out of Giant hands for touchdowns. Detroit won, 26-7, and the Giants knew how upset the Bears had felt a year earlier.

```
┌─────────────────────────────────────┐
│           — 1936 —                    │
│             5-6-1                      │
│        3rd Eastern Division           │
│            Steve Owen                 │
│                                       │
│   L   Philadelphia      7-10   A      │
│   L   Pittsburgh        7-10   A      │
│   W   Boston            7-0    A      │
│   T   Brooklyn          10-10  H      │
│   W   Chicago Cardinals 14-6   H      │
│   W   Philadelphia      21-17  H      │
│   W   Detroit           14-7   H      │
│   L   Chicago Bears     7-25   H      │
│   L   Detroit           0-38   A      │
│   L   Green Bay         14-26  H      │
│   W   Brooklyn          14-0   A      │
│   L   Boston            0-14   H      │
└─────────────────────────────────────┘
```

An avid sports-page reader, nineteen-year-old Wellington Mara, a Fordham junior, read about Tuffy Leemans, a George Washington University halfback who scored touchdowns in bunches. Wellington went to Washington to talk to Tuffy. In February 1936, at the NFL's first draft, the Giants picked Ohio University tackle Art Lewis in the first round, Tuffy Leemans in the second. Wellington signed Tuffy to a three-thousand-dollar-a-year contract.

Tuffy was one of the lucky ones. Most Giant backs got $150 a game, linemen $100. When a new league, the American Football League, offered more princely sums, Ken Strong and Harry Newman leaped to the AFL.

Injuries slowed Mel Hein, Johnny Dell Isola and Ed Danowski for much of the season. But a victory over the renamed Boston Redskins in the season's last game would have given the Giants a fourth straight Eastern title. On a muddy Polo Grounds field, in front of 15,000 drenched spectators, Boston won, 14-0.

As one solace to the Giants, Tuffy Leemans led the league in rushing with 836 yards. The Maras and Steve Owen came to a decision—they would rebuild the team around Leemans and Hein.

Meanwhile, young Wellington was staring at movies in darkened rooms. His mother had given him a movie camera as a gift. From the press box he trained the camera on the playing field, filming each play. "I knew the plays," he said later, "so I knew what was coming." He showed the movies to Giant coaches—and for the first time in the NFL, movies were being employed to spot opponents' strengths and weaknesses.

In Steve Owen's A-formation, the two guards were placed left or right of the center, creating an unbalanced line. The backs were positioned so that any one of three could take the long snap from the center; the fourth back was set as a wingback to catch the short, quick pass or act as a blocker on sweeps.

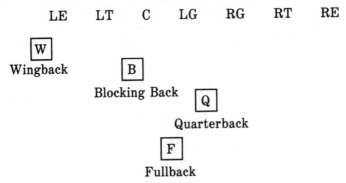

LE   LT   C   LG   RG   RT   RE

W
Wingback

B
Blocking Back

Q
Quarterback

F
Fullback

The key player was center Mel Hein, who had to block opponents as they tried to ram the weak side. "Without Hein," an opposing coach once said, "the A was not nearly as effective. As a result, no other team used it." The advantage of the A was that defenders could not know who the ballcarrier or passer would be, since any one of three backs could run left of right. And either the quarterback or the fullback could pass.

— 1937 —
6-3-2
2nd Eastern Division
Steve Owen

L	Washington	3-13	A
W	Pittsburgh	10-7	A
W	Philadelphia	16-7	A
W	Philadelphia	21-0	H
W	Brooklyn	21-0	H
T	Chicago Bears	3-3	H
W	Pittsburgh	17-0	H
L	Detroit	0-17	H
W	Green Bay	10-0	H
T	Brooklyn	13-13	A
L	Washington	14-49	H

New faces swarmed into the Giants' training camp at a Westchester Country Club. Among them: ends Jim Poole and Jim Lee Howell, tackle Ed Widseth, guard Tarzan White, center Kayo Lunday and backs Hank Soar and Ward Cuff—all later to become cherished names in Giants history.

Steve Owen gave the rebuilt team a new look—his A-formation. The A showed a line unbalanced to one side, the backfield unbalanced to the other side (see diagram).

The new Giants lost their opener to the new Washington Redskins, transplanted from Boston, and their rookie quarterback, transplanted from Texas, Slingin' Sammy Baugh. But down to the season's final game they had lost only to the Lions, and that final game against the Redskins would decide the division winner.

The Redskins came to New York led by 8,000 rooters and a fifty-five person band, the musicians dressed in Indian war bonnets. Some 58,000 spectators filled the Polo Grounds, and for most Giant fans, the afternoon stretched long and dreary. Baugh flipped for touchdowns and halfback Cliff Battles ran for more in a 49-14 rout. "The Giants used a 5-3-2-1 defense," Stanley Woodward wrote in the Herald Tribune. "They should have used a 12-7-5-4."

Second-place Mara Tech, as New York sportswriters dubbed the collegians-turned-pros, had one consolation. They drew 260,000 fans, the most ever for a Giant team and tops in a league that, for the first time, drew more than a million.

— 1938 —
8-2-1
1st Eastern Division
NFL Champions
Steve Owen

W	Pittsburgh	27-14	A
L	Philadelphia	10-14	A
L	Pittsburgh	10-13	H
W	Washington	10-7	A
W	Philadelphia	17-7	H
W	Brooklyn	28-14	H
W	Chicago Cardinals	6-0	H
W	Cleveland	28-0	H
W	Green Bay	15-3	H
T	Brooklyn	7-7	A
W	Washington	36-0	H

NFL Championship

W	Green Bay	23-17	H

By 1938 only five Giants—Mel Hein, Dale Burnett, Ed Danowski, Elvin Richards and Johnny Dell Isola—had been on the team long enough to have played on the 1934 championship team. And only two others—Tuffy Leemans and back Leland Shaffer—had been Giants more than one season. Several of last year's rookies, including ends Jim Poole and Jim Lee Howell, were starters.

Youthful mistakes, however, caused a stumbling start, the team losing two of its first three games. In Washington to play last year's champion Redskins, the Giants trailed 7-3. Ed Danowski threw to Jim Lee Howell for a touchdown and a 10-7 triumph.

By mid-season Stout Steve had so much talent he split the team into two squads, playing one for a quarter, then inserting a second platoon for the next quarter. The Giants raced unbeaten through their schedule, tied only once in a snowstorm by the Brooklyn Dodgers. In a grand finale, they got revenge for the previous year's 49-14 beating by blanking Sammy Baugh's Redskins, 36-0.

Green Bay (8-3-0) had won the West, its strong suit a passing attack from Arnie Herber to the lanky Don Hutson. A rugged Packer front wall knocked Mel Hein and Johnny Dell Isola out of the game early. As more than 65,000 watched in a packed Polo Grounds, the Packers took a 17-16 lead midway through the third period.

Owen shuffled his two platoons to put his best eleven on the field for the rest of the game. On a fourth and one at midfield, Hank Soar bucked over the middle for a first down. That seemed to crack the Green Bay defense. Four plays later Soar caught a pass from Danowski in the end zone. The Giants staggered off the field 23-17 victors and winners of their third NFL championship, their second playoff victory in three appearances.

Ed Danowski again led NFL passers, completing 70 of 129. Running out of the A-formation, he gained an average of better than 4 yards a carry. Mel Hein, six times an All-Pro center, won the league's first Most Valuable Player award. And Mara Tech looked at a balance sheet number of $200,000, its biggest profit ever.

9-1-1
1st Eastern Division
Steve Owen

W	Philadelphia	13-3	A
T	Washington	0-0	A
W	Pittsburgh	14-7	A
W	Philadelphia	27-10	H
W	Chicago Bears	16-13	H
W	Brooklyn	7-6	A
L	Detroit	14-18	A
W	Chicago Cardinals	17-7	H
W	Pittsburgh	23-7	H
W	Brooklyn	28-7	H
W	Washington	9-7	H

NFL Championship

L	Green Bay	0-27	A

"A top college team will beat most pro football teams because the college kids have more spirit. The pros play only for money."

That was a popular belief in the 1930s. In the annual game between the NFL champions and the College All-Stars, the collegians had seemed to prove that the popular belief was correct. The All-Stars had won four of the five previous battles with the NFL's champions.

The 1939 College All-Stars boasted TCU passer Davey O'Brien and Pitt runner Marshall Goldberg. The Giants' huge, young line bottled up both and won, 9-0, with three field goals by Ward Cuff and Ken Strong, who had come back from the wreckage of the disbanded American Football League.

The Giants had not lost at the Polo Grounds since early the previous season. That streak seemed likely to be severed by George Halas's Bears, who came to Manhattan with a fearsome offense, sparked by young quarterback Sid Luckman. He was a Columbia graduate who had escaped the grasping tentacles of Mara Tech. By now Wellington Mara was rated by his NFL peers as the game's shrewdest judge of college talent.

In four games the Bears had totalled 157 points. The Giants built up a 16-0 lead. Luckman fired two touchdown passes in the closing minutes, but the Giants escaped with a 16-13 victory.

Again the Eastern Division title would be decided by a Washington-New York battle in the Polo Grounds, Sammy Baugh testing the Giant defense. More than 62,000 sat in a freezing rain and watched as both defenses stalled the other side's mud-mired offense. Ward Cuff and Ken Strong kicked three field goals, and as the fourth period began the Giants led, 9-0.

The Redskins' Frank Filchock replaced the injured Baugh at quarterback and threw a touchdown pass to close the lead to two, 9-7. The Giants looked tired as the Redskins drove to the Giant 5. A penalty set the ball back to the 10. There were only forty-five seconds to play.

Ray Flaherty, now the Redskins coach, sent in rookie Bo Russell to kick a field goal. The ball sailed toward the goal posts. Redskin players leaped into the air, indicating that the kick was good. But referee Bill Halloran waved his arms across his chest—no good!

Flaherty and his Redskins stormed around Halloran. "It was eight inches inside the post," one Redskin said later. "It was twelve inches outside," countered Halloran, and his view prevailed.

The Giants ran out the clock. As the game ended, fistfights broke out between players and spectators. A fist whizzed by Halloran's chin. Cops rushed onto the field, broke up fights and pushed the players toward the clubhouse. The regular season ended with a riot. Later, Washington owner George Preston Marshall plaintively asked Tim Mara, "Tim, what church do you go to?"

Again Green Bay had won in the West. The Giants went to Milwaukee as a thousand fans cheered them aboard their train. In Milwaukee a two dollar and twenty cent ticket sold for twenty-five dollars. More than 32,000 fans and more than a hundred reporters crowded into a small park, its jerry-built press box swaying in a strong wind.

Cuff missed a field goal early—and that was about the only good news for the Giants. They never again got close to scoring. Big Clarke Hinkle slammed through the Giant line as if it were a swinging door. Arnie Herber and Cecil Isbell threw passes over the confused Giants. The Packers won, 27-0. "Come on, fellows," Jim Lee Howell said to the dejected Giants as they boarded their bus to leave the park. "We're lucky to have escaped alive."

	— 1940 — 6-4-1 3rd Eastern Division Steve Owen		
T	Pittsburgh	10-10	A
L	Washington	7-21	A
W	Philadelphia	20-14	A
W	Philadelphia	17-7	H
W	Pittsburgh	12-0	H
L	Chicago Bears	21-37	H
W	Brooklyn	10-7	A
L	Cleveland	0-13	H
W	Green Bay	7-3	H
W	Washington	21-7	H
L	Brooklyn	6-14	H

The Giants got a message early in the 1940 season that the glory days were gone for a while. They could only tie the perennially weak Steelers, 10-10, in their first game. They won their next three, but then lost Tuffy Leemans, their best rusher, after he injured his back.

Injuries also cut down quarterback Ed Danowski and halfback Ward Cuff. Mel Hein had to call the plays in the huddle. The Giants lost three of their next seven, the season ending with a 14-6 beating by the Dodgers, Brooklyn's first victory over the Giants since 1930.

Steve Owen's conservative formula had been a success during the 1930s, winning two championships and five Eastern titles. Stout Steve liked to build an early lead, often with field goals, then play a safe offense while his defense forced the other team into errors. That kind of solid, old-time football tired players and, worse, bored fans.

Speed. That was the buzz word around the NFL at season's end after the Bears' speedy, explosive T-formation racked up touchdown after touchdown in a 73-0 rout of the Redskins in the championship game. Said Steve Owen as he pondered the coming season: "I've got to find us someone who can run like Jesse Owens."

— 1941 —
8-3
1st Eastern Division
Steve Owen

W	Philadelphia	24-0	A
W	Washington	17-10	A
W	Pittsburgh	37-10	A
W	Philadelphia	16-0	H
W	Pittsburgh	28-7	H
L	Brooklyn	13-16	A
L	Chicago Cardinals	7-10	H
W	Detroit	20-13	H
W	Cleveland	49-14	H
W	Washington	20-13	H
L	Brooklyn	7-21	H

NFL Championship
L	Chicago Bears	9-37	A

On December 7 the Giants met the Dodgers in a game at the Polo Grounds. The game was meaningless — the Giants had clinched the Eastern championship a week earlier with a 20-13 victory over Washington.

The Dodgers took a 14-7 lead midway through the first half. In the press box a Western Union man stared at his chattering machine and said to a nearby reporter, "How do you like that — the Cards are beating the Bears by one touchdown."

A minute later the machine clacked again. "Oh, my God!" the Western Union man said.

"The Cards score again?" the reporter asked.

"No. The Japs have attacked Pearl Harbor!"

Minutes later the nation heard that America was marching toward World War II. New Yorkers clicked off their radios to talk worriedly about their future. The Giants and their game against the Bears for the championship two weeks later were forgotten.

Steve Owen had put speed in the defense, adding three fleet rookie running backs: Fordham's Lenny Eshmont, Minnesota's George Franck and Pennsylvania's Frank Reagan.

Two light (205-pound) but quick guards, Monk Edwards and Len Younce, flanked the thirty-five-year-old Mel Hein, who was no longer an All-Pro. Younce and Edwards helped the old man throw back rushers and, on offense, open holes for Owen's new lightning bolts. The Giants had a brief mid-season slump, losing 16-13 to Brooklyn and 10-7 to the Cardinals, but swept everyone else under the rug—until December 7.

The Giants heard about Pearl Harbor on clubhouse radios at halftime. The men knew they would be carrying guns within months. In a quiet Polo Grounds, they lost the game, 21-7.

The Giants went to Wrigley Field to play a Bear team that many thought the best ever. Spinning out of the T, Sid Luckman arched passes to Ken Kavanaugh and Ray McLean. When defenders dropped back, three speedy and tricky runners—Norm Standlee, George McAfee and Bill Osmanski—streaked up the middle or swept around end. The Bears had stormed through a 10-1-0 season and piled up a record 396 points.

Only 13,341 came to see the game in a time when Americans were hearing only bad news from the Pacific. The Giants contained the Bear juggernaut in the first half, but the Bears broke loose to pour in 28 points in the second half for a 37-9 victory, winning their second straight NFL title.

— 1942 —
5-5-1
3rd Eastern Division
Steve Owen

W	Washington	14-7	A
L	Pittsburgh	10-13	A
W	Philadelphia	35-17	H
L	Chicago Bears	7-26	A
L	Brooklyn	7-17	A
L	Pittsburgh	9-17	H
W	Philadelphia	14-0	A
L	Washington	7-14	H
T	Green Bay	21-21	H
W	Chicago Cardinals	21-7	H
W	Brooklyn	10-0	H

Eighteen Giants had gone to war. The Duke of Mara, Wellington, now wore Navy officer's blue. He read happily that his latest discovery, the six-six, 245-pound Al Blozis, a world champion shotputter, bowled over tacklers in preseason games. Spectators stared, gaping, at Blozis, a giant among pygmies. Most players of the time stood only to his armpits.

Veterans like Tuffy Leemans, Ward Cuff and Hank Soar, some on military leave, could not hope to replace the speedy but departed George Franck, Lenny Eshmont and Frank Reagan. A rookie fullback, Mississippi's Merle Hapes, showed promise of being a breakaway runner, but for this season Steve Owen's number-one gun on offense was the arm of Tuffy Leemans.

The Giants opened by beating Washington, 14-7, with a 50-yard Leemans pass and a 65-yard return of an interception. Then they lost four of their next five, eventually coming even keel by winning their last two. Their record was the worst, up to then, in Giants history.

— 1943 —
6-3-1
Tied 1st Eastern Division
Steve Owen

L	Phil/Pitt	14-28	A
W	Brooklyn	20-0	A
W	Phil/Pitt	42-14	H
L	Green Bay	21-35	H
T	Detroit	0-0	A
L	Chicago Bears	7-56	H
W	Chicago Cardinals	24-13	H
W	Brooklyn	24-7	H
W	Washington	14-10	H
W	Washington	31-7	A

Divisional Playoff

L	Washington	0-28	H

Mel Hein retired to become a college coach. But he promptly "unretired" and came back at thirty-six for his thirteenth season. He would retire for good in 1945. Steve Owen got a tip about a Georgia Tech dropout, Bill Paschal, and the fleet twenty-two-year-old won a job in the Giants' first preseason game by running back a kickoff 99 yards.

The Giants lost their opener to the Steagles, a team made up of Eagles and Steelers. The last touchdown in the Steagles' 28-14 victory was scored by a little quarterback who sneaked over to score. His name was Allie Sherman.

The Giants began to surprise teams with Paschal's long runs and passes by Leemans and rookie Emery Nix, of TCU, to Cuff and Hank Soar. They ran off five victories in eight games. Their last two games were against Washington. If the Giants could win both, they would face a playoff with Washington for the Eastern championship.

In the first game, at the Polo Grounds, they trailed 10-0 in the third period. Paschal slammed over for a touchdown. In the fourth period, running behind the titanic Al Blozis, home on weekend leave from the army, Paschal whizzed 47 yards for the winning touchdown.

The next Sunday, in Washington, Paschal won the rushing title as he galloped for 91 yards. Cuff scored 13 points in a 31-7 Giant rout. The Giants and Redskins met a third straight Sunday, this time in the playoff for the title. In the first two games Sammy Baugh's passes had been batted away or picked off by Soar, Cuff or Paschal. But on this Sunday Baugh threw straight arrows into Redskins jerseys. The Redskins won, 28-0.

"Well," said a resigned Tim Mara, "at least I will get to spend Christmas with my grandchildren."

— 1944 —
8-1-1
1st Eastern Division
Steve Owen

W	Boston	22-10	A
W	Brooklyn	14-7	A
W	Card/Pitt	23-0	H
L	Philadelphia	17-24	H
W	Boston	31-0	H
T	Phildelphia	21-21	A
W	Green Bay	24-0	H
W	Brooklyn	7-0	H
W	Washington	16-13	H
W	Washington	31-0	A

NFL Championship

L	Green Bay	7-14	H

"I honestly don't see how we're going to win a single game this season." Speaking was Steve Owen at the Giant training camp at Bear Mountain. Ex-Packer Arnie Herber, 34, hadn't thrown a pass in three years. Thirty-eight-year-old Ken Strong had not kicked a football in two years. Both joined the Giants. Herber confused the players in preseason by calling Packer plays.

Also on hand were Mel Hein (35), Ward Cuff (31) and Hank Soar (30). Young Bill Paschal came back on weekend passes from the army to play, along with another GI, tackle Al Blozis. In one game the Bears' Bulldog Turner charged at Ken Strong, then stopped. "Hell," said the Bulldog, "I can't block you—you're too old."

But Herber could still loft a ball into a receiver's hands, and he had a fleet end, Howie Livingston, as a target. Blozis blew holes in opposing lines, and Paschal sprinted through for touchdowns. The Giants won their first three games to disprove Owen's doleful prediction, lost to Philadelphia, 24-17, then won five of their last six, tied only by the Eagles, 21-21.

The Packers came to the Polo Grounds for the championship game. Lanky end Don Hutson had caught a league-leading 58 passes during the season, about one of every three thrown by the Packers. Ted Fritsch plunged up the middle and averaged 4 yards a crack.

A crowd of 46,016 filled most of the Polo Grounds, the Sunday papers telling of allied armies coming at Germany from east and west. On the first play, Bill Paschal's knee gave way and he collapsed, through for the day. Hutson snared a pass for one touchdown, Fritsch went over for another. A long pass, Herber to Frank Liebel, put the Giants on the 1, and Ward Cuff crashed over to make the score 14-7. The Giants started a game-tying drive, but another long pass from Herber was picked off at the Giant 20. In seven attempts to win the NFL championship since 1933, the Giants had won two, lost five.

Al Blozis had played his last game. Two months after the championship game, a German gun in France felled the giant forever.

— 1945 —
3-6-1
3rd Eastern Division
Steve Owen

W	Pittsburgh	34-6	A
T	Boston	13-13	A
L	Pittsburgh	7-21	H
L	Washington	14-24	H
L	Cleveland	17-21	H
L	Philadelphia	17-38	A
W	Detroit	35-14	H
L	Green Bay	14-23	H
W	Philadelphia	28-21	H
L	Washington	0-17	A

Steve Owen got a letter from a fan complaining about how terrible this team was. Stout Steve wrote back, "All you have to do is turn off your radio or walk out of the Polo Grounds. I have to sit here every Sunday and watch them."

Arnie Herber was back to pass, aided by an ex-Mississippi tailback, Junior Hovious. The best catcher was slim end Frank Liebel. Bill Paschal, Ward Cuff and a service returnee, George Franck, could run with the ball, but seldom very far. One reason, said Owen, "is the worst line I ever had," his best the thirty-six-year-old Mel Hein. The Giants played defense as though runners were slippery eels. A college coach offered to loan Owen some tackling dummies.

"No," Owen said, "I have too many tackling dummies already."

The Giants won their first game, tied the second, then lost six of their remaining eight. They played their last game at Washington. General Dwight Eisenhower, returning from victory in Europe, sat in the stands. He saw a Giant offense that could move the ball into Redskin territory only once—to the 49, where it lost the ball. The Redskins won, 17-0. Ike left early.

— 1946 —
7-3-1
1st Eastern Division
Steve Owen

W	Boston	17-0	A
W	Pittsburgh	17-14	A
L	Washington	14-24	A
W	Chicago Cardinals	28-24	H
W	Chicago Bears	14-0	H
L	Philadelphia	14-24	A
W	Philadelphia	45-17	H
T	Boston	28-28	H
W	Pittsburgh	7-0	H
L	Los Angeles	21-31	H
W	Washington	31-0	H

NFL Championship

L	Chicago Bears	14-24	H

"It's amazing," said Steve Owen, "what a difference one man can make for a ball club."

The one man was Frank Filchock, who had played in Washington in the shadow of Sammy Baugh. Filchock could run out of Owen's A-formation, pass from the T—newly installed by Stout Steve—or run or pass from the single wing. Filchock did not come cheap. He demanded a three-year contract worth about thirty-five thousand dollars — a new high in price and duration at Mara Tech.

The Giants won three of their first four, one victory a spectacular showing at home against the Cardinals. Chicago led 17-7 in the third period. Filchock threw left, right and up the middle. He hit Bill Paschal for a 20-yard touchdown, then threw to Paschal again for a 40-yard TD strike and a 21-17 lead.

The Cardinals scored to go ahead, 24-21, but Filchock coolly let loose a pass to Frank Liebel that covered 55 yards and put the Giants in front for good, 28-24.

Sid Luckman and the Bears arrived the following Sunday. A crowd of more than 62,000 filled every seat and spilled over onto the field. Another 10,000 milled outside. Filchock passed for one touchdown and ran for another. A big Giant line (the square face of Mel Hein absent for the first time since 1931) rushed Luckman so fiercely that the Bears did not score, losing 14-0. It was only the second shutout suffered by the Bears since George Halas sprang the T on the NFL before the war.

The Giants once more had to beat the Redskins in the final game to win the Eastern championship. Filchock showed his old master, Sammy Baugh, how much he had learned, the Giants winning a 31-0 laugher. The Giant line — Jim Poole, Jim White, Kayo Lunday, Frank Cope, Tex Coulter, Len Younce, Monk Edwards and Jim Lee Howell among them — had once again given Steve Owen what he wanted most in a team: the big D.

Filchock was picked as the Giants' most valuable player. He had set Giant records for completions, 87 of 169, and touchdowns (12), and also led the team in rushing with 371 yards.

The Bears again came to town, this time for the championship game. Fewer than twenty-four hours before the game, police reported that Filchock and fullback Merle Hapes had been offered bribes to allow the Redskins to win. Hapes said he had rejected the bribe, but conceded he had not reported the criminal action, as NFL regulations required. Filchock denied knowing anything about the bribe. NFL commissioner Bert Bell ordered Hapes out of the game but allowed Filchock to play.

The Bears scored quickly on a 21-yard pass by Luckman. Then they grabbed a pass by Filchock. His nose smashed, blood streaming down his face, Filchock came off the field hearing the boos of an angry and suspicious crowd. The Bears scored again to lead 14-0.

Face still bloodied, Filchock came back to throw a 38-yard pass to Frank Liebel for a touchdown. In the third period, the Giants on the Bear 5, he drilled a pass to Steve Filopowicz for the touchdown that tied the game, 14-14.

Sid Luckman steered the Bears to the Giant 19. Luckman rarely ran, but this time he faked a handoff, then skirted around end to trot unmolested into the end zone as the Giants ran the wrong way. The Bears won, 24-14.

Filchock later admitted being offered the bribe and was barred from playing until 1950.

Tim Mara and his two sons, Jack and Wellington, had more than bribe offers to worry about. Millionaire Dan Topping, the owner of the Dodgers, wanted to play in nearby Yankee Stadium, but the Maras wouldn't let him. So he jumped from the NFL to join a new league, the All-American Football Conference. AAFC teams were owned by millionaires like Topping. The AAFC began to outbid the NFL for college stars like Otto Graham and for established NFL stars like the Giants' Len Eshmont.

The Maras had to boost their salaries. Once more, as in the Red Grange twenties, star players began to ask for double and triple what they had been paid. Giant salaries soared from four thousand dollars for linemen to twelve thousand dollars, from ten thousand dollars for backs to twenty thousand dollars.

The Giants had won the NFL's Eastern title but lost the championship. Topping's Yankees had won the AAFC's Eastern title. For the first time, Mara Tech could not brag that it unarguably had the best pro team in town.

	— 1947 —		
	2-8-2		
	5th Eastern Division		
	Steve Owen		
T	Boston	7-7	A
L	Philadelphia	0-33	A
L	Washington	20-28	A
L	Boston	0-14	H
L	Pittsburgh	21-38	H
L	Detroit	7-35	A
L	Philadelphia	21-41	H
L	Pittsburgh	7-24	A
T	Green Bay	24-24	H
W	Chicago Cardinals	35-31	H
W	Washington	35-10	H
L	Los Angeles	10-35	A

Steve Owen figured he had a strong bunch up front—Lou De Filippo, Chet Gladchuk, Frank Cope, Jim White, Len Younce, Tex Coulter and Kayo Lunday. The running backs looked big and fast—Bill Paschal, George Franck, Choo Choo Roberts, Frank Reagan. Old reliable Ken Strong trotted out to kick field goals for one more season. The Giants had three sure-fingered pass-catchers—Frank Liebel, Ray Poole and Jim Lee Howell.

What the Giants didn't have, with Frank Filchock banned, was a passer.

Young Jerry Niles, given the ball as the team's number-one passer, could complete only 19 of 57. A desperate Stout Steve began to look elsewhere.

The Giants tied Boston, 7-7, then lost seven in a row, the longest losing streak up to then in Giant history. The Giants sent their best runner, Bill Paschal, to Boston to get Paul Governali, a former Columbia star.

Governali set a raft of Giant records in only eight games, completing 72 of 186 passes for 1,350 yards and 13 touchdowns. But too often, at critical moments, his blocking broke down, and Governali stared upward at the November sky.

The Giants seemed to flash a signal that 1948 would be brighter by winning two of their last four, including a 35-31 upset of the Cardinals. Overall, though, this was the worst Giant record ever—and their first basement finish.

— 1948 —		
4-8		
3rd Eastern Division		
Steve Owen		
W Boston	27-7	A
L Washington	10-41	A
L Philadelphia	0-45	A
L Chicago Cardinals	35-63	H
W Pittsburgh	34-27	H
L Chicago Bears	14-35	A
L Philadelphia	14-35	H
L Los Angeles	37-52	H
W Green Bay	49-3	A
W Boston	28-14	H
L Pittsburgh	28-38	A
L Washington	21-28	H

Washington had sent Frank Filchock—and a 1946 Eastern title—to New York. Now, loaded with passers, the Redskins dispatched a richer prize—Charlie Conerly, a hawk-faced rookie quarterback out of Mississippi. Steve Owen installed Conerly as his starting quarterback, Paul Governali going to the bench. In the Giants' first game Conerly tossed passes to rookie Bill Swiacki, another former Columbia star, and Ray Poole for a 27-7 victory over Boston.

Owen had brought twenty rookies to his thirty-five-man team, one a former Iowa halfback, Emlen Tunnell, who became the Giants' first black player. Slender as a stick at six-foot and 180, Emlen hit ball carriers like a bullet. Stout Steve decided to play Tunnell only on defense, making him one of the first pass-defending specialists in a league soon filled with them.

Owen's young defense — Joe Sulatis, Tex Coulter and Jim White were among the few veterans — cracked wide open in 41-10, 63-35 and 52-37 losses. Conerly tried to keep the Giants even by firing passes, 22 flying for touchdowns, a Giant record. And running out of Owen's A, he gained an average of 4 yards a dash.

Those whopping enemy scores — the Giants gave up 35 or more points in seven games — brought boos rolling out of the Polo Grounds stands. The Giants gave up 388 points in twelve games, their most ever.

To keep Conerly out of the grasps of the All-America Football Conference, the Giants gave him a four-year, fifty-five-thousand-dollar contract. The boos — and flat attendance figures — put frowns on faces at Mara Tech. Only one league, the Maras realized, could survive. Other NFL owners agreed. They offered to take in some of the stronger AAFC teams, notably the Cleveland Browns. But when other AAFC teams demanded entry, the war raged on.

— 1949 —
6-6
3rd Eastern Division
Steve Owen

L	Pittsburgh	7-28	A
W	New York Bulldogs	38-14	A
W	Washington	45-35	A
L	Pittsburgh	17-21	H
W	Chicago Bears	35-28	H
W	Chicago Cardinals	41-38	A
L	New York Bulldogs	24-31	H
W	Green Bay	30-10	A
L	Detroit	21-45	H
W	Washington	23-7	H
L	Philadelphia	3-24	H
L	Philadelphia	3-17	A

A Navy All-American end, Dick Duden, played the 1949 season for the Giants, catching two passes. Years later he filled out a questionnaire about his pro career. Under *Pro Honors Received,* he wrote, "None. Lucky to be alive."

Stout Steve Owen believed that football could only be played one way — violently. "You play football down in the dirt," he often said, "and in the dirt is where it belongs." His beloved A-formation required players who knew how to play down in the dirt. But A-formation football could often be dull, the off-tackle slant not nearly as exciting as T-formation razzle-dazzle. Stout Steve heard the boos of bored fans. He brought in a wiry ex-Eagle quarterback, Allie Sherman, to teach the T to his backs. Allie taught the T so well that Charlie Conerly completed more than half his passes, 17 for touchdowns. Choo Choo Roberts sped out of the A or T to score 17 touchdowns and lead the league.

By 1949 substitution rules had been loosened to allow two-platoon football. Some players performed on both the offense and defense; Joe Sulatis, for example, was a fullback and defensive end. But defensive back Emlen Tunnell and young tackle Al De Rogatis played only on defense. The sixty-minute player had become an endangered species.

Charlie Conerly and Choo Choo Roberts couldn't score enough touchdowns, especially during the first nine games, to match the number being given up by a porous defense. In six of those first nine games, the Giants gave up 28 or more points. The team had a 6-4 record with two games to go but lost both to the Eagles, the 1948 and 1949 NFL champions.

At season's end the AAFC's millionaires gave up and agreed that four of their teams would come to the NFL. The teams were the Baltimore Colts, the New York Yankees, the San Francisco 49ers and the team that would keep the Giants under their heels for the next three years—Otto Graham's Cleveland Browns.

```
             — 1950 —
                10-2
     Tied 1st American Conference
            Steve Owen

     W  Pittsburgh         18-7   A
     W  Cleveland           6-0   A
     W  Washington         21-17  A
     L  Pittsburgh          6-17  H
     W  Cleveland          17-13  H
     L  Chicago Cardinals   3-17  A
     W  Washington         24-21  H
     W  Chicago Cardinals  51-21  H
     W  Baltimore          55-20  A
     W  Philadelphia        7-3   H
     W  New York Yanks     51-7   H
     W  Philadelphia        9-7   A

          Conference Playoff
     L  Cleveland           3-8   A
```

The NFL split into two conferences to make room for the four AAFC teams. The Giants joined the American Conference with the Browns, Redskins, Eagles, Cardinals and Steelers.

Steve Owen could pick any five Yankees as part of the deal that allowed the former AAFC team to stay in New York. Owen knew he needed defense. He picked the six-foot-four 240-pound tackle Arnie Weinmeister. Arnie's strength astounded even other linemen. He once hoisted a two-hundred-pound teammate on his shoulders and piggybacked him half a mile up a hill so steep that some players could not run up it with nothing on their backs. Of Owen's other four choices, three were defensive backs — Otto "The Claw" Schnellbacher, Harmon Rowe and a vicious, speedy tackler who had flown bombers during World War II — Tom Landry.

Owen designed what would soon be called the umbrella defense against the pass. In passing situations he dropped his two ends to help out his four backs — Tunnell, Schnellbacher, Rowe and Landry. A diagram, positioning the six, formed spokes like those of an umbrella.

Rookie Eddie Price won the fullback job; Choo Choo Roberts was the halfback. The Giants won their opener, beating the Steelers, 18-7, and went to Cleveland to face the Browns, AAFC champions from 1946, when the AAFC began, to its demise in 1949. NFL fans labeled the Browns the champions of a bush league, but Owen had to treat them with respect. In their opener, the Browns had demolished the Eagles, two-time NFL champions, 35-10.

Otto Graham passed defenders dizzy. When the defenses laid back, Graham sent his huge fullback, Marion Motley, charging up the middle. Lou (the Toe) Groza kicked field goals whenever Otto fell short of the end zone. And the Brown defense seldom yielded more than three touchdowns.

The Giants' umbrella did not allow a Graham pass to touch a Browns' player's hand in the first half. The Giants won, 6-0, the first time the Browns had ever been shut out.

The Browns did not lose again (while Pittsburgh beat the Giants, 17-6) until their next meeting, this time at the Polo Grounds. "We knew that a lot of people thought that first win was a fluke," said the outspoken Arnie Weinmeister. "We knew it wasn't and were determined to prove it to everybody else."

The Browns took a 6-3 lead into the second period. Then a Giant rookie messed up a kickoff and the Browns pounced on the ball on the 1. They scored to lead 13-3 at the half. In the second half, Charlie Conerly hit on two long passes for one touchdown to trail, 13-10. On fourth and one at the Cleveland 2, the Giants could have kicked a game-tying field goal. Instead they went for the touchdown. Joe Scott whipped around end for the 6 points and a 17-13 victory.

The Giants and Browns clashed in Cleveland in a playoff for the Eastern title. With the score 3-3, Conerly lobbed a pass to Bob McChesney, alone in the end zone, and McChesney grabbed the ball for what seemed to be a go-ahead touchdown. But a Giant was offside, and the touchdown nullified.

Lou Groza then kicked a field goal and the Browns scored a safety to win the game, 8-3, and the title. They went on to win the NFL championship in their first NFL season. The Giants could go home only with bragging rights after beating the new champions two out of three.

	— 1951 — 9-2-1 2nd American Conference Steve Owen		
T	Pittsburgh	13-13	A
W	Washington	35-14	A
W	Chicago Cardinals	28-17	H
W	Philadelphia	26-24	H
L	Cleveland	13-14	A
W	New York Yankees	37-31	H
W	Washington	28-14	H
L	Cleveland	0-10	H
W	Chicago Cardinals	10-0	A
W	Pittsburgh	14-0	H
W	Philadelphia	23-7	A
W	New York Yankees	27-17	A

Sticking his large hand into a hat held by Commissioner Bert Bell, Steve Owen pulled out a slip of paper. So did other team officials, but Stout Steve had pulled out the name the others wanted in this special draft.

"Kyle Rote!" shouted the ruddy-faced coach. "We picked Kyle Rote!"

A shifty SMU tailback, Kyle Rote passed, kicked field goals, punted and ran—"the wildest thing I ever tried to tie onto," said a Notre Dame tackler. Owen hoped that Kyle would be the explosive scorer who could streak by the Brown defense.

But Rote injured a knee early in the season and played little. Charlie Conerly, arm aching, could not throw long. Stocky Eddie Price turned into a workhorse, and the fullback led the league with 271 rushes for 971 yards.

The front defensive wall, spearheaded by Arnie Weinmeister and Al De Rogatis, was backed by the umbrella secondary of Harmon Rowe, Tom Landry, Otto Schnellbacher and Emlen Tunnell. The defense gave up 18 or more points only twice all season. But the Browns lost only once. The Giants were tied by the Steelers, 13-13, and lost the two games they couldn't lose, 14-13 and 10-0, to those mighty Browns, again the conference winner.

		— 1952 —	
		7-5	
		2nd American Conference	
		Steve Owen	
W	Dallas Texans	24-6	A
W	Philadelphia	31-7	A
W	Cleveland	17-9	A
L	Chicago Cardinals	23-24	H
L	Philadelphia	10-14	H
W	Chicago Cardinals	28-6	A
W	San Francisco	23-14	H
L	Green Bay	3-17	H
W	Washington	14-10	A
L	Pittsburgh	7-63	A
L	Washington	17-27	H
W	Cleveland	37-34	H

"You've been drafted by the New York Giants."

"The *baseball* Giants?" Frank Gifford asked. Later he explained his confusion: "You have to really know how small-time pro football was in those days. In 1952 the football Giants didn't mean much to someone at USC."

The handsome tailback, the first of a long line of dashing runners out of the University of Southern California, could also pass and kick. He was the quintessential triple threat of the time. But Steve Owen rejected him as a ball carrier, calling him "Tippy Toes" because Gifford didn't seem to run with abandon. A first-round choice, Gifford won a job—but as a defensive back.

The Giants won six of their first nine, beating Cleveland, 17-9. But Charlie Conerly had some off days, especially on the road, games that New York fans saw; away games were being telecast back to the city for the first time. And when the Giants came home, Charlie heard the boo-birds.

Conerly hurt his throwing shoulder before the season's tenth game. Tom Landry, who had filled in at quarterback, took over the team and threw one touchdown pass, the only one of his career. It was also the only one of the day for the Giants in a 63-7 pasting by the Steelers.

The Browns again won the Eastern Conference title, even though the Giants beat them once. In the season's last game, against Cleveland, Conerly threw four touchdown passes, New York winning 37-34.

But a third straight second-place finish to the Browns had come close to exhausting the patience of New York fans. They compared Paul Brown's flashy split-end offense to Owen's stodgy A and old-fashioned T. Signs hung from the upper tiers of the Polo Grounds. Some said, "Conerly Must Go!" and others demanded, "Owen Must Go!"

— 1953 —
3-9
5th Eastern Conference
Steve Owen

L	Los Angeles	7-21	A
L	Pittsburgh	14-24	A
L	Washington	9-13	A
W	Chicago Cardinals	21-7	H
L	Cleveland	0-7	H
W	Chicago Cardinals	23-20	A
L	Philadelphia	7-30	A
L	Pittsburgh	10-14	H
L	Washington	21-24	H
W	Philadelphia	37-28	H
L	Cleveland	14-62	A
L	Detroit	16-27	H

"I know it isn't fair to you," Steve Owen was saying, "and I'm sorry about it, but I am so short of material that I can't do anything else."

Stout Steve was telling Frank Gifford that the jut-jawed defensive back would have to play halfback on offense while playing safety on defense. The Giant offense had been crippled by injuries to Kyle Rote and Eddie Price. The defense had also come apart. Otto Schnellbacher and Harmon Rowe had left and Arnie Weinmeister was so unhappy that he would leave the next season for Canada.

The umbrella blew away in a game against the Browns. Otto Graham passed almost at will to his split ends, Dante Lavelli and Mac Speedie. The Giants limped out of Municipal Stadium the battered 62-14 losers. Detroit ended their season with a 27-16 thumping.

Giant fans had one player to cheer even as they cussed Steve Owen and Charlie Conerly. Frank Gifford, playing an average of fifty minutes a game, led the team in scoring as he kicked field goals, passed, ran and raced back kickoffs and punts. He had become that rarity — a triple-threat college star who became a triple-threat as a pro, one of the last in the ever-more-specialized NFL.

After the season, Steve Owen was asked to come into the office of Tim Mara. Waiting for him, sad-faced, were Tim, Wellington and Jack. "You've got a place with the Giants as long as you live, Steve," Jack said, but no longer as a coach.

So the Owen Era had ended after twenty-eight seasons as a player and a coach. An ex-Marine would now usher in an era that began almost immediately with a championship.

	— 1954 —		
	7-5		
	3rd Eastern Conference		
	Jim Lee Howell		
W	Chicago Cardinals	41-10	A
L	Baltimore	14-20	A
W	Washington	51-21	A
W	Chicago Cardinals	31-17	H
W	Washington	24-7	H
L	Cleveland	14-24	A
W	Pittsburgh	30-6	A
W	Philadelphia	27-14	H
L	Los Angeles	16-17	H
L	Cleveland	7-16	H
W	Pittsburgh	24-3	H
L	Philadelphia	14-29	A

"Vince Lombardi teaches the style of football I like and believe in. Vinny is daring and he's brainy."

Jim Lee Howell, the old end, a former Marine officer and now the Giants' head coach, was explaining to reporters why Vince Lombardi, most recently a West Point assistant (and a member of Fordham's Seven-Blocks-of-Granite team of the 1930s), would be his backfield coach. Tom Landry, continuing as a player, would coach the defense. Together, Lombardi and Landry, two who would later conjure up championship teams far from New York, began to build New York's first championship team since 1938.

Mara Tech drafted and traded for new faces for the new head coach. Among the new ones were halfback Dick Nolan, quarterback Don Heinrich, ends Bob Schnelker and Barney Poole, and linebacker Bill Svoboda. End Ken MacAfee and linebacker Cliff Livingston came back from military duty. Huge lineman Roosevelt Brown, along with flashy Jack Stroud and center Ray Wietecha, rookies last year, seemed ready to dig in as starters on the offensive line.

Charlie Conerly had told the Giants he would not come back after the beatings and booings of a year ago. But for Jim Lee Howell, a down-home boy from the south like himself, Chuckin' Charlie agreed to return.

Lombardi immediately made Frank Gifford a ball carrier only and gave Charlie Conerly snappier plays for a snappier T. Dick Nolan fitted neatly with Em Tunnell, Dick Rich and Tom Landry in a deep four.

The Giants' revved-up offense and tighter defense won the season opener against the Cards, 41-10. The defense gave up 22 or more points only twice all season. Conerly pitched to Schnelker, MacAfee and Kyle Rote for 17 touchdowns in the season's first nine games. The Giants, 6-3, hung close to the Browns.

Then Charlie went down, his knee giving way. Young Don Heinrich could not carry the load. The Giants lost two of their last three as the Browns sprinted ahead to a fifth straight division title (the division's name had been changed from American Conference to Eastern Conference the year before).

Attendance had been flat or dipping during the early 1950s, but the Maras saw a sign of good times to come — more than 50,000 filled the Polo Grounds for the last game of the season, and hope filled the arena below Coogan's Bluff that a time for winning was at hand.

— 1955 —
6-5-1
3rd Eastern Conference
Jim Lee Howell

L	Philadelphia	17-27	A
L	Chicago Cardinals	17-28	A
L	Pittsburgh	23-30	A
W	Chicago Cardinals	10-0	H
L	Pittsburgh	17-19	H
W	Washington	35-7	H
L	Cleveland	14-24	A
W	Baltimore	17-7	H
W	Philadelphia	31-7	H
T	Cleveland	35-35	H
W	Washington	27-20	A
W	Detroit	24-19	A

The Giant coaches met in the office high above centerfield in the windswept Polo Grounds. The Giants had lost four of their first five games. Jim Lee Howell had offered to resign — the Maras turned him down. The bespectacled Vince Lombardi, hair iron-gray at the temples, said that he and line coach Ed Kolman had an idea — powerhouse running plays for short yardage.

"Ed and I," said Lombardi, rubbing his brick of a jaw, "thought if we put double-team blocking into our running game, we'd catch a lot of teams by surprise. I don't think there is a lineman in the game today who can handle a double-team block."

The Giants modified two plays. One was called a Forty-seven Power in which Frank Gifford carried the ball and Ken MacAfee and Dick Yelvington double-teamed the end; the other was called a Twenty-six Power in which Alex Webster, a fullback recently lured from Canada, cut through the opposite side with two blockers teaming on the other end.

Webster, a six-foot-three, 210-pound bull, had arrived in New York with Mel Triplett, a six-foot-one, 215-pound flash, to join Gifford as the Giant runners. Kyle Rote had been shifted to flanker and would be primarily a pass-catcher.

The defense added a new battering ram, six-foot-five, 275-pound Rosey Grier, who joined the front four. Harland Svare came to the team as a linebacker. The secondary—Dick Nolan, Tom Landry, Jimmy Patton and Emlen Tunnell—began to meld into a fluid-motion unit. But on defense the Giant right often didn't know what its left was doing. The confusion showed in the early going, with games lost 27-17, 28-17 and 30-23.

Then the defense firmed. Conerly threw daggers to Gifford, Rote, Schnelker, Webster and MacAfee. Webster and Gifford pounded through lines and skirted around ends, Gifford averaging 5 yards, Webster 4.

The Giants won five of their last seven, tying the Browns, who were on their way to a sixth straight Eastern title. "Over the last few games," Gifford said, "we were really beginning to move."

Move toward a championship.

— 1956 —
8-3-1
1st Eastern Conference
NFL Champions
Jim Lee Howell

W	San Francisco	38-21	A
L	Chicago Cardinals	27-35	A
W	Cleveland	21-9	A
W	Pittsburgh	38-10	H
W	Philadelphia	20-3	H
W	Pittsburgh	17-14	A
W	Chicago Cardinals	23-10	H
L	Washington	7-33	A
T	Chicago Bears	17-17	H
W	Washington	28-14	H
L	Cleveland	7-24	H
W	Philadelphia	21-7	A

NFL Championship

W	Chicago Bears	47-7	H

Retiring as a player, defensive coach Tom Landry pieced together a new defensive unit with old and new faces. He got Ed Hughes from Los Angeles to replace him in the deep four. Hughes joined Em Tunnell, Dick Nolan and Jimmy Patton. Landry convinced a worried rookie out of West Virginia, Sam Huff, that he was good enough to play in the NFL. When the cherubic-faced Sam proved to himself and the Giants that he could be a fierce line-backer despite his lack of size (six feet and 210 pounds), Landry inserted Huff as the team's middle linebacker between Cliff Livingston and Harland Svare.

For the front four the Giants drafted or swapped for people who within a year would be among the city's idols — end Jim Katcavage, tackle Dick (Little Mo) Modzelewski and end Andy Robustelli, a fierce rusher with hands that swept bigger men left, right or onto their rears. In the middle of that front four stood a mountain — the six-foot-five, 275-pound tackle Rosey Grier.

Offensively, few changes were made. Charlie Conerly threw to flanker Kyle Rote or end Ken MacAfee. The two big backs, Alex Webster and Mel Triplett, shared the ball-carrying with Frank Gifford, the halfback who could go inside or outside.

A big offensive line — it averaged 234 pounds — swept aside defenders. Anchoring it at center was Ray Wietecha. Bill Austin and Jack Stroud were the guards, Rosey Brown (the biggest and fastest lineman) and Dick Yelvington the tackles.

Playing their first three games on the road, the Giants won two. They beat the Browns, playing without Otto Graham for the first time in their history, 21-9. They came to New York and a new home — Yankee Stadium. The Polo Grounds, soon to be abandoned by the westward-bound baseball Giants, had become dilapidated. The Giants won the Stadium opener, beating Pittsburgh, 38-10. Giant tickets suddenly became rare finds, most every Sunday a last-minute sellout.

Giant fans bandied new "in" words among themselves: "blitz" and "red-dog" were two favorites. When a Giant blitzer dumped a passer for a 20-yard loss, the stadium roared as loudly — *dee-fense! dee-fense!* — as it did for a Giant touchdown.

The Giants lost to the Cardinals, Redskins and Browns, and were tied by the Bears. But that 8-3-1 record was good enough for first in the NFL East. They went into their first NFL playoff for a championship since 1946. Facing them for the NFL title: The same bad news they fought in 1933, 1934 and 1946 — the Chicago Bears.

The 9-2-1 Bears dazzled foes with long passes from Ed Brown or George Blanda to the long-striding end, Harlon Hill. A crashing fullback, Rick Casares, topped the NFL with 1,126 yards and 12 touchdowns. On defense, the Midway Monsters sent their biggest monster, the six-eight, 265-pound Doug Atkins, bowling by blockers on the pass rush to terrorize quarterbacks.

On a cold, gray day at Yankee Stadium, 56,836 spectators watched the Giants trot onto a frozen field wearing sneakers. Unlike 1934, the Giants didn't have to chase all over town to find their footwear; the always-prepared Andy Robustelli, hearing a forecast of icy eighteen-degree weather, had ordered them from a Connecticut dealer.

The sneakers made the Giants surer of foot than the Bears, but the Giants also seemed to be faster, stronger and better prepared than George Halas's Bears. The Giant backs bumped Harlon Hill at the line, never letting him get loose on one of his fly patterns down the sideline. Sam Huff and the linebackers bottled up Rick Casares for most of the Bears' series, and only once — on a 9-yard rumble up the middle — did he crash into the end zone for a touchdown. Mel Triplett scored the first touchdown on a 17-yard dash, Ben Agajanian kicked two field goals, and at the half the Giants, scoring three more touchdowns, led 34-7.

By the second half the Giant pass-catchers, especially Frank Gifford and Kyle Rote, had found they could snake around rookie back J. C. Caroline. Charlie Conerly pitched pass after pass to open receivers, the Giants scoring two more touchdowns. They won their fourth NFL championship, 47-7. With a young, yet experienced and talented team, Mara Tech looked ahead to a string of championships. But Wellington Mara, then a sprightly forty, would be a graying seventy before the Giants would win another.

— 1957 —
7-5
2nd Eastern Conference
Jim Lee Howell

L	Cleveland	3-6	A
W	Philadelphia	24-20	A
W	Washington	24-20	A
W	Pittsburgh	35-0	H
L	Washington	14-31	H
W	Green Bay	31-17	A
W	Chicago Cardinals	27-14	H
W	Philadelphia	13-0	H
W	Chicago Cardinals	28-21	A
L	San Francisco	17-27	H
L	Pittsburgh	10-21	A
L	Cleveland	28-34	H

Wherever there was a gathering of that new breed of sports fan — the "in" pro-football fan who knew an outside pass pattern from a fly — the talk focused on a Giant dynasty. The Conerlys, Rotes, Giffords, Huffs, Tunnells, et al could only improve. While that would prove to be true for most of the Giant players, Cleveland's Paul Brown had found an athlete who would once again make his Browns the best of the East. Big at six-foot-two and

230 pounds, he had a track sprinter's speed and the ramming power of an ice-breaker. His name was Jim Brown and in the next few years he would put his name all across the pages of the NFL record book.

Before the first Giant-Jim Brown confrontation, defensive coach Tom Landry told middle linebacker Sam Huff to go wherever Brown went. "Follow him," as the old joke went, "even if he goes to the bathroom." The quick, slashing Huff knifed through blockers to keep Brown out of the end zone, but the Browns won, 6-3.

Playing a soft schedule in the middle of the season, the Giants won seven of their next eight, but lost to a strong 49ers team, 27-17, to Pittsburgh, 21-10, and to Cleveland, 34-28, as the Browns double-teamed Huff and Jim Brown ran wild. Cleveland finished first in the East. Brown and Huff, however, would see much more of each other.

— 1958 —

9-3

1st Eastern Conference
Jim Lee Howell

W	Chicago Cardinals	37-7	A
L	Philadelphia	24-27	A
W	Washington	21-14	A
L	Chicago Cardinals	6-23	H
W	Pittsburgh	17-6	H
W	Cleveland	21-17	A
W	Baltimore	24-21	H
L	Pittsburgh	10-31	A
W	Washington	30-0	H
W	Philadelphia	24-10	H
W	Detroit	19-17	A
W	Cleveland	13-10	H

Conference Playoff

W	Cleveland	10-0	H

NFL Championship

L	Baltimore	17-23	H

This would be a miracle kind of season. And even though it ended in sudden-death defeat for the Giants—the first sudden death in pro football—the Giants could brag of playing in a game that would propel pro football on a rocketlike climb toward a popularity that would match or exceed that of the nation's grand old game, baseball.

In the offseason, the Giants traded two defensive backs for a young pass defender, Lindon Crow. To make it a two-for-two deal, the Cardinals threw in a twenty-eight-year-old field goal kicker with an indifferent record—Pat Summerall.

Jim Lee Howell drafted for fullback Phil King. He got Rosey Grier back from the army and put him back into the trenches with the front four.

In the Giants' first six games—they won four and lost two—Pat Summerall missed 7 of 10 field goals and talked of quitting. He changed his mind on the eve of a game against the Baltimore Colts. The next day he kicked a twenty-eight-yard field goal at 1:59 to beat the Colts, 24-21.

The Giants lost to the Steelers the next Sunday, 31-10. At 5-3, they had to win all of their last four games to hope to catch Cleveland. They beat Washington, Philadelphia and Detroit, that 19-17 victory over the Lions saved when Harland Svare blocked a last-minute field goal from the 25.

Next came the season's last game—against the Browns. On the game's first play, Jim Brown evaded Sam Huff and shot 65 yards for a touchdown. The Giants came back to tie the game, 10-10, but a tie would give Cleveland the title. With four minutes to go the Giants pushed to the Brown 31. On fourth down Pat Summerall tried a field goal—and saw it twist to the side. "I'd have liked to have gone anywhere but back to the bench," he said later.

Two minutes later the Giants again elbowed their way into Brown territory. On fourth down Pat again came in to try for a field goal—from 49 yards away. "I knew I had to hit it good," he said. It went straight and true between the goal posts—and the Giants and the Browns would meet again a week later at Yankee Stadium to wrestle in a playoff for the Eastern title.

Huff and his wrecking crew revved themselves up to stop Jimmy Brown. As the packed stadium roared, Giant tacklers flattened Brown within split seconds whenever he touched the ball. He gained only 8 yards and the Giants, winning, 10-0, went to their second championship game in three years.

The Colts had won the Western title by relying on the passing and playcalling of a burr-headed, spindly quarterback named Johnny Unitas. He threw to a favorite receiver, the quick Raymond Berry. He handed off to a crashing fullback, Alan Ameche, and to a mercurial halfback, L.G. (Long Gone) Dupre. A take-no-prisoners defense was led by three-hundred-pound Big Daddy Lipscomb, who, it was said, threw blockers left and right "until he sorted everyone out and found the guy carrying the ball."

Amid a city in a frenzy for tickets, many Giant fans climbed into their cars, knowing the game would not be shown on TV screens within fifty miles of the stadium. They drove north, south, east and west to find TV sets in motels or the homes of friends.

No one came away from that game sorry that they had seen it. As New York fans chanted, *goooo Giii-ants*, the Colts went, taking a 14-3 lead at halftime. In the third period the Giants stopped what could have been the clinching Colt touchdown. The Colts had the ball at the Giant 3, first down and goal to go. But the Giants threw back the Colts and took over at the 5.

Conerly arched a short pass to Kyle Rote, who shot ahead of his man and sped all the way to the Giant 25. A Colt caught him from behind. As Rote hit the ground, the ball pinched out of his arm and bounced crazily toward the goal line. Giants and Colts chased after it. Alex Webster won the race, falling on the ball at the 1. Mel Triplett then leaped into the end zone and the Giants trailed, 14-10.

Up in a press box Wellington Mara had been taking Polaroid pictures of the Colt defense. He dropped the prints in a weighted sock to the Giant bench. Landry and Lombardi looked at the photos and saw a hole in the Colt secondary. Bob Schnelker swerved into those holes and caught two passes, one for 46 yards. From the 15 Conerly looked to Schnelker on the right, then lobbed to Frank Gifford on the left for a touchdown. The crowd's roar rose into the darkening sky above Yankee Stadium. The Giants led, 17-14.

The Colts took the ball but had to punt it back to the Giants. There were two minutes to play when the Giants' Gifford, on third down, battled for a first down and fell short by inches on the Giant 43.

"Go for it! Go for it!" screamed Giant fans. But Jim Lee Howell decided to be conservative, knowing a failure to make those inches could cost the game or at best give the Colts a shot at a tying field goal. Don Chandler got off a long punt that was downed at the Colt 14.

Out came the stony-faced Unitas. He had 120 seconds or so to score. He knew the Giants would fall back to stop the long pass that could beat them. Unitas darted four short passes, Ray Berry catching three for gains of 25, 15 and 22 yards. There were only seven seconds to go, the ball on the Giant 13. Steve Myhra kicked a field goal that tied the game and left Yankee Stadium hushed.

A 1955 NFL rule had mandated a sudden-death overtime to decide an NFL champion in a playoff tie, a situation that had never happened — up to now. In pro football's first overtime game, the Giants won the coin toss and took the kickoff. But the Colts forced a punt, the Colts taking over at their 20. In twelve plays, Unitas tossing left and right and his backs stabbing up the middle, the Colts reached the 1. In a quiet Stadium, the small band of Colt fans could be heard for the first time, shrieking and yipping as Ameche plunged over for the winning touchdown.

The Colts took home almost five thousand dollars a man, the Giants about three thousand, which seemed a huge reward for one game's work. Of the game itself, Vince Lombardi — soon to go to Green Bay and glory as Packer head coach — said of the game from a Giant viewpoint, "It was a couple of inches too short and seven seconds too long."

— 1959 —
10-2
1st Eastern Conference
Jim Lee Howell

W	Los Angeles	23-21	A
L	Philadelphia	21-49	A
W	Cleveland	10-6	A
W	Philadelphia	24-7	H
W	Pittsburgh	21-16	A
W	Green Bay	20-3	H
W	Chicago Cardinals	9-3	H
L	Pittsburgh	9-14	H
W	Chicago Cardinals	30-20	A
W	Washington	45-14	H
W	Cleveland	48-7	H
W	Washington	24-10	A

NFL Championship

L	Baltimore	16-31	A

Vince Lombardi went to Green Bay. Allie Sherman, the assistant who had taught the T to Charlie Conerly in the early 1950s, became the offense coach. His passer was Charlie Conerly, his runners Frank Gifford, Alex Webster, Mel Triplett and rookie Joe Morrison. The word out on the Giants was: no breakaway speed.

The Giants opened by edging the Rams, 23-21, the game won on a Pat Summerall field goal, his second. Short passes by Conerly, bursts up the middle by the Giant runners for 10 or 15 yards, and the Summerall field goal would be the essence of the Giant offense. The defense massed Rosey Grier up front, with Sam Huff roving behind the line and Jim Patton, Dick Lynch and Lindon Crow covering in the secondary. The defense broke down in a 49-21 thumping by the Eagles. But only once for the rest of the season did it give up more than 16 points in a game.

The Giants had the number of an old nemesis that season — Paul Brown and his Browns. The Giant pass rush scurried after quarterback Milt Plum before he could lob one of his dinks to Jim Brown or another back. And Sam Huff plastered himself to Brown wherever he went on a rushing play. "We hit him," Huff said, "with as much as we can."

The Giants humbled the Browns at Yankee Stadium, 48-7, to clinch a third Eastern title in four years. Winners in the West were Johnny Unitas and his Colts. The outcome of this championship game, like the memorable 1958 battle, would hinge on a play of inches.

At Baltimore's Municipal Stadium, the Giants led, 9-7, in the third period on three Pat Summerall field goals. Late in the third period, the Giants jabbed to the Colt 29, where they faced a fourth down and inches to go. Last year Jim Lee Howell had chosen to punt. This time, at Baltimore's Memorial Stadium, he chose to go for the first down. Alex Webster slammed into the line—but the Colts held.

The Colts moved to a quick touchdown. Intercepting two Conerly passes, the Colts banged over 24 points in less than fifteen minutes to win their second straight NFL title, 31-16.

The Giants had lost two straight titles by a total of 21 points. In his history of the Giants, *The Giants of New York,* Barry Gottehrer wrote that for Howell and his Giants, "it was more a matter of fifteen inches."

— 1960 —
6-4-2
3rd Eastern Conference
Jim Lee Howell

W	San Francisco	21-19	A
W	St. Louis	35-14	A
W	Pittsburgh	19-17	A
T	Washington	24-24	H
L	St. Louis	13-20	H
W	Cleveland	17-13	A
W	Pittsburgh	27-24	H
L	Philadelphia	10-17	H
L	Philadelphia	23-31	A
T	Dallas	31-31	H
W	Washington	17-3	A
L	Cleveland	34-48	H

Tim Mara, the happy bookie who had bought the Giants for five-hundred-dollars when there wasn't even a team, died in 1959. Ownership of the team went to his two sons, Jack and Wellington.

The Duke of Mara still had his nose for talent, both on and off the field. When NFL commissioner Bert Bell died, the owners could not decide between two candidates. Wellington startled the owners by offering the name of a relatively unknown Ram official, Pete Rozelle. Since neither of the two prime candidates could get enough votes to win, the weary owners decided on Wellington's choice, no one having any strong feelings pro or con about Rozelle. The Rozelle Era—in football and in pro sports—began. In the next two decades, pro sports rose from smokey backrooms to the boardrooms of twentieth-century corporate America.

Mara Tech had its comings and goings. Tom Landry went off to coach the Dallas Cowboys. Charley Conerly, Frank Gifford, Kyle Rote and Alex Webster stumbled in and out of games on legs aching from injuries. In their first five games the Giants were tied by a weak Washington team and beaten by the mediocre Cardinals.

Jim Lee Howell's temper flared, already inflamed by the pressures of coaching in New York. Millions now second-guessed the decisions concerning their favorite pro team. He and the Maras announced he would become the team's personnel director at season's end. He barked at the Giants. They responded by savaging the Browns in a brutal head-butting contest, limiting Jim Brown and the rushing offense to 6 yards, the game won, 17-13, by New York.

But a speedy Eagle team flew by the Giants two games in a row, 17-10 and 31-23. In one of those games lineman Chuck Bednarik blindsided Frank Gifford, knocking him cold. Gifford, treated for a concussion, came back to play the next week, but by season's end he had decided to retire.

The Eagles won the Eastern title and beat Vince Lombardi's Green Bay Packers for the NFL title. Wellington Mara could look at the young Eagles with envy in his eyes. His Giants averaged almost thirty.

The Maras made one of Howell's assistants, Allie Sherman, the new head coach, just as Howell and Steve Owen had been raised from assistants to head coach. Both the Maras and the thirty-eight-year-old Sherman knew what was needed: new faces, preferably ones sitting on speed.

— 1961 —
10-3-1
1st Eastern Conference
Allie Sherman

L	St. Louis	10-21	H
W	Pittsburgh	17-14	A
W	Washington	24-21	A
W	St. Louis	24-9	A
W	Dallas	31-10	A
W	Los Angeles	24-14	H
L	Dallas	16-17	H
W	Washington	53-0	H
W	Philadelphia	38-21	H
W	Pittsburgh	42-21	H
W	Cleveland	37-21	A
L	Green Bay	17-20	A
W	Philadelphia	28-24	A
T	Cleveland	7-7	H

NFL Championship

L	Green Bay	0-37	A

"I call Wellington Mara 'Pretzel,' " said Dan Reeves, owner of the Rams. "He twists and turns every which way, but he always comes up with a winner."

After a welter of deals, the Duke brought to New York the names that would still make eyes shine in New York more than twenty-five years later: The Bald Eagle, quarterback Y.A. Tittle; the skinny pass-catcher, Del Shofner; stocky tight end Joe Walton; and a slashing tackler, defensive back Erich Barnes. The draft blew in a flashy runner, Bobby Gaiters. All told, sixteen of the thirty-six Giants of 1961 were new arrivals.

Charlie Conerly had to know his days as number-one quarterback were numbered now that Y.A., a semilegend during his years with the 49ers, had come east. But the two veterans got along well.

Allie didn't wait long to call on Y.A. after the Giants lost their opener, 21-10. Y.A. came into the second game to rally the Giants for a 17-14 victory over Pittsburgh. Later in the season Y.A. seemed to lose his touch against the Rams. Allie Sherman sent in Chuckin' Charlie, who threw two touchdown passes for a come-from-behind 24-14 victory.

But Y.A. took over as number one after that game. The Eagles met the Giants near season's end, the two old rivals tied for first place. The Eagles led, 10-7, and the Giant offense seemed draggy. Allie sent in Charlie to replace Y.A. so, as he explained later, "Y.A. could see the Eagle defense from the sideline" for a few plays.

Y.A. never left that study hall. Conerly threw a 35-yard touchdown pass to Joe Walton, then hit the Ichabod Crane-like Del Shofner for two more. The Giants won, 28-24, grabbing their fourth Eastern title in six years.

Y.A. was chosen the league's Most Valuable Player after throwing 17 touchdown passes. Del Shofner had caught 68 passes to become an All-Pro. Allie Sherman was picked NFL Coach of the Year.

Out west Vince Lombardi had built a machine that would terrorize the league for much of the decade. Bart Starr slung passes to gluey-fingered speedsters. Defenses were overwhelmed by the Green Bay power sweep, which sent Jim Taylor or Paul Hornung slashing around end behind a wave of blockers. Vince had not forgotten what double-team blocking could do to even the toughest tacklers.

The Giants went to Green Bay and, as in 1939, were ploughed under by a Packer juggernaut. Paul Hornung scored one touchdown and kicked a field goal during a 24-point Packer explosion in the second period. The Packers' front wall hounded Y.A., who completed only 6 of 20 and threw 4 into the hands of Packers. The Giants limped off Lambeau Field the 37-0 losers.

"It was," said Pat Summerall, counting his $3,339.99 loser's share, "the most profitable humiliation I ever participated in."

Allie had a more positive outlook. "Today," he said, "they were the better team. Maybe next time we'll be better."

Next time was only a year away.

12-2

1st Eastern Conference
Allie Sherman

L	Cleveland	7-17	A
W	Philadelphia	29-13	A
W	Pittsburgh	31-27	A
W	St. Louis	31-14	A
L	Pittsburgh	17-20	H
W	Detroit	17-14	H
W	Washington	49-34	H
W	St. Louis	31-28	H
W	Dallas	41-10	A
W	Washington	42-24	A
W	Philadelphia	19-14	H
W	Chicago	26-24	A
W	Cleveland	17-13	H
W	Dallas	41-31	H

NFL Championship

L	Green Bay	7-16	H

Charlie Conerly and Kyle Rote retired before the season began. But one of the Giants' backfield stars returned. Frank Gifford, missing football, came back after a one-year retirement. The new Three Musketeers, as Rote, Gifford and Conerly had once been called, were now Gifford, Sam Huff ("Huff! Huff! Huff!" Giant fans shouted whenever he made a tackle), and the seemingly phlegmatic quarterback, Y.A. Tittle.

Y.A. was not as retiring as the grandfatherly image he projected. Once he saw a Giant running back hesitate as he approached the line of scrimmage. A tackler spilled the runner. Y.A. charged over to the fallen back and screamed into his ear, "You charge into that line or you get off this football field!"

"When our younger players see a thirty-six-year-old man get so fired up," Gifford said, "they have to get excited. Hell, so do I."

The Giants had built a legion of followers so devoted that season tickets were a status symbol. Gifford had to smuggle his son into a game at Yankee Stadium as an assistant waterboy because he couldn't buy the boy a seat.

Those fans worried as the Giants lost two of their first six. Unbeaten Washington came to town. After that game, in the minds of many Giant fans, Y.A. Tittle — The Bald Eagle — was the greatest Giant quarterback ever. He completed 27 of 39 passes, seven for touchdowns, while gaining 505 yards.

Don Chandler, who had been the team's punter, had learned to kick field goals, replacing the retired Pat Summerall. Chandler rammed four over the bar as the Giants beat the Bears, 26-24, to clinch a second straight Eastern title. For the first time ever, all Giant home games had been sellouts.

Tittle had tossed 33 touchdown passes, a league record, to become the Player of the Year. Chandler kicked 104 points, a Giant record. Allie Sherman won his second straight Coach of the Year award.

Vince Lombardi and his Packers won a second straight Western title. The Packers came to Yankee Stadium on a day that seemed more Green Bayish than New Yorkish. The temperature dropped to ten degrees but most of the 64,892 who attended that day will remember it as the coldest day of their lives. Fifty-mile-an-hour gusts snapped flags until they were as straight as a sheet of ice. "The temperature itself wasn't that bad," Packer quarterback Bart Starr said later after fearing his ears had been frozen. "We practiced in fifteen-below-zero weather in Green Bay and it didn't seem as cold as it was out there today. The wind was brutal."

"The ball was like a diving duck," Y.A. Tittle said. "I threw one pass and it almost came back to me."

The action turned as brutal as the numbing winds as the Packers' big runners, Jim Taylor and Paul Hornung, slammed into the violent world of Sam Huff and the Giant defense, which was rated the most savage in the league. On one play five Giants slammed Jim Taylor to the frozen ground. "All of a sudden," Dick Modzelewski said later, "I felt a terrible pain. Taylor bit me."

Numbed Giant fingers bobbled balls that turned into Packer scores. Ahead 3-0, the Packers ripped the ball from the hands of ball carrier Phil King at the Giant 28. On two plays, a halfback pass by Hornung for 22 yards and a 6-yard charge into the line by Taylor, the Packers scored to lead, 10-0.

Early in the second half the Giants' Erich Barnes blocked a Green Bay punt. The ball bounced into the end zone where the Giants' Jim Collier fell on it for the Giants' first and only score. A little later the Packers pounced on a Giant fumble at the Giant 40. Jerry Kramer kicked a 29-yard field goal. In the last period he kicked another, a 40-yarder, his third of the day, to ice a 16-7 Packer triumph and a second straight NFL championship. Since 1956 the Giants had lost four of five NFL title games. This team of Y.A. and Sam Huff would have one more chance before the Long Darkness dropped on Mara Tech.

```
    — 1963 —
        11-3
  1st Eastern Conference
      Allie Sherman

W   Baltimore      37-28  A
L   Pittsburgh      0-31  A
W   Philadelphia   37-14  A
W   Washington     24-14  A
L   Cleveland      24-35  H
W   Dallas         37-21  H
W   Cleveland       33-6  A
W   St. Louis      38-21  A
W   Philadelphia   42-14  H
W   San Francisco  48-14  H
L   St. Louis      17-24  H
W   Dallas         34-27  A
W   Washington     44-14  H
W   Pittsburgh     33-17  H

      NFL Championship
L   Chicago        10-14  A
```

The Giants had a weapon that soon would be *de rigeur* for any team with championship hopes — the quick touchdown strike. With Y.A. tossing to the flying wide receiver, Del Shofner, on what were called fly patterns or "bombs," the Giants could strike for a big-play touchdown from as far away as their 10. Frank Gifford, Phil King and Joe Morrison ran mostly for short yardage behind an offensive line spearheaded by Rosey Brown and Jack Stroud. The defense, cemented by Sam Huff in the middle; Andy Robustelli, Dick Modzelewski and Jim Katcavage up front; and Dick Lynch and Jim Patton guarding the rear, allowed 22 or more points only three times in the Giants' last twelve games. After a 31-0 loss to the Steelers and a 1-1 start, the Giants won ten of twelve to win their fourth Eastern Conference title in five years.

Papa Bear Halas and his newest model of the Monsters of the Midway had won in the West. This latest clash between the two old rivals, who had met in the first championship game thirty years earlier, created a familiar question: Could a great defense stop a great offense? Y.A. had thrown 36 touchdown passes in the 1963 season; the Giants offense had scored 30 or more points in ten of its fourteen games. The Bear defense, coached by George Allen, had limited opponents to 17 or fewer points in twelve of its fourteen games.

Icicles hung from Wrigley Field rafters as a packed house of more than

45,000 shivered in eight-degree cold. The Giants got a break when the Bears, after driving to the Giant 17, fumbled and lost the ball. The Giants then marched 83 yards, scoring when Y.A. tossed a 14-yarder to Frank Gifford.

Another Bear fumble gave the Giants the ball on the Bear 31. Y.A. stepped back and saw his favorite receiver, Del Shofner, shoot ahead of a Bear defender. Tittle threw a perfect pass that Shofner caught in the end zone — but then dropped, his fingers numbed by the cold.

That break seemed to stiffen the confidence of the Bear defenders. Deep back Larry Morris grabbed a Tittle screen pass and scooted to the Giant 5. Quarterback Billy Wade sneaked over to tie the game, 7-7.

In the second period Don Chandler kicked a field goal from 13 yards out to put the Giants ahead at the half, 10-7. But in the third period, the Bears' Ed O'Bradovich snatched another Tittle screen pass and ran it to the New York 14. The Bears scored in three plays, Wade twisting over from the 1.

The Bears led for the first time, 14-10. Tittle had twisted his knee in the second period and had to leave the game. But Glynn Griffing, his backup, couldn't move the team, so Y.A. limped back into the game. He badly wanted the championship he had never won with the 49ers and the Giants. He knew this might well be his final season. But so far the Bears had picked off 4 of his passes. With ten seconds to go, the Giants got to the Bear 39. On the game's final play, Y.A. arched a long pass to Del Shofner cutting across the end zone. Richie Petibon leaped high to pull the ball away from Shofner.

Tittle jerked off his helmet and slammed it against the ground, anger and frustration plain on his bony face. That championship would never be his. This would be the last championship for Papa Bear, George Halas, who had won his first in 1921. The Bears would not win another championship for twenty-two years. The Giants would have to wait one year longer.

	— **1964** —		
	2-10-2		
	7th Eastern Conference		
	Allie Sherman		
L	Philadelphia	7-38	A
L	Pittsburgh	24-27	A
W	Washington	13-10	H
L	Detroit	3-26	A
T	Dallas	13-13	A
L	Philadelphia	17-23	H
L	Cleveland	20-42	A
W	St. Louis	34-17	H
L	Dallas	21-31	H
T	St. Louis	10-10	A
L	Pittsburgh	17-44	H
L	Washington	21-36	A
L	Minnesota	21-30	H
L	Cleveland	20-52	H

As this season began, the Giants owned a 33-8-1 record over the previous three championship seasons. But no one needed any great expertise to see that the players who had won those three straight Eastern titles were now sliding toward the exit door as athletes. Andy Robustelli, on defense, and Y.A. Tittle, on offense, told a story by reciting their ages — thirty-eight and thirty-seven — that the higher-ups at Mara Tech read too late.

Wellington Mara and Allie Sherman began to make moves that backfired in their faces. They traded Sam Huff, the most popular defensive player on the team, to Washington in the hope of getting younger players. While the average age of the team did decline, so did its talent. And the anger among fans over the loss of Huff began to be aimed at the guy on the field who had made the trade — Allie Sherman. When Sherman was introduced before games, boos mixed with cheers for the winningest (up to 1964) coach in Giant history.

Sherman and Wellington Mara were grooming Gary Wood, a rookie out of Cornell, to replace Y.A. But Wood stood only five-ten and often had to run to escape taller rushers. A huge rookie fullback, Ernie Wheelwright, was picked to be the lead horse on the ground. But while he gained 407 yards on 100 tries, Wheelwright needed blocking for long gainers, blocking that the Giants didn't have. Allie counted on establishing a running game, but his only other reliable back was thirty-three-year-old Alex Webster.

A shocking reminder to the Giants that they had grown old suddenly came early in the season. A pass rusher flattened Y.A. He arose on his knees, then keeled over. His helmet was taken off, exposing to the world his bald skull and fringe of gray hair. He could have been a grandfather suddenly hurt trying to play ball with his grandsons.

The defensive secondary of Dick Lynch, Jimmy Patton and Erich Barnes had also grown too old. Giant fans stared mournfully at scoreboards showing losses of 38-7, 42-20 and 44-17. Of the team's last six games, it lost five and tied the other.

And high in the upper tiers at Yankee Stadium came a chant that soon would become a demanding roar:

Good-bye Allie!, Good-bye Allie!

```
        — 1965 —
            7-7
    3rd Eastern Conference
        Allie Sherman

   L  Dallas        2-31   A
   W  Philadelphia  16-14  A
   W  Pittsburgh    23-13  A
   L  Minnesota     14-40  A
   W  Philadelphia  35-27  H
   L  Cleveland     14-38  H
   W  St. Louis     14-10  H
   L  Washington    7-23   H
   L  Cleveland     21-34  A
   W  St. Louis     28-15  A
   L  Chicago       14-35  H
   W  Pittsburgh    35-10  H
   W  Washington    27-10  A
   L  Dallas        20-38  H
```

Yelverton Abraham Tittle retired. Aware that Gary Wood would not be a second Y.A., the Giants got Earl Morrall from the Lions. And they trotted out what the press called the Baby Bulls — a quartet of rookie running backs: Tucker Frederickson, Steve Thurlow, Ernie Koy and Chuck Mercein.

Big (six-two and 220 pounds) and fast, Tucker Frederickson came to the Giants hailed as the next Jim Brown. An Auburn All-American, he was the first pick of the draft, the last-place Giants picking first. In camp the Giant veterans stared in awe at his bullish speed. "The first time I hit him," said Dick Lynch, "I thought I hit a truck."

Earl Morrall looked to some choice targets, notably a fleet flanker, Homer Jones, who caught 26 passes and ran them 709 yards, an average of 27 yards a catch. Joe Morrison caught 41 for 4 touchdowns, Aaron Thomas 27 for 5 scores. All told, Morrall threw 22 touchdown passes.

At times the defense looked porous, giving up 40 points to Minnesota and 31 to Dallas. But as Frederickson blew by tacklers, gaining 659 yards for the season, the Giants won three of their last five.

The finish surprised experts; they had thought the Giants dead after the team lost all five preseason games. Had the Giants turned around? Mara Tech thought so — it signed Allie Sherman to a ten-year contract.

```
┌─────────────────────────────────┐
│         — 1966 —                 │
│           1-12-1                 │
│    8th Eastern Conference        │
│        Allie Sherman             │
│                                  │
│   T  Pittsburgh      34-34   A   │
│   L  Dallas           7-52   A   │
│   L  Philadelphia    17-35   A   │
│   L  Cleveland        7-28   H   │
│   L  St. Louis       19-24   A   │
│   W  Washington      13-10   H   │
│   L  Philadelphia     3-31   H   │
│   L  St. Louis       17-20   H   │
│   L  Los Angeles     14-55   A   │
│   L  Atlanta         16-27   H   │
│   L  Washington      41-72   A   │
│   L  Cleveland       40-49   A   │
│   L  Pittsburgh      28-47   H   │
│   L  Dallas           7-17   H   │
└─────────────────────────────────┘
```

Earl Morrall broke his wrist and missed almost half the season. Tucker Frederickson banged up his knees. Surgeons dug into his knees, but never again would Tucker be hailed as the new Jim Brown. "I just couldn't do it anymore," he said years later.

What came after the losses of Morrall and Frederickson was the worst Giant season ever. Gary Wood threw to the whiz, Homer Jones, who caught 48 passes, 22 of them ending up in the end zone, tops in the league. A rookie defensive back, Spider Lockhart, pulled down 6 interceptions. But he couldn't hold back the avalanches as the Giants were buried by scores of 52-7, 55-14 and 72-41. The Giants' humiliation was completed when they finished in last place behind Atlanta, the expansion team's first year.

```
——— 1967 ———
               7-7
        2nd Century Division
           Allie Sherman

W   St. Louis        37-20   A
L   Dallas           24-38   A
L   Washington       34-38   A
W   New Orleans      27-21   H
W   Pittsburgh       27-24   A
L   Green Bay        21-48   H
W   Cleveland        38-34   H
L   Minnesota        24-27   A
L   Chicago           7-34   A
W   Pittsburgh       28-20   H
W   Philadelphia     44-7    H
L   Cleveland        14-24   A
L   Detroit           7-30   H
W   St. Louis        37-14   H
```

The Giants had a cross-town rival, the New York Jets. The Jets (originally the Titans) played in the American Football League, which began in 1960. Up to 1964 the Jets had played before thousands of empty seats in the Polo Grounds. Then a new owner, showman Sonny Werblin, signed a University of Alabama quarterback, Joe Namath, for $400,000 — an unheard-of sum in those days. Fans began to pour into the Jets' new home, Shea Stadium, to watch Broadway Joe. The Jets rose to second in their AFL division this season. Mara Tech had to worry once again about losing its place as Gotham's number-one football team.

The Giants bought scrambling quarterback Fran Tarkenton, a future Hall-of-Famer, from the Vikings. Wellington Mara, the Duke, now ran the team by himself, his brother Jack having died. Jack's 50 percent of the team went to his son, Tim. Tim would let uncle Wellington have his way — but not forever.

The Giants' offense was Fran Tarkenton. Although one of the Baby Bulls, Ernie Koy, averaged 4.8 yards a rush, the Giants scored 16 touchdowns rushing, 33 by passing. Fran threw to wide receiver Aaron Thomas and the deep threat, Homer Jones, who led the league with 13 TD catches.

An Olympic sprinter, Henry Carr, had joined Spider Lockhart in the secondary. But the defense was so threadbare that only once all season did it limit the opposition to fewer than 14 points. The Packers, rolling toward the first Super Bowl and a victory over the AFL's Oakland Raiders, feasted on that defense, walloping the Giants, 48-21.

One solace: soccer-style kicker Pete Gogolak, "who kicks funny," said Giant fans. Wellington Mara had lured him away from the AFL's Buffalo Bills. He put 6 of 10 tries through the uprights and became the NFL's first sidewinder, a breed that would soon make almost extinct the straight-ahead kicker.

The NFL now had 16 teams. The league split into two conferences— Eastern and Western. Each conference had two divisions. The Giants joined the Eastern Conference's Century Division and finished two games shy of catching the Browns for the division title.

But second place, as Allie Sherman was about to discover, was not good enough for all those ticket holders chanting, "Goodbye, Allie!" Taking his children to school one morning, Wellington Mara heard schoolboys throw the chant at his kids—and winced.

— 1968 —
7-7
2nd Capitol Division
Allie Sherman

W	Pittsburgh	34-20	A
W	Philadelphia	34-25	A
W	Washington	48-21	H
W	New Orleans	38-21	H
L	Atlanta	21-24	A
L	San Francisco	10-26	H
W	Washington	13-10	A
L	Baltimore	0-26	H
W	Dallas	27-21	A
W	Philadelphia	7-6	A
L	Los Angeles	21-24	A
L	Cleveland	10-45	A
L	St. Louis	21-28	H
L	Dallas	10-28	H

The Giants were switched from the Eastern Conference Century Division to the Capitol, whose best was Tom Landry's Dallas Cowboys. The Giants beat Dallas, 27-21, in Dallas, but lost to Dallas, 28-10, in New York. For the second straight season, the Giants finished in second place.

A rookie runner, Bobby Duhon, ranked third in the league in rushing, but the Giants needed Fran Tarkenton's strong right arm to score. He threw to Homer Jones for 7 touchdowns and to Joe Morrison for 6. On defense, Spider Lockhart picked off 8 interceptions, and newcomer Willie Williams snatched 10.

The team won its first four, then stumbled through its next six by winning only three. It finished with a four-game losing streak. The chanting grew loud enough to sound like a lynch mob's roar:

Good-bye, Allie, Good-bye Allie!

	— 1969 — 6-8 2nd Century Division Alex Webster		
W	Minnesota	24-23	H
L	Detroit	0-24	A
W	Chicago	28-24	H
W	Pittsburgh	10-7	H
L	Washington	14-20	A
L	Dallas	3-25	A
L	Philadelphia	20-23	H
L	St. Louis	17-42	A
L	New Orleans	24-25	H
L	Cleveland	17-28	A
L	Green Bay	10-20	A
W	St. Louis	49-6	H
W	Pittsburgh	21-17	A
W	Cleveland	27-14	H

The Jets, fresh from their triumph in the Super Bowl in January, knocked over the Giants, 37-14, in a preseason game. That was all the Maras could take: They said goodbye to Allie.

Hired as head coach was the Giants now-retired running back, Alex Webster. Big Red, as Giant fans called him, had no head coaching experience. Alex let the Giants' offense go on doing what it had been doing so well—Fran Tarkenton throwing to Homer Jones and Joe Morrison. Tarkenton threw 23 touchdown passes while the Giant rushers dived into end zones only nine times. The Giants still lived or died with Tarkenton.

Ernie Koy and Tucker Frederickson were hobbled by injuries. The Giants got Junior Coffey from the Falcons. He earned his pay, rushing 131 times for 511 yards, but he seldom broke away on long runs—the threat the Giants needed to keep defenses honest as defenders spread wide to swallow Tarkenton passes.

— 1970 —
9-5
2nd NFC Eastern Division
Alex Webster

L	Chicago	16-24	H
L	Dallas	10-28	A
L	New Orleans	10-14	A
W	Philadelphia	30-23	H
W	Boston	16-0	A
W	St. Louis	35-17	H
W	New York Jets	22-10	A
W	Dallas	23-20	H
W	Washington	35-33	H
L	Philadelphia	20-23	A
W	Washington	27-24	A
W	Buffalo	20-6	H
W	St. Louis	34-17	A
L	Los Angeles	3-31	H

The ten-year-old American Football League vanished into the history books. The ten AFL teams, along with Pittsburgh, Baltimore and Cleveland from the NFL, formed the new American Football Conference of the merged NFL. The Giants joined the Eastern Division of the new National Football Conference.

In one of Wellington Mara's best moves since he acquired Y.A. Tittle and Del Shofner almost ten years earlier, he traded away the erratic flanker, Homer Jones, who had scored only once in 1969, to Cleveland for running back Ron Johnson. Ron reminded people of perhaps the greatest breakaway runner of his day, Gale Sayers. In his first season in scarlet and blue, the six-one, two-hundred-pounder sped for 1,027 yards, becoming the first Giant to go over a thousand.

Fran Tarkenton used a lot of play-action passes, freezing defenses that had to watch Johnson. No rushers clinging to his neck, Tarkenton completed 56 percent of his passes as he threw to Clifton McNeil (50 catches), Johnson (48), Tucker Frederickson (40) and Bob Tucker (40). Pete Gogolak, the soccer-style kicker, convinced doubters that the sidewinder kick was here to stay by making 25 of 41 attempts.

The Giants needed a win in their last game, against the Rams, to stay even with Dallas in the NFC's Eastern Conference. The Rams blew them out, 31-3. "We had a sprinkling of great individuals," Ron Johnson later said, "Tarkenton, Spider Lockhart, Clifton McNeil—but we weren't really that deep in talent. The record surprised all of us."

There would be fewer and fewer such pleasant surprises in the decade that had just begun.

— 1971 —
4-10
5th NFC Eastern Division
Alex Webster

W	Green Bay	42-40	A
L	Washington	3-30	H
W	St. Louis	21-20	A
L	Dallas	13-20	A
L	Baltimore	7-31	H
L	Philadelphia	7-23	A
L	Minnesota	10-17	H
W	San Diego	35-17	H
W	Atlanta	21-17	A
L	Pittsburgh	13-17	A
L	St. Louis	7-24	H
L	Washington	7-23	A
L	Dallas	14-42	H
L	Philadelphia	28-41	H

Ten years earlier the Giants boasted the league's best defense. Now it had the worst. Typical games were the opener, a 42-40 victory over Green Bay, and the finale, a 41-28 loss to Philadelphia. The Giant defense gave up 21 or more points in eight of the season's fourteen games.

Tarkenton had little choice except to pass—rather than run—for touchdowns. Bobby Duhon, his best runner, carried the ball behind a line nearly always overmatched; Bobby gained only 344 yards.

Fran's number-one target was end Bob Tucker, who caught 59 passes to lead the league, 13 of them good for touchdowns. Wide receiver Don Herrmann caught 27, and four others caught 20 or more.

The Giants had a powerful bombing attack—but no air-raid shelter when the other side bombed.

```
            — 1972 —
                8-6
     3rd NFC Eastern Division
          Alex Webster

   L   Detroit         16-30   A
   L   Dallas          14-23   H
   W   Philadelphia    27-12   A
   W   New Orleans     45-21   H
   W   San Francisco   23-17   A
   W   St. Louis       27-21   H
   L   Washington      16-23   H
   W   Denver          29-17   H
   L   Washington      13-27   A
   W   St. Louis       13-7    A
   W   Philadelphia    62-10   H
   L   Cincinnati      10-13   A
   L   Miami           13-23   H
   W   Dallas          23-3    H
```

Fran Tarkenton was gone, traded to the Falcons. But the Giants were still a rushing team second, a passing team first. The thrower was veteran Norm Snead, obtained from the Vikings. More than one observer noted that the Giants had not drafted for a successful quarterback since before World War II. (Filchock and Conerly came from Washington, Tittle from San Francisco, Tarkenton from Minnesota.)

In 1972 the Giants established a running game to bring up linebackers and leave working room for the receivers. Ron Johnson, the running sensation of 1970, had been hobbled by bad knees, but he came back this season to finish second in NFL rushing, averaging 4 yards a try. Snead connected on 3 of every 5 passes and led the league with 17 touchdowns. Tight end Bob Tucker grabbed 55 passes and Johnson caught 45. When Johnson or Snead ran or passed the Giants within field goal range, Pete Gogolak could usually get three points, kicking 21 field goals in 31 tries.

The defensive line had been fortified by the arrivals of two highly praised rookies: defensive tackles John Mendenhall and Larry Jacobson, who had won the Outland Trophy. Soon both were starting. Old reliable Spider Lockhart pulled down 4 interceptions, tying for best in the NFC.

The Giants lost their first two games, 30-16 and 23-14. But then the defense firmed, and the Giants won seven of their next nine, including a 62-10 pasting of the Eagles and a 23-3 whipping of the Cowboys.

"In 1973," Alex Webster said, "we need a stronger pass rush to cut down the number of TD passes thrown against us."

Alex, if only it could have been that easy.

2-11-1
4th NFC Eastern Division
Alex Webster

W	Houston	34-14	H
T	Philadelphia	23-23	H
L	Cleveland	10-12	A
L	Green Bay	14-16	H
L	Washington	3-21	H
L	Dallas	28-45	A
L	St. Louis	27-35	A
L	Oakland	0-42	A
L	Dallas	10-23	H
W	St. Louis	24-13	H
L	Philadelphia	16-20	A
L	Washington	24-27	A
L	Los Angeles	6-40	A
L	Minnesota	7-31	H

Alex Webster had sought: 1) a running attack to match his aerial attack; 2) a pass defense. After the season's opener at Yankee Stadium, he seemed to have attained his goals. The Giants beat the Oilers, 34-14, as the defense picked off 4 passes by Dan Pastorini; the runners, Ron Johnson and Vin Clemens, gained almost 200 yards. Norm Snead, facing an honest defense, completed 17 passes.

The rest of the season's news was grim. The next week the Giants played what would be their last game at Yankee Stadium for a while, a 23-23 tie with the Eagles. The city of New York shut down the Stadium for a restructuring job. Mayor John Lindsay and Wellington Mara barked at each other when word came from Mara Tech that the Giants would jump across the Hudson to New Jersey where a new stadium was being built.

The Giants were grateful when offered a temporary home in the Yale Bowl in New Haven, seventy-seven miles from New York. There they lost four of their final five "home" games.

The Giants, along the way, suffered through a seven-game losing streak, including a 42-0 disaster to Oakland, the most lopsided defeat in Giant history. Injuries to Ron Johnson slowed the offense; and injury to front-line bulwark John Mendenhall opened holes in the defense. The Giants averaged only 12 points a game in their final seven games. The defense gave up 21 or more points in nine of their fourteen games.

In the glare of the spotlight from the media stood Wellington Mara. The Duke had to answer critics pointing to a long line of high draft choices who had flopped. They included running back Rocky Thompson, defensive tackle Rich Glover, linebacker Jim Files and tackle Francis Peay.

Alex Webster quit after a 40-6 loss to Los Angeles, the next-to-last game of the season. The Giants ended the season by being blasted off the field in the Yale Bowl, 31-7, by the Super Bowl-bound Vikings. Never had the Giants gone more than ten years without winning a divisional title. But the Giants, alas, were only halfway through a 20-year nightmare.

```
                — 1974 —
                   2-12
         5th NFC Eastern Division
               Bill Arnsparger

    L   Washington        10-13   H
    L   New England       20-28   H
    W   Dallas             14-6   A
    L   Atlanta             7-14  H
    L   Philadelphia        7-35  A
    L   Washington          3-24  A
    L   Dallas              7-21  H
    W   Kansas City        33-27  A
    L   New York Jets      20-26* H
    L   Detroit            19-20  A
    L   St. Louis          21-23  H
    L   Chicago            13-16  A
    L   Philadelphia        7-20  H
    L   St. Louis          14-26  A

    *Overtime
```

"The Pope" had returned. The champion Giants of the early 1960s had dubbed Andy Robustelli the Pope because he was their spiritual leader both on and off the field. At the behest of a beleaguered Wellington Mara, assailed for his failed draft choices, Andy returned to the Giants as director of operations. He would oversee drafts, trades and the picking of a new head coach. He picked Bill Arnsparger, acclaimed as the defensive genius who had molded Miami's No-Name Defense. That unit had spearheaded the Dolphins' drive to two straight Super Bowl triumphs.

While Robustelli looked for talent in the colleges, Arnsparger began to try to build a New-Name Defense in New York. He had a promising linebacker, Brad Van Pelt, a Michigan All-American and the Giants' number-one pick of 1973, along with John Mendenhall up front and Spider Lockhart in the secondary.

Arnsparger started the season with Norm Snead at quarterback. But after the offense looked dull in a 14-7 loss to the Falcons, he brought in young Jim DelGaizo. Ron Johnson, spelled by young Doug Kotar and veteran Joe Dawkins, were the runners.

The Yale Bowl jinx continued to haunt the Giants. They lost all seven of their home games in the Bowl, including their first regular-season overtime game, a 26-20 defeat inflicted by Joe Namath and his Jets.

Pete Gogolak kicked field goals, young Dave Jennings punted tall and long. But Ron Johnson went down with an injury and the Giants' best rusher, Joe Dawkins, could gain only 561 yards. Giving up on DelGaizo and Snead, the Giants got ex-Cowboy Craig Morton. In his first start, he threw a 51-yard strike to Joe Dawkins for a 33-27 triumph over Kansas City. Tight end Bob Tucker and wideout Don Herrmann were two of the pass catchers. But it was a measure of the Giants' stunted passing attack that the catching leader was back Joe Dawkins, who led the team with 46 catches of dinks.

The Giants said a farewell to their luckless home field, the Yale Bowl, losing 20-7 to the Eagles in a downpour in front of 30,000 empty seats. Only 18,000 or so came to see the curtain fall on another Giant tragedy or farce, depending on your point of view.

The Giants lost their last six games. But help, promised Robustelli, would soon be coming from future college draft choices and a horde of free agents he would bring to the 1975 preseason camp. Leading the alphabetical list of rookies would be Mike Ajello, a linebacker from Fordham. If that name didn't make you sit up and take notice, how would you have reacted to the name George Martin? A defensive end out of the University of Oregon, he was drafted eleventh, a member of nobody's All-America team.

— 1975 —
5-9
4th NFC Eastern Division
Bill Arnsparger

W	Philadelphia	23-14	A
L	Washington	13-49	A
L	St. Louis	14-26	A
L	Dallas	7-13	H
W	Buffalo	17-14	A
L	St. Louis	13-20	H
W	San Diego	35-24	H
L	Washington	13-21	H
L	Philadelphia	10-13	H
L	Green Bay	14-40	A
L	Dallas	3-14	A
L	Baltimore	0-21	H
W	New Orleans	28-14	H
W	San Francisco	26-23	H

The Giants returned to New York after a two-year stay in New Haven, playing at Shea Stadium. They came back to town to meet the Cowboys after two on-the-road wallopings from Washington (49-13) and St. Louis (26-14), their offensive line weakened by injuries. The defense, fortified by two fiery youngsters, linebacker Brad Van Pelt and rookie defensive end George Martin, gave the Cowboys' Roger Staubach fits. He completed only 8 of 22. But Craig Morton threw an interception that turned into a Cowboy touchdown, their only one of the day, and the Cowboys' 13-6 triumph spoiled the homecoming.

The Giants had no rushing offense. Joe Dawkins led the team with a measly 438 yards. Craig Morton zeroed in on newcomer Walker Gillette, a fleet wideout, and tight end Bob Tucker. Craig threw 363 passes, completing 186; Walker Gillette caught 43 to lead the team.

Fumbles, mistakes and plain ineptitude caused a five-game losing streak in which the Giants scored a grand total of 40 points, an average of 8 per game. "We would go into the fourth period, wondering what was going to happen to make us lose this one," Brad Van Pelt said years later. "We didn't wonder whether we would win."

"It just wasn't fun any more," said Ron Johnson of that season. "The hurting part of that period was that it just seemed we didn't get any help in the draft. Rocky Thompson, Rich Glover, we just didn't seem to get the talent to sustain a winning tradition. It was frustrating."

And it would get worse.

— 1976 —
3-11
5th NFC Eastern Division
Bill Arnsparger (0-7)
John McVay (3-4)

L	Washington	17-19	A
L	Philadelphia	7-20	A
L	Los Angeles	10-24	A
L	St. Louis	21-27	A
L	Dallas	14-24	H
L	Minnesota	7-24	A
L	Pittsburgh	0-27	H
L	Philadelphia	0-10	H
L	Dallas	3-9	A
W	Washington	12-9	H
L	Denver	13-14	A
W	Seattle	28-16	H
W	Detroit	24-10	H
L	St. Louis	14-17	H

As workmen polished the shiny, spectacular new Giants Stadium in the Meadowlands, the Giants opened the season with four away games. In the opener, Washington beat them, 19-17, on a Billy Kilmer pass with forty-five seconds to play.

A rookie linebacker, Harry Carson (out of South Carolina State), made the team to join end George Martin, linebacker Brad Van Pelt and tackle John Mendenhall, giving the Giants a respectable up-front defense. The secondary, however, was picked apart by the Eagles, Rams and Cardinals. The Giants came to Giants Stadium for their first game ever in New Jersey licking their wounds, their record 0-4.

"Every year we'd draft defense, defense, defense," Mendenhall said years later. "But defense wasn't the problem. We needed talent on offense."

Desperate for a big runner, Bill Arnsparger and the Pope, Andy Robustelli, got the bearish but slowing Larry Csonka, once a thousand-yard rusher, from Miami. But stumpy Doug Kotar led the team with 731 yards. Craig Morton threw mostly to tight end Bob Tucker and wideout Walker Gillette, but in the first four games the Giants could score only 55 points, an average of about 14 a game.

That was exactly the number the Giants scored in their opener at the new stadium. The Cowboys built a 17-0 halftime lead. The Giants scored in the third period on a 30-yard pass play, Craig Morton to wideout Jimmy Robinson. Norm Snead came in to steer a 74-yard drive, Larry Csonka smashing over from the 6 for the Giants' last score of the day in a 24-14 loss. The huge crowd of 76,042 went away disappointed.

Then came four more losses to Minnesota, Pittsburgh, Philadelphia and Dallas. The defense gave up only 19 points in two of those losses, but in those eight quarters the Giant offense racked up a total of three points. Over five straight losses the Giants' offense could muster only 24 points.

The seventh straight loss, a 9-3 defeat in Dallas, cost Arnsparger his job. John McVay, a former head coach in the disbanded World Football League and now a Giant assistant, took over. The Giants came home to the Meadowlands to play the Redskins. Late in the game the score was tied 9-9, the Giants' three field goals kicked by Joe Danelo, who had joined the team in 1975 out of Washington State.

One Danelo field goal came after end George Martin recovered a fumble. The third came after linebacker Harry Carson pounced on another fumble. The stocky Danelo then rammed home a fourth, a 50-yard field goal for a 12-9 victory, the Giants' first at Giants Stadium. Under McVay the Giants seemed to straighten to even keel, winning two of their last four.

The Giants offense had scored 27 or more points only once all season. By contrast, the defense had yielded only 85 points in its last seven games — an average of 12 points a game. Whom did the Giants draft first? A defensive tackle, of course, but he would prove good enough to start — Gary Jeter. Robustelli and McVay also drafted for offense, taking wide receiver Johnny Perkins and quarterback Randy Dean, but for a while to come, the Giants' best offense would be their defense.

— 1977 —
5-9
4th NFC Eastern Division
John McVay

W	Washington	20-17	H
L	Dallas	21-41	A
L	Atlanta	3-17	A
L	Philadelphia	10-28	H
W	San Francisco	20-17	H
W	Washington	17-6	A
L	St. Louis	0-28	A
L	Dallas	10-24	H
W	Tampa Bay	10-0	A
L	Cleveland	7-21	H
L	Cincinnati	13-30	A
W	St. Louis	27-7	H
L	Philadelphia	14-17	A
L	Chicago	9-12*	H

*Overtime

Great teams often first show their coming dominance with a knockout defense. The Giants showed that defense in the 1977 opener against the Redskins. A record crowd of 76,086 filled the stadium. Early in the game defensive end George Martin leaped high to pull down a Billy Kilmer screen pass. Martin dashed 30 yards for a touchdown and a 7-0 lead. For the rest of the half the Giant defense stalled the Redskin attack, and at the half the score was still Giants 7, Washington 0.

The Redskins exploded in the fourth period to go ahead, 17-10. Giant quarterback Jerry Golsteyn hit Ed Marshall on a 47-yard pass play that tied the game, 17-17. With less than two minutes to play, middle linebacker Harry Carson dived on a Redskin fumble at the Redskin 19. Joe Danelo kicked a 30-yard field goal for a 20-17 victory.

But the Giant offense, its three young quarterbacks, Golsteyn, Joe Pisarcik and Randy Dean, trying to win the number-one job, lacked the runner to tie up defenses. Larry Csonka was near the end of the road. Young Bob Hammond, with only 577 yards in 154 tries, led the rushers. That offense was so insipid that Jimmy Robinson, with 22 catches, led the receivers. During a stretch of five games, the Giants scored only 27 points. The season high was 27 against St. Louis. In only four games did the Giants score 20 or more.

The Giant defense rated among the league's best. It gave up only 36 points in the last three games (two of them losses). In the season's finale, a 12-9 loss in overtime to the Bears, it held Walter Payton, on his way to NFL rushing records, to 47 yards in 15 carries.

```
┌─────────────────────────────────────┐
│            — 1978 —                  │
│               6-10                   │
│      5th NFC Eastern Division        │
│            John McVay                │
│                                      │
│   W  Tampa Bay      19-13   A        │
│   L  Dallas         24-34   H        │
│   W  Kansas City    26-10   H        │
│   W  San Francisco  27-10   H        │
│   L  Atlanta        20-23   A        │
│   L  Dallas          3-24   A        │
│   W  Tampa Bay      17-14   H        │
│   W  Washington      17-6   H        │
│   L  New Orleans    17-28   A        │
│   L  St. Louis      10-20   A        │
│   L  Washington     13-16*  A        │
│   L  Philadelphia   17-19   H        │
│   L  Buffalo        17-41   A        │
│   L  Los Angeles    17-20   H        │
│   W  St. Louis       17-0   H        │
│   L  Philadelphia    3-20   A        │
│                                      │
│   *Overtime                          │
└─────────────────────────────────────┘
```

The Pope's reign had come to an end. Before the start of the season, Andy Robustelli told Wellington Mara that he would resign at season's end as director of operations. His family, he said, wanted him to return to the family's travel business in New Haven. So far the Robustelli Era had hardly been a roaring success. Since 1974, when Andy took the reins, the Giants had won 15 and lost 41.

And the worst defeat was yet to come.

Robustelli tried to knit together an offensive line that could clear the way for the breakaway runner the Giants didn't have. He had signed free agent guard Brad Benson in 1977, and his number-one pick in the 1978 draft was another offensive lineman—Stanford's All-American, Gordon King.

John McVay picked Joe Pisarcik to open the season at quarterback. Larry Csonka, in his last season, started at running back along with Doug Kotar, who would lead the team with 625 yards. Pisarcik threw to a flock of young and fast receivers, notably Johnny Perkins and Jimmy Robinson, who each caught 32 to lead the team.

Helped by three interceptions, the Giants knocked over Tampa Bay, 19-13, to open the season. The Giants won three of their first four, the offense rolling up 382 total yards in subjugating the 49ers, 27-10. But then that offensive yardage began to shrink; only once during the rest of the season would the Giants score more than 17 points in a game.

The defense kept the Giants in most games, including a 16-13 overtime loss to Washington that put the Giants record at 5-6.

Then the Eagles came to Giants Stadium. On Sunday, November 19, the 70,318 spectators saw one of the most bizarre finishes in football history — the finish variously described as The Fumble, The Play and The Dumbest Thing You Ever Heard Of.

The Giants led, 17-12. There were 31 seconds to play, and the Eagles had used up all their timeouts. The ball sat on the Giant 26. The Giant players expected Pisarcik to kneel and let the clock run out. Instead an assistant coach sent in a play calling for Pisarcik to hand off the ball to Csonka.

"Somebody in the huddle said, 'Let's just fall on it,'" Joe remembered some eight years later. Other players said they agreed. But Pisarcik cut them off. "Let's do what the coaches want," he told the Giants. "Let's run the play and go home."

Pisarcik took the snap, turned and handed the ball to Csonka. The ball hit Csonka's hip, popped into the air and bounced onto the turf. It rebounded up into the outstretched hands of a charging Eagle lineman. He hugged the ball to his chest and ran 26 yards for the winning touchdown.

That night in hundreds of thousands of homes, Giant fans stared, stunned, asking over and over, "But why didn't they..."

Anger smoldered in the chests of season ticket holders. A Giant fan came to the stadium parking lot and burned about a hundred tickets for the next game. "We're not gonna take it anymore!" he cried as the tickets blazed and another season turned as black as the ashes. The Giants lost three of their remaining four games. Banners floated in Giants Stadium: "Ten years of lousy football — we've had enough."

Robustelli left. The Duke still believed the Pope had turned the team around. His nephew, Tim, did not agree. For the first time, although they had bickered for several years, Tim challenged the Duke's authority to run the team. The Giants had two masters. Each wanted to steer the Giants down his road. The Giant, pulled one way and the other, stood paralyzed.

```
—1979—
6-10
4th NFC Eastern Division
Ray Perkins

L   Philadelphia      17-23   A
L   St. Louis         14-27   H
L   Washington         0-27   A
L   Philadelphia      13-17   H
L   New Orleans       14-24   A
W   Tampa Bay         17-14   H
W   San Francisco     32-16   H
W   Kansas City       21-17   A
W   Los Angeles       20-14   A
L   Dallas            14-16   H
W   Atlanta            24-3   H
L   Tampa Bay          3-31   A
W   Washington         14-6   H
L   Dallas             7-28   A
L   St. Louis         20-29   A
L   Baltimore          7-31   H
```

Uncle and nephew would not budge. Each owned 50 percent of the shares of the team, so neither Mara could outvote the other. But each could stop the other from making a major decision like the naming of a new general manager to succeed Andy Robustelli.

Pete Rozelle, the NFL commissioner who owed his job to Wellington Mara's intercession two decades earlier, stepped into the gap between Uncle Wellington and nephew Tim. The Maras agreed he could find someone acceptable to both. Rozelle came back with the name George Young, and both Maras said yes.

George Young? An unknown to New York fans, he was a former high school teacher and coach who had worked for Don Shula at Baltimore and Miami as an assistant coach and personnel director. George Young, the warring Maras agreed, could oversee the picking of a new coach, the drafting of players and the trading for players.

Young picked Ray Perkins as the coach. Perkins had the steely-eyed look of a gunfighter. A former NFL pass-catcher, Perkins had been an assistant coach with the Patriots and Chargers. To Giants fans, they now had a Ray Who? to go with a George Who?

As their number-one draft choice Young and Perkins picked a little-known passer from a little-known school—Phil Simms out of Morehead State in

Kentucky. When the Giants announced that Simms was their number-one choice, fans booed. Phil Who?

Ray Perkins's icy stares chilled the Giant clubhouse. "It was a country club before he came," one Giant said. "It became a place full of tension whenever he walked in."

Perkins stayed with Pisarcik at quarterback. Newcomer Billy Taylor and veteran Doug Kotar were the running backs, Johnny Perkins and rookie Earnest Gray the pass-catchers. Phil Simms watched from the sideline as the offense slipsided its way through five straight defeats. Total point production in those games: 58.

In the season's sixth game, against Tampa Bay at home, Perkins started Phil Simms, who had made his debut a week earlier by replacing Pisarcik and throwing 8 completions in 19 attempts for 115 yards. Billy Taylor also made his first start at halfback. Taylor plunged over for two touchdowns in the second period, and the Giants hung on to win their first game of the season, 17-14. The game-winner was a 47-yard Joe Danelo field goal. Simms had passed sparingly — 6 hits in 12 tries for 37 yards. But Taylor's 148 yards were the most for a Giant runner since 1967.

Simms had a sensational afternoon the next week, hitting 17 or 32, his favorite target fellow-rookie Earnest Gray, and the Giants buried the 49ers, 32-16. Simms racked up 300 yards, the most for a Giant passer since 1973. The Giant defense stopped the legendary O.J. Simpson; he gained only 24 yards on 12 carries.

The Giants won four of their next six. But fumbles, interceptions and other mistakes by Simms and his youthful offense put pressure on the defense, and the Giants lost their last three games. In that stretch of five games, the offense scored only 51 points. Giant fans had to wonder if Simms was as good as he, at times, had seemed.

Billy Taylor gained 700 yards that year, more than any Giant back (except Doug Kotar in 1978) since 1973. Simms threw 13 touchdown passes in two-thirds of a season, the most by any Giant since 1972.

Could Phil Simms bring the offense up to the level of the defense? There soon would be good reasons to answer with a resounding "No!"

```
     — 1980—
         4-12
5th NFC Eastern Division
      Ray Perkins

W  St. Louis        41-35  A
L  Washington       21-23  H
L  Philadelphia      3-35  A
L  Los Angeles       7-28  H
L  Dallas            3-24  A
L  Philadelphia     16-31  H
L  San Diego         7-44  A
L  Denver            9-14  H
L  Tampa Bay        13-30  A
W  Dallas           38-35  H
W  Green Bay        27-21  H
L  San Francisco     0-12  A
L  St. Louis         7-23  H
W  Seattle          27-21  A
L  Washington       13-16  A
L  Oakland          17-33  H
```

This was the year in which the Giants, specifically Ray Perkins but later Bill Parcells, began to have doubts about Phil Simms.

Fourth-year man Billy Taylor was the number-one runner, Doug Kotar the halfback. In the opener against the Cardinals, however, Ray Perkins showed where he seemed to have the most of his confidence offensively — in the passing of Phil Simms. Phil completed 16 of 31 for 280 yards, throwing five touchdown passes, four of them to Earnest Gray, a Giant record for TD catches in a single game. But the game was won not by passing; two field goals by Joe Danelo proved the winning margin in the 41-35 victory.

At home the next week, the Giants held a 21-20 lead against Washington with two minutes to play, but lost 23-21. Simms — and the offense — sagged visibly in a 35-3 loss to Philadelphia. When the offense couldn't score a point for three periods against the Rams, Perkins lost patience with Simms and injected rookie Scott Brunner into the game. Scott got the Giants' lone touchdown with a 19-yard pass to Johnny Perkins, but the Giants had lost their third straight, 28-7.

The Giants were locked onto a losing track that would stretch through eight straight games. In seven of those games, the offense could score only 58 points, not quite 9 a game. A desperate Ray Perkins tried Simms, then Brunner, and usually both. In one game the Giants' best rusher gained only 33 yards, in another only 48.

The defensive picture looked just as dark. During that losing streak the

Giants gave up 30 or more points in four of the eight games. The loss of middle linebacker Harry Carson, out with an injury the last half of the season, left a hole in the middle that rookie Joe McLaughlin tried to fill. It may have been around this time that Perkins and Young decided that their number-one draft choice should be that terror down in North Carolina, Lawrence Taylor.

The Giants, now 1-8, finally won by upsetting the 7-2 Cowboys at home, 38-35. The inconsistent Simms had a sparkler, completing 18 of 33 and throwing for three touchdowns. His 40-yard pass on a flea flicker to rookie Mike Friede set up the 27-yard Joe Danelo field goal that won the game.

The Giants beat Green Bay the next week, 27-21, as Simms passed for 300 yards, the most by a Giant since 1961 and Y.A. Tittle. But Simms could put the Giants on the scoreboard only once in the next two games, then he was hurt. Scott Brunner took over but looked just what he was, a rookie, and the Giants finished a miserable season by losing four of their last five.

Simms had completed fewer than 50 percent of his passes. Billy Taylor, the top runner, gained only 580 yards. Now an eight-year veteran, Brad Van Pelt talked openly about wanting to leave a team that seemed to be painted with a color no one could wash off after almost twenty years. If that color had a name, you would call it loser's blue.

— 1981—
9-7**
3rd NFC Eastern Division
Ray Perkins

L	Philadelphia	10-24	H
W	Washington	17-7	A
W	New Orleans	20-7	H
L	Dallas	10-18	A
L	Green Bay	14-27	H
W	St. Louis	34-14	H
W	Seattle	32-0	A
W	Atlanta	27-24*	A
L	New York Jets	7-26	H
L	Green Bay	24-26	A
L	Washington	27-30*	H
W	Philadelphia	20-10	A
L	San Francisco	10-17	A
W	Los Angeles	10-7	H
W	St. Louis	20-10	A
W	Dallas	13-10*	H

*Overtime
**Wild Card Finish

PLAYOFFS

W	Philadelphia	27-21	A
L	San Francisco	24-38	A

While Ray Perkins mulled over who should be his starting quarterback, Phil Simms or Scott Brunner, he came quickly to another decision: his slumping defense had to improve. The Giants had slid to twenty-fifth in overall defense in 1980. Perkins hired a new defensive coordinator who had been a Giant assistant in 1979 before going into private business. His name was Bill Parcells.

Perkins told the bulky, square-faced Parcells to change the Giant defense from a 4-3 to a 3-4. Right from the start of preseason camp, Parcells knew who one of those four linebackers would be—the six-foot-three, 240-pound rookie out of North Carolina, the Giants' number-one draft choice, Lawrence Taylor. In his first camp scrimmage, Taylor sacked the quarterback four times and recovered one fumble.

Parcells put Taylor on the outside of the linebackers. Brian Kelley, a veteran, stood on the other side. Harry Carson and Brad Van Pelt roamed the middle, with another rookie, Byron Hunt from SMU, a backup.

Up front Parcells had veterans Gary Jeter, one of the few number-one Giant draft choices to succeed, and George Martin at the ends. Bill Neill crouched in the middle as the nose guard. His backup was a rookie free agent, Jim Burt out of Miami.

Parcells shook up the secondary. He put Terry Jackson and Mark Haynes at the corners; Beasley Reece and Bill Currier were the safeties.

Perkins had to be happy about his kicking. Dave Jennings had become an artist at dropping punts into coffin corners. Joe Danelo had proved to be reliable kicking field goals; his 55-yarder later this season would be a Giants record.

Perkins frowned when he talked about his offense. Neither Billy Taylor nor Doug Kotar could flash for the long gain or quick touchdown. Neither Simms nor Brunner looked impressive in preseason. Tight end Gary Shirk and wide receivers Johnny Perkins and Earnest Gray had the good hands and acceptable speed. Ernie Hughes centered the line with Brad Benson, a Giant since 1977, at one tackle post and Gordon King, last year's number-one draft pick, on the other side. Rookie Billy Ard would take over at guard with Jeff Weston and Roy Simmons sharing work on the other side. But this line, Perkins knew, did not open holes for runners. Nor did it give his two young quarterbacks the time young passers need to see what defenses were doing. Offensive lines always need more time to mature than defensive units; but this unit would need not only time, it would need new faces.

Predictably enough, the defense looked promising in the first two games, while the offense chugged along like a flivver needing new spark plugs. The Giants split those two games, then blasted the Saints, 21-7, as the offense piled up 421 yards and Phil Simms, after two so-so games, hit on 21 of 28 attempts. Tight end Gary Shirk tied a club record with 11 catches.

But the Giants had no running game. Doug Kotar had gained only 76 yards in two games—and he led the team both times. Early in the season Perkins got big Rob Carpenter from the Oilers, and in his first game, against the Cardinals, he broke loose for 104 yards, the first time a Giant runner had gained more than 100 this season.

In mid-November the Giants lost Phil Simms for the year, his throwing shoulder separated. Scott Brunner stepped in but threw too many interceptions. Carpenter continued to pound out 100-yard days. The Giants, with a 6-7 record, needed to win all three remaining games to grab a wild-card playoff berth.

The Giants' fast-improving defense, which would allow only one 100-yard rushing day all season, dug in. It gave up only 27 points in those final three games. Scott Brunner and the offense didn't blow away any teams, but three straight wins — a 10-7 victory over the Rams, a 20-10 victory over St. Louis and a nail-biting 13-10 overtime victory over Dallas at Giants Stadium — put the Giants in their first playoff game since 1963. The offensive hero was Joe Danelo with his game-winner against the Rams and two field goals against Dallas. One was a 40-yarder into the wind with thirty seconds left in regulation, the second a 35-yarder for the win in overtime.

As a wild-card team, the Giants journeyed to Philadelphia to face the defending NFC champions. The Giants jumped out to a 20-0 lead in the first period, two of the three touchdowns coming on short passes by Brunner, the third on a fumble recovery by Mark Haynes in the Eagle end zone.

The Giants led 27-7 at the half, the fourth TD a 27-yard pass from Brunner to tight end Tom Mullady. The Eagles stormed back to score two touchdowns and come within one of winning. But the Giants ran out the clock.

Brunner had passed sparingly (9 or 14 for 96 yards, 3 for touchdowns). Carpenter had gained 161 yards, while the defense, recovering two fumbles, had scored one touchdown and set up another.

The Giants went to San Francisco minus the injured Beasley Reece. Joe Montana picked at the Reeceless secondary. The 49ers went ahead, 7-0, Montana passing 8 yards to ex-Giant Dave Young. Brunner hit Earnest Gray for a 72-yard bomb that tied the score. The 49ers got a field goal, then intercepted Brunner. Montana hit Freddie Solomon for a 58-yard strike and a 17-7 lead. A Giant fumble set up another 49er touchdown, and at the half the 49ers led, 24-10. But after Bill Currier picked off a Montana pass, Brunner threw to Johnny Perkins, who weaved his way into the end zone for a 59-yard TD that closed the gap to a touchdown, 24-17.

That was all she wrote for the 1981 Giants. The Giants drove to the 4, but Earnest Gray dropped a pass in the end zone. Joe Danelo missed a chippie from 21 yards out, and the air hissed out of the Giants' balloon.

The 49ers punched over another touchdown, then intercepted a Brunner pass to score a second and lead, 38-17. Brunner tossed a touchdown pass late in the game, but the Giants flew home the 38-24 losers. Their lunge for the Super Bowl had fallen two victories short.

Brunner, Simms and the rushing offense obviously needed to improve. (Carpenter had gained only 61 against the 49ers; Brunner, while gaining

290 yards, had completed only 16 of 37.) But the Giant defense had lifted eyebrows: From twenty-fifth in the league a year earlier, it now ranked third. Bill Parcells had done a job.

```
┌─────────────────────────────────────┐
│          — 1982—                    │
│              4-5*                    │
│     4th NFC Eastern Division         │
│           Ray Perkins                │
│                                      │
│   L   Atlanta        14-16   H       │
│   L   Green Bay      19-27   H       │
│   L   Washington     17-27   H       │
│   W   Detroit        13-6    A       │
│   W   Houston        17-14   H       │
│   W   Philadelphia   23-7    H       │
│   L   Washington     14-15   A       │
│   L   St. Louis      21-24   A       │
│   W   Philadelphia   26-24   A       │
│   *—9-game season due to players'    │
│     strike.                          │
└─────────────────────────────────────┘
```

Ray Perkins and George Young showed what was foremost in their minds when draft time came. Their first pick was Michigan running back Butch Woolfolk. Their second choice: a small package of speed and power, the guy who broke the Syracuse rushing records of people like Larry Csonka and Jim Brown—Joe Morris.

In his first run with a ball in a regular-season game, Joe swept around end for 3 yards and a touchdown. Scott Brunner, having won the number-one job after last season's streak for the playoffs, pitched for 310 yards in the opener against Atlanta. But he fumbled away the ball on one drive. On another, with the Giants ahead 14-7 and at the Atlanta 9, fullback Leon Perry hit the line and fumbled. An Atlanta safety picked up the ball and ran 91 yards to tie the game. The Falcons won, 16-14.

The Giants lost their first two games before the eight-week players' strike. When activity began again in November, Scott Brunner still was throwing for an offense that could produce only 3 points in the first half of a 27-17 loss to the Redskins. The Giants made their first Thanksgiving Day game appearance on TV in the annual game at Detroit. Lawrence Taylor showed the nation why he would one day become the NFL's Most Valuable Player. The Giants were losing 6-0 in the second half, their offense stalled, when L.T. forced a pass that was intercepted, setting up a field goal by Joe Danelo. Then he hit a Lion runner, who fumbled the ball—a second Danelo field goal. The Lions drove to the Giant 4. Lion quarterback Gary Danielson flipped a short pass. L.T. stepped in front of the receiver, grabbed the ball and ran 97 yards for the winning touchdown.

The Giant offense coughed, off again and on again, for the rest of the abbreviated season, its best production a 26-point total in the final game against the Eagles. The Giants won three of their last five, but that wasn't good enough to make the playoffs.

The defense, notably its linebacker unit, had become one of the league's most feared. But Butch Woolfolk, Rob Carpenter and Joe Morris had not given the Giants the lightning-bolt touchdown threat that would hold back defenses and discourage them from blitzing Scott Brunner.

There was, however, a bigger question facing George Young after Ray Perkins announced he would return to his alma mater, Alabama, as head coach: Who would be the Giants' eleventh head coach?

— 1983—
3-12-1
5th NFC Eastern Division
Bill Parcells

L	Rams	6-16	H
W	Atlanta	16-13*	A
L	Dallas	13-28	A
W	Green Bay	27-3	H
L	San Diego	34-41	H
L	Philadelphia	13-17	H
L	Kansas City	17-38	A
T	St. Louis	20-20*	A
L	Dallas	20-38	H
L	Detroit	9-15	A
L	Washington	17-33	H
W	Philadelphia	23-0	A
L	Raiders	12-27	A
L	St. Louis	6-10	H
L	Seattle	12-17	H
L	Washington	22-31	A

*Overtime

"There are two things in New York," Bill Parcells said of the season. "Euphoria and disaster. This year was disaster."

The choice of Bill Parcells to be head coach seemed a conventional one for the Giants. No Giant head coach had ever been a head coach for any other pro team. But more than one Meadowlands fan wondered: Couldn't the Giants find someone with a name? Bill Who?

To fortify a defense that seemed the team's strongest unit, the Giants' first pick was safety Terry Kinard (from Clemson). The second choice was defensive end Leonard Marshall, who became, at 285 pounds before dinner, the biggest Giant. Lower draft choices included two linebackers, Andy Headen from Clemson and Robbie Jones from Alabama.

The Giants' third choice added more weight and quickness to an offensive line that had let in too many pass rushers. The newcomer, all six-six and 272 pounds of him, was Karl Nelson.

Young and Parcells knew they had to build up the team's passing yardage. Five free-agent pass-catchers were brought to camp. Only one would survive — tight end Zeke Mowatt.

Another rookie, Ali Haji-Sheikh, won the job of kicking field goals. His future looked bleak when he missed 2 tries in the Giants' opener, a 16-6 loss to the Rams. But he clinched the job by kicking 3 against the Falcons, the last a 30-yard kick in overtime that beat Atlanta, 16-13. Apart from Ali, the only shining spot in the Giants' offense during the first two games was Rob Carpenter, who had two straight 100-yard games. Scott Brunner, with Phil Simms and Jeff Rutledge watching from the bench, threw 5 interceptions in those two games.

Turnovers continued to haunt the Giants as they split their first four games. Brunner passed for 395 yards but fumbled twice, and the Chargers took both into the end zone for touchdowns, winning 41-34. In the next game, against the Eagles, Parcells replaced Brunner with Phil Simms, who hit on 4 straight passes as the Giants rocketed 78 yards for a touchdown. But a minute later an Eagle fractured Phil's thumb and he was through for the season.

So were the Giants. They lost eight of their final ten games. They managed a 20-20 tie against the Cardinals in a Monday night game that neither team seemed capable of winning. The game was so dull that when the Cardinals came to Giants Stadium a month and a half later, the memory of that stinker lingered: 51,000 ticket holders stayed home.

The season's last game was typical. The Giants' defense held the Redskins to 1 touchdown until late in the third quarter. The Giants led, 22-17, in the final minutes. Then Jeff Rutledge fumbled and the Redskins scored to go ahead and, after another TD, win, 31-22.

The defense had intercepted Joe Theismann 4 times and sacked him 6 times. But a fumbling offense and a weak-kneed running attack (Joe Morris led in the game against the Redskins with only 69 yards — his best of the season), and inconsistent passing had dragged this team down to where it seemed to belong — the pits.

```
         — 1984—
           9-7*
   2nd NFC Eastern Division
        Bill Parcells

W   Philadelphia      28-27   H
W   Dallas            28-7    H
L   Washington        14-30   A
W   Tampa Bay         17-14   H
L   L.A. Rams         12-33   A
L   San Francisco     10-31   H
W   Atlanta           19-7    A
L   Philadelphia      10-24   A
W   Washington        37-13   H
W   Dallas            19-7    A
L   Tampa Bay         17-20   A
W   St. Louis         16-10   H
W   Kansas City       28-27   H
W   New York Jets     20-10   A
L   St. Louis         21-31   A
L   New Orleans        3-10   H

*Wild Card Finish
          PLAYOFFS
W   L.A. Rams         16-13   A
L   San Francisco     10-21   A
```

Bill Parcells knew that George Young had considered hiring a new coach to replace him. "Bill and I had a talk in my office after the season ended," Young said later. "The next day I told him he was still the coach."

But in the next three years, twenty-eight of the forty-five players who would go to the Super Bowl would be added to the team that had won only three of sixteen in 1983.

The Giants had two number-one draft choices and picked, in order, linebacker Carl Banks (Michigan State) and offensive tackle Bill Roberts, a six-five, 280-pound tackle from Ohio State. Other draft choices included linebacker Gary Reasons (Northwest Louisiana State) and wideout Lionel Manuel (Pacific), who outran all the Giant receivers in speed drills. Early in the season Young swung deals that brought safety Kenny Hill from the Rams and running back Tony Galbreath, a onetime 1,000-yard runner, from the Vikings. After looking over players seeking employment as the United States Football League came apart, Young picked up guard Chris Godfrey, cornerback Elvis Patterson and wide receiver Bobby Johnson. By the next season, three of the four draftees—Banks, Reasons and Manuel—would be starting. And four of the five players picked up in trades or as free agents would start.

Parcells had made what would probably be his most important decision. He got rid of Scott Brunner and told Phil Simms that he was the team's number-one quarterback. Playing his first full game in almost two seasons, Simms passed for 409 yards—second highest in Giant history—as the Giants opened with a 28-27 victory over the Eagles. He completed 23 of 30 passes, 4 of them scoring the Giants' touchdowns. Rookie Bobby Johnson caught 2 of those TD throws.

The Giant rushing game would still be a headache for Parcells. In the Eagle game, Butch Woolfolk led the team with only 39 yards. During a 30-14 loss to Washington in which Simms passed for 347 yards, Rob Carpenter led the team with 41 yards. Joe Morris was next with 5 yards in 3 tries.

And that, it seemed, was a good day for the Giant runners. During a 33-12 loss to the Rams, Carpenter could gain only 6 in 9 tries, Woolfolk only 2 yards in 3 tries for a grand total of 8 yards in an entire game.

No Giant runner—Carpenter and Morris getting most of the calls—could gain more than 86 yards in any game until Little Joe Morris exploded for 107 in 16 tries during a 31-21 loss to the Cardinals.

But Phil Simms's passing—he would set club records for passing yardage and completions—kept the Giants near the top of the NFC Eastern Conference. With a 6-5 record, the Giants had to beat St. Louis to hope for a wild-card playoff position. They were losing 7-0 when rookie Gary Reasons jumped on a Cardinal fumble to set up a field goal by Ali Haji-Sheikh. Then Reasons pulled down a Cardinal pass to put the Giants in position for a second field goal. A third Sheikh field goal moved the Giants ahead, 9-7.

The Giant defense then intercepted Neil Lomax twice in the fourth period, their third and fourth interceptions of the day. Simms got the offense's first and only touchdown, an 11-yard pitch to Lionel Manuel, to ice a 16-10 victory.

The Giants split their last four games, but they backed into the playoffs on the season's last day when both the Cardinals and Cowboys lost.

The Giants went west to Anaheim to play the Rams, the team that had trounced them earlier, 33-12, and held their rushers to a paltry 8 yards. The Giants still couldn't run against the Rams—Morris and Carpenter could gain only 41 yards in 23 tries. But Phil Simms sent his backs on short curling patterns and his wideouts and tight ends on sharp cuts inside and outside. He completed 22 of 31 daggerlike passes for 179 yards. The Giants jumped out to a 10-0 lead in the first quarter. The Giants still led, 10-3, as the Rams drove to the Giant 4. But on second and goal from the 4, Leonard Marshall sliced through to drop a Ram runner for a loss. The Rams had to settle for a field goal that left them short, the Giants winning, 16-13.

Once more the San Francisco 49ers dashed Giant hopes in the divisional playoff a week later. The 49ers jumped out to a 14-0 lead. A field goal and Harry Carson's 14-yard return of an intercepted Joe Montana pass put the Giants close, 14-10. Undaunted, Montana fired a 29-yard pass to Freddie Solomon for a touchdown and a 21-10 halftime lead.

The Giants still couldn't run. Morris and Galbreath gained only 80 yards. Morris was held to 46 yards in 17 tries. Knowing Simms had to pass, the 49ers pasted themselves to his receivers. He completed 25 of 44 but for only 218 yards, and 2 were intercepted.

A 1,000-yard running back. The Giants needed one if they were to be any better than a wild-card team. George Young and Bill Parcells would bring more new faces to this Giant team for the 1985 summer camp, but they already had the runner who would be the breakaway threat the Giants needed so badly.

— 1985 —
10-6**
2nd NFC Eastern Division
Bill Parcells

W	Philadelphia	21-0	H
L	Green Bay	20-23	A
W	St. Louis	27-17	H
W	Philadelphia	16-10*	A
L	Dallas	29-30	H
L	Cincinnati	30-35	A
W	Washington	17-3	H
W	New Orleans	21-13	A
W	Tampa Bay	22-20	H
W	Los Angeles Rams	24-19	H
L	Washington	21-23	A
W	St. Louis	34-3	A
L	Cleveland	33-35	H
W	Houston	35-14	A
L	Dallas	21-28	A
W	Pittsburgh	28-10	H

**Wild Card Finish
*Overtime

PLAYOFFS

W	San Francisco	17-3	H
L	Chicago	0-21	A

Five straight preseason victories in which his offense sparkled gave Bill Parcells reason to think he might have an offense that at least would come closer to matching the efficiency of his defense. He decided to try to solve his biggest problem—the rushing attack—by teaming rookie George Adams, the Giants' number-one draft choice, with Joe Morris, who had begun to hit holes with the rapidity the Giants had long expected of him.

Parcells and George Young had drafted with their eyes on the offense. Wide receiver Stacy Robinson (North Dakota State) was a number-two choice, center Brian Johnston a number-three (North Carolina), tight end Mark Bavaro (Notre Dame) a number-four, even though scouts said he was slow getting off the line. Running back Lee Rouson (Colorado) came in the eighth round. The only defensive draftee to make the team was safety Herb Welch, a twelfth-round choice from UCLA.

Young and Parcells added free agents to the offense: Maurice Carthon, a burly runner and devastating blocker out of the USFL; tackle Damian Johnson; and center Bart Oates, along with punter Sean Landeta. Of these ten newcomers, three—Oates, Landeta and Bavaro—would soon be starters.

The strength of the Giants, however, rested within the linebackers. After an argument with Parcells, Brad Van Pelt had gotten his longtime wish— to be traded. Parcells still had depth even when he went with five linebackers: Lawrence Taylor and Carl Banks on the outside, Harry Carson and Gary Reasons or Andy Headen on the inside, with Robbie Jones and Byron Hunt among the reserves.

The front three were: Jim Burt at nose tackle and veterans George Martin and Leonard Marshall on either side of him. The coming of Kenny Hill in a 1984 trade had changed the look of the secondary. Hill and young Terry Kinard roamed deep as the safeties, with Elvis Patterson and Mark Haynes the corners.

Phil Simms, now a highly respected NFL passer, looked to a flock of receivers. He had always liked to throw to his backs circling out of the backfield, and most had good hands, especially Tony Galbreath. He could throw to either of two glue-fingered, bull-like tight ends—Zeke Mowatt and the rookie, Mark Bavaro. His wideouts included a feisty former Navy helicopter pilot, Phil McConkey, a free agent pickup in 1984; and the jet-fast Bobby Johnson and Lionel Manuel.

The Giants opened with the kind of balanced showing that any coach would love. The defense shut out the Eagles—and at home!—21-0. Taylor and Co. sacked Eagle quarterback Ron Jaworski 8 times and held his team to only 168 yards total offense. Simms hit on 8 of 21 for 133 yards. And Joe Morris, scoring 2 touchdowns, rushed for 88 yards while George Adams gained 47 and the Giants racked up 192. No longer could opponents say that Phil Simms's arm was the Giant offense.

The Giants won three of their first four even though the rushing yardage shrank and place-kicker Ali Haji-Sheikh was lost for the season (and, as it turned out, for a career) with an injured leg. Rookie Eric Schubert became the first of a line of place-kickers to be tried and found not good enough.

After winning three of their first four, the Giants lost two squeakers, 30-29 to Dallas, 35-30 to Cincinnati. Leading 29-27 late in the Dallas game, Phil Simms fumbled in his backyard, and the Pokes won with a field goal. He fumbled again on his one against Cincinnati—and the Cincinnati touchdown a few moments later was the Bengals' margin of victory.

When he held onto the ball, Phil connected with his receivers long, short and across the middle. He gained 432 yards passing against Dallas, completing 18 of 26, and 513 against the Bengals (40 of 62), setting club and NFL records. Phil *had* to pass—Giant runners could gain only 33 yards against the Bengals, not much more against Dallas.

Then the Giants took off on a four-game winning streak. During that streak Joe Morris suddenly began to grow into the All-Pro runner he would one day be.

Joe gained 100 or more yards in two of the four games. Brad Benson, Billy Ard and the other "Suburbanites," Bill Parcells's name for his offensive line, mowed down tacklers to spring Little Joe on sweeps left and right. Joe had learned how to stick close to his blockers, look for the opening and, with his explosive bursts of speed, veer left or right to dash into daylight. "Nobody in this league," said Redskin defensive end Dexter Manley, "cuts and swerves any better than Joe Morris."

Manley and his Redskin confederates snapped the Giant winning streak in a Monday night game during which Lawrence Taylor hit Joe Theismann so hard he broke the quarterback's leg and ended his career. But Joe Morris sped through the Washington line for another 100-yard game.

Their record 9-5, the Giants went to Dallas to fight the Cowboys for first place in the NFC East. They lost another squeaker, 28-21, their fourth loss in which the margin of defeat was 7 or fewer points. In that game the Giant defense became the true terrors of the league, knocking out not one quarterback but two—Danny White and Gary Hogeboom.

Back home against the Steelers, the Giants clinched a wild-card playoff spot—and the wild-card home-field advantage. Joe Morris took off on a 65-yard touchdown run, and longtime Giant fans asked each other when was the last time a Giant back had run more than 50 yards for a TD. All told, Little Joe gained an awesome 202 yards, the second highest in Giant history. Phil Simms could rest his arm, throwing only 16 passes—and completing 10. The defense sacked the Steeler quarterback, Scott Campbell, 3 times to finish with a club record of 68, tops in the NFL.

The Super Bowl champion 49ers, who had knocked the Giants out of the playoffs in 1981 and 1983, came to Giants Stadium. The Giants were playing host in a playoff game for the first time since they played the Packers in 1962. After a field goal by Eric Schubert from 47 yards out, Phil Simms hit Mark Bavaro in the end zone, the burly Notre Damer grabbing the ball with one hand as he fell to the turf. The Giants led 10-3 at the half, a packed house of 75,842 roaring on every play. Early in the third period Simms mixed short passes with a 30-yard burst off-tackle by Joe Morris to move the Giants 77 yards for a touchdown and a 17-3 lead. The defense shut down Joe Montana and his crew the rest of the way. The Giants won, 17-3.

Once again, as had been true in Giant victories all season, the offense had produced a balanced blend — Joe Morris gained 141 yards, Simms hit 15 of 31 for 181 yards. And he had thrown his passes to his wideouts (Manuel caught 3 for 56 yards), his tight ends (Bavaro nabbed 5 for 67) and backs (Rob Carpenter caught 3 for 36).

Once more the season ended for the Giants in the divisional playoff, this time on a freezing day in Chicago. Early in the game Sean Landeta stood near his goal line to punt. As he dropped the ball, he saw — to his horror — that a gust of wind had swirled the ball sideways. Landeta's foot grazed the ball. The ball hit the ground, bouncing upward into the hands of a Bear lineman who scurried into the end zone for as easy a touchdown as the Giants had ever given up.

The picture got bleaker for New York. Simms snapped two passes, a 31-yarder to George Adams and a 17-yarder to Bobby Johnson. The Giants crouched at the Bear 2, first down and goal to go for the TD that could tie the score. But 3 passes missed connections. Eric Schubert then hit the goal post with a 19-yard chip shot and the Giants went off with nothing.

The Giants never got closer. Jim McMahon hit receivers for two touchdowns in the third period for a 21-0 Bear lead. The defense would give up no more points. But Joe Morris could gain only 32 yards in 12 tries and Phil Simms hit on only 14 of 35 passes. The Giants trudged off the field 21-0 losers, their first loss by a shutout in 83 games.

The Giants sat glumly in their locker room. "We knew we had played one of our worst games of the season," safety Kenny Hill said later. Before he let in the reporters, Bill Parcells spoke to his team. In his hoarse voice, Parcells, after pointing to his veterans George Martin and Harry Carson, rasped: "They don't deserve what happened here today. They deserve to be champions."

He walked over to where Martin and Carson sat. "We'll get there next year," he said. "I'm not going to rest until we get there."

"There" was the Super Bowl. The Giants team of 1986 started its trek to the Super Bowl on that afternoon in Chicago on January 5, 1986. "We knew we had let ourselves down," Kenny Hill said. "I think, on the trip back home, we all promised ourselves we wouldn't let ourselves down again."

"January 5, 1986," the team's exuberant cheerleader, Phil McConkey, would say a year later. "That's where our success in 1986 had its roots."

In a deeper sense, however, this team could trace its roots back to 1979 and the arrival in East Rutherford of a man who liked to think of himself as an educator.

Year	Draft	Trade	Free Agent
1979 6-10 4th, NFC East	QB Phil Simms (1)		
1980 4-12 5th, NFC East			
1981 10-8 3rd, NFC East	LB Lawrence Taylor (1) G Billy Ard (8C) LB Byron Hunt (9)		NT Jim Burt
1982 4-5 4th, NFC East Regular Season	RB Joe Morris (2)	QB Jeff Rutledge (from L.A. Rams)	NT Jerome Sally
1983 3-12-1 5th, NFC East	S Terry Kinard (1) DE Leonard Marshall (2) T Karl Nelson (3A) CB Perry Williams (7) LB Andy Headen (8) LB Robbie Jones (12A)		TE Zeke Mowatt
1984 10-8 2nd, NFC East	LB Carl Banks (1A) T William Roberts (1B) LB Gary Reasons (4B) WR Lionel Manuel (7)	RB Tony Galbreath (from Minnesota) S Kenny Hill (from L.A. Raiders)	G Chris Godfrey WR Bobby Johnson CB Elvis Patterson WR Phil McConkey
1985 11-7 1st, NFC East	WR Stacy Robinson (2) C Brian Johnston (3B) TE Mark Bavaro (4) RB Lee Rouson (8) S Herb Welch (12)		RB Maurice Carthon R Damian Johnson P Sean Landeta C Bart Oates
1986 17-2 NFL Champions	DE Eric Dorsey (1) CB Mark Collins (2A) NT Erik Howard (2B) LB Pepper Johnson (2C) S Greg Lasker (2D) WR Solomon Miller (6A)	RB Ottis Anderson (from St. Louis) WR Phil McConkey (from Green Bay)	K Raul Allegre S Tom Flynn

The Giants: 1986-1987
The Lunch Pail Guys

George Young
Vice President and General Manager

George Young came to the Giants as general manager and vice president on Valentine's Day of 1979. On that day, of the forty-five players who trotted onto the field for Super Bowl XXI almost nine years later, only these three wore the New York Giant uniform: defensive end George Martin, linebacker Harry Carson and tackle Brad Benson. The table on the opposite page shows how George Young, keen hunter of talent, brought the other 1986 Giants to East Rutherford to pursue a championship.

Despite that track record, this bulky man (he admits to 300 pounds), a former college defensive tackle and history major, frowns when he hears talk that he "built" this team. "Don't call me a builder," he says. "Don't call me an architect. This is a 'we' operation. I'm just a contributor."

Yes, boss, we will not call you a builder. Yes, boss, we will not call you an architect. We will agree with your perception of yourself—"an educator first." But let us now praise a suddenly famous man by looking at his two most important decisions in the making of a championship season—the drafting of Lawrence Taylor and Phil Simms.

On the drafting of Taylor: "We had wanted him ever since he was a junior, certainly when he was a senior. We had second pick in the 1981 draft. George Rogers was the guy most everyone wanted, but our choice was L.T. We got lucky when we heard at the last minute that the Saints, who had the first pick, would draft Rogers. We picked second and took L.T. We would have been very disappointed if New Orleans had taken him."

On Simms: "Once you get the quarterback, you give the fans hope and they can sleep better. You can also build an offense around him. Until you do, you try to get stronger on defense. When it was our turn to draft in 1979, Ray Perkins [hired by George in 1978] and I felt the two best guys were Phil Simms and Ottis Anderson. Ray had worked with quarterbacks as an assistant in New England and with Dan Fouts in San Diego. Ray was a guy who could make it a little easier to pick at a lower level for a college quarterback if we decided to take a shot with one." George decided to take that shot after Perkins told him that Phil Simms could carry the team to a Super Bowl.

Not all the number-one picks were great ones. In 1982 the number-one pick was Butch Woolfolk, later shipped to Houston. "There were nine good running backs in 1982," George says. "We wanted two of the nine. Woolfolk had all the ability; he just didn't work out. But we hit on Joe."

Joe was the Giants' number-two pick that year — Joe Morris.

George Bernard Young, born in Baltimore on September 22, 1930, is the son of a Baltimore tavern-owner who separated from his wife when George was a boy. George attended a Catholic high school.

"He came from a broken home and it was a very painful experience," says George's wife, Kathryn. "The Christian Brothers gave him a good support system and through them he learned the values of male leadership."

He attended Bucknell, where he played defensive tackle and made several Little All-Americas. The Dallas Texans drafted him but cut him before the 1952 season. He went back to Baltimore to teach history at a public high school and coach football at Calvert Hall, his alma mater.

The team and its coach caught the eye of Don Shula, the Colts' young head coach. Shula asked George to scout college players. Later George joined Shula in Miami as a member of the Dolphins' personnel department. He negotiated contracts and scouted players. When Pete Rozelle was called in by the warring Maras — Wellington and nephew Tim — to find a general manager acceptable to both, Rozelle called Shula, who recommended George.

"He had a great background to be a general manager," Shula says. "His education background made him a natural for coaching. He was also a good mediator, very organized. And he had tremendous patience. He used to wear guys out during contract negotiations. He loves to talk. He would talk on any subject."

As a general manager, says George, he is guided by the Golden Rule — doing unto others as he would want them to do to him. "*By the grace of God, there goeth I* is something else I'm very sensitive about," he adds. "I am sensitive about the shortness of a football career. Basically, I'm an educator first and I still feel a responsibility to young people. I hate to see a mind or a physical ability go to waste. You only get one shot at something like this."

But after hiring Bill Parcells to replace the gone-to-Alabama Ray Perkins at the start of the 1983 season, George's patience and his belief in the Golden Rule were put over fire. The new coach came up with a dismal 3-12-1 record. George and Bill sat down for a chat.

Bill Parcells
Head Coach

Bill Parcells walked into George Young's office on a December day in 1983 not knowing whether he would be hired for the next year or fired. Wellington Mara had told people that he thought the 3-12-1 team of this 1983 season "had taken two steps backward" from the 9-7 playoff team of 1981. "After we had that 3-12-1 season," Parcells would say later, "I didn't know if I would make it. If you lose, you go, so you must win. We'd had a bad year, but I thought I knew what I was doing."

In that chat with George Young, Bill convinced the general manager that he did know what he was doing. "I also convinced the powers that be," he now says, "that certain things had to be done."

A strength coach was added, for starters. But more important, the Giants began to get what Parcells said they had to get — better players. At the next three drafts in 1984, 1985 and 1986, and by signing USFL refugees as free agents, the Giants added twenty-eight of the forty-five players who would go to the Super Bowl. Only seventeen players remained of that 1983 club. Of those seventeen, thirteen were starters by 1986 — Phil Simms, Harry Carson, George Martin, Brad Benson, Lawrence Taylor, Billy Ard, Byron Hunt, Perry Williams, Jim Burt, Joe Morris, Leonard Marshall, Karl Nelson and Zeke Mowatt.

"Bill likes to put labels on us," Jim Burt once said. His offensive linemen, for example, are the Suburbanites because they have yuppie sounding names like Benson, Oates and Ard. But Parcells's favorite nickname for his team is "The Lunch Pail Guys."

His best friends away from football are lunch-pail guys — a truck driver, a deep-sea fisherman. His father was a U.S. Rubber executive, but Bill was a lunch-pail guy very early. Bill grew up in the suburbs, Oradell, New Jersey. (He was born in Englewood, New Jersey, on August 22, 1941.) He played basketball and football at River Dell High in Oradell. Six-foot and brawny, he worked summers on roofing jobs for a construction company.

"I carried a lunch pail to work just like the rest of the guys. I used to carry the shingles up to the roof. And if anybody dropped anything off the scaffold, I was the guy who had to go down and get it. In college I was still carrying a lunch pail. I worked in meat-packing plants. I used to push the dead hogs along. The biggest thing was to count how many hogs you pushed through by the end of the day. I'd push 1,300.

"You need one of those lunch-pail guys at quarterback on a football team. I got one. The guys who aren't lunch-pail guys, you put 'em with the guys who are and they convert 'em. I think Pepper Johnson will be a lunch-pail guy. Erik Howard definitely is."

This lunch-pail guy went to Wichita State, where Lion scouts liked him enough to recommend that Detroit draft him. The Lions picked him on the seventh round of the 1964 draft.

But Bill thought his future was in coaching. From 1964 to 1977 he was an assistant at six colleges, including Army and Wichita State, before becoming the Air Force Academy head coach in 1978. The team lost eight of eleven, and Bill left to become, in 1979, a Giant defensive coach.

By then, his wife had become tired of bouncing around the country with their three daughters. She talked him into taking a job with a Colorado real estate firm as a salesman.

Life away from football quickly became a bore. In 1980 he joined the Patriots as a linebacker coach. In 1981 he rejoined the Giants as defensive coordinator, improving the defense from twenty-fifth in the league to third in just a season. That jump got him the job as head coach when Ray Perkins resigned late in the 1982 season.

Remodeling a 3-12-1 team into a 17-2 team in three years, he says, was accomplished the way any good team has to be improved. "Where you have to start is with defense," he says. "Then you need a quarterback and a good punter, but a good defense keeps you in a game."

"He's two people," says tackle Brad Benson. "The one side of him knows how to handle the stars as well as knowing how to handle the people like the offensive linemen who may not be stars.

"The other side of him is that he loves being one of the boys. He can't resist getting into the jousting in the locker room."

"I like kidding around with them," says the coach. "It makes me feel like I'm twenty-six again."

He obviously relishes the shower under a barrel of Gatorade that he gets near the end of every Giant victory. "A lot of people think it shows disrespect," says Brad Benson. "And maybe if we had another group of players, he might not let it happen. But he has enough security in himself as a coach to show he can allow that and know he can have control when the game is over and he talks to us in the meeting room." It has been said of Parcells, however, that while some coaches rule by intimidation, he rules by what has become close to being affection.

But he can be curt as he lights a fire under the feet of his players. Once, after the offense failed to score a touchdown against Denver, he saw Bart Oates, the center of that line, smiling. "What have you got to smile about?" Parcells growled. "They shut you out, didn't they?"

That is the intense side of Parcells. "That is the most difficult thing for me as coach," he once said. "It's just after a game, even sometimes after a win, because you know what happened and what went wrong and you better fix it. My players understand that. They know I will do everything I can to win. To me, the most fun in pro football is winning on the road and the ride back."

His players shake their heads when they talk about all of Bill's superstitions. He will never pick up a penny tails-up. He once hit a black cat on the highway on the way to a game. He veered off the highway, made a U-turn and went by the cat a second time—this time being careful not to hit the body. On the way to the stadium for practice, he drinks a cup of coffee at one diner, then picks up a container in a second diner — always the same ones. Ask him why he makes the unnecessary second stop and he tells you with his devilish grin, "Because that's the way it is, that's why."

On game day he insists that guard Billy Ard be the first Giant to enter the dressing room. Ard is not the first Giant if you list them alphabetically — Raul Allegre is. But now, as we look at the Lunch Pail Guys, we start with Billy Ard. We start with Ard because, we suspect, Bill Parcells would have it no other way.

67 Ard, Billy
Guard   6-3   270
Born: 3/12/59
NFL Exp.: 6 Yrs.
College: Wake Forest

He is one of the Suburbanites, as Bill Parcells likes to call his offensive line. "We don't have any linemen from tough city streets," Parcells says. "Our guys are from Watchung, New Jersey."

At least one is. Billy went to Watchung Hills High. He has been a Giant fan since he was five and sat next to his father, a season ticket holder since 1964, in a seat high in Giants Stadium. His father never dreamed he'd see his son down on the field wearing scarlet and blue — at least not until the 1980 season. That year Syd Kitson, another Wake Forest guard like Billy, was picked during the third round of the NFL draft. Bill Ard, Sr., president of a New Jersey real estate firm, said to himself, "My God, if he's a third-round draft choice, Billy's going to play in the pros." Suddenly he stopped watching the quarterback and started watching the offensive line.

When the 1981 draft began in a Manhattan hotel room, Billy's Watchung neighbors came bearing a banner that read: "Let Ard Be Your Guard." The Giants, to the delight of Ard, Sr., picked Billy midway through the eighth round, but he was their third pick in that round. Nothing daunted by being picked low, Billy made the starting team midway through his rookie season.

Of his mates on the offensive line, Ard says they indeed are not tough city brawlers. "We're the kind of guys," he says, "our mothers drove us to football practice." He grins when Parcells tells people, "Ard, Oates, Godfrey and Benson, they sound like a law firm."

Now a stockbroker, Billy spends at least part of each day being pulled away from stocks and bonds to talk about the Super Bowl victory. He doesn't mind. "In ten years or so," he says, "it'll be nice to have people point to me and say, 'There's Billy Ard. He played on that Super Bowl team.' That's why I plan on living here in New Jersey all my life. A guy from Nebraska or someplace like that will always have that Super Bowl ring and that pride, but it's not the same as playing in what's more or less your home town."

Ard tries to be nice—aren't all stockbrokers?—to everyone, even opposing players. As the Giants destroyed the 49ers in the 1986 playoff game, says Ard, "I looked over at their sideline and it was tough. I started feeling bad. I didn't know what to say to them after the game. So I said, 'Gee, there's nothing I can say.' They were good about that—they said they could accept that."

When not selling stocks, Billy pumps iron to keep his weight between 255 and 270. And where does he live in Jersey? Where else but Watchung?

2 Allegre, Raul
Kicker 5-10 167
Born: 6/15/59
NFL Exp.: 4 Yrs.
College: Texas

When the 1986 season began, Raul was lacing on work boots to go to his job as a civil engineer at a building site in Indianapolis. How he got from the mud of that job to the green grass of the Super Bowl reads like the script of a soap opera.

Raul grew up in Torreon, Mexico. He came to the U.S. in 1977 to attend a high school in Shelton, Washington, as part of an exchange program. His soccer-style kicks caught the attention of University of Texas scouts. At Texas he majored in civil engineering.

The Indianapolis Colts drafted him. After three seasons he lost his job at the start of the '86 season. He went to what he thought would be his future—a civil engineering job.

Bill Parcells, meanwhile, had gone through five place-kickers in two years, the most recent Joe Cooper. The Giants decided to give Allegre a tryout. Parcells liked what he saw, and the Giants began to draw up a contract. The Colts had given Allegre bonuses depending on how many field goals and extra points he kicked. Raul and his agent were going over the contract to see if those bonus clauses could be inserted into the Giant contract. At a practice one day, Parcells asked if Raul had signed his contract. Raul said no. Parcells told an aide that Raul was trying to hold up the Giants. "Put him on the next plane back to Indianapolis," Parcells growled.

The Giants stayed with Joe Cooper. But early in the season he missed on 2 of 2 beyond the 30.

Civil engineer Allegre, meanwhile, had written to Parcells explaining that he had not tried to ask too much of the Giants. Allegre was called back, hanging up his engineer's boots and putting on his kicking shoe. He made 24 of 32 field goal tries, including 18 of 19 from inside the 40 yardline. He made all 33 extra points to score 105 points in thirteen weeks, fifth in NFL kicking scoring.

But Raul didn't feel that he was an integral part of the team until well after mid-season. "I really didn't feel I had done anything. I wanted to be able to do something so that it didn't seem like I was just going along for the ride."

The night before a game in Minnesota, he sat alone in a hotel coffee shop. Linebacker Gary Reasons, the special-teams captain, invited him to join several other Giants for dinner. Allegre told the players he didn't feel he was contributing.

The next afternoon he kicked 5 field goals, including the game-winner with fifteen seconds left. After the game Reasons asked that Allegre be given the game ball. Allegre felt very much a part of the team. That game ball was another reason why Raul, at the end of the season, had a look that lived up to what his last name means in Spanish — happy.

24 Anderson, Ottis
Running Back   6-2   225
Born: 11/19/57
NFL Exp.: 8 Yrs.
College: Miami

The leading all-time rusher for the Cardinals with 7,845 yards in seven seasons, Ottis came to the Giants in a mid-season trade. He stepped willingly into the shadows, no longer a starter, but he said he didn't mind being a backup. He ran only 24 times, usually in goal-line situations or to give Joe Morris a breather. He gained 81 yards and scored 1 touchdown. He caught 9 passes for 46 yards.

"I'm happy to be on the team that made it to the Super Bowl," he said. "In all those years with St. Louis, we never came close. I'm not in an uproar about not playing. If I came here and they had an offense that wasn't producing, and the running back position wasn't producing, then I would probably be more upset. But the fact is, the running back situation is producing very well.

"I'm an older guy on the way out of the game, and what I'd like to do now is to be the Giants' Reggie Jackson. I've got to prepare myself mentally so that when I go in there, I can make something happen to ignite the team."

58 Banks, Carl
Linebacker   6-4   235
Born: 8/29/62
NFL Exp.: 3 Yrs.
College: Michigan State

Near the end of the 1986 season, two astute observers — Denver coach Dan Reeves and TV commentator John Madden — came up with the same summary judgement: The Giants' best linebacker was Carl Banks.

Carl Banks? How could that be? The Giants' other outside linebacker, Lawrence Taylor, was the National Football League's Most Valuable Player, wasn't he? But L.T. or no L.T., Madden and Reeves said that, at season's end, Carl Banks was doing more things better than any other NFL linebacker.

"I'm very thankful for the compliment," Carl said. "I just go out and play. I can't worry about what they think of me. I think the best is yet to come.

"It takes eleven guys out there and I'm part of the eleven. We have some great individual efforts, but it's eleven men working."

Carl grew up in Flint, Michigan. "I was a fair-weather fan. I rooted for all the good teams, the Cowboys, the Vikings. I naturally did not root much for the Giants. They were nowhere in the 1970s. But when I got picked number one by them [in the 1984 draft], I was very excited. My friends asked, 'How can you be so excited? They have so many great linebackers. Where are you going to play?' 'I didn't worry about that. To me, it was a chance to learn from the best. And they all helped me, Harry, Lawrence, Andy Headen and Byron Hunt."

In 1985, after sharing the outside linebacking with Byron Hunt in 1984, he won the starting job. In 1986 he led the Giants in tackles with 120 (L.T. had 105).

Unlike the often-glowering L.T., Carl is a wisecracking smiler off the field. Interviewed before the Super Bowl, he told reporters, "You guys look like you need something to smile about." And he gave them some smiles.

"I was a troubled child. I spent three years in prison at the age of four. I murdered an aunt."

"How did you kill her?"

"It was a horseshoe."

"How did you get the nickname Killer?"

"I used to work in a cemetery. I dug graves and buried people. It was a good job. People were dying to get in."

When you dare to make bad jokes like that, you *have* to be the league's best linebacker.

89 Bavaro, Mark
Tight End   6-4   245
Born: 4/28/63
NFL Exp.: 2 Yrs.
College: Notre Dame

Listen to the raves about Mark Bavaro:

"Toughest kid I ever coached in twenty-five years of college coaching" — Ex-Notre Dame coach Gerry Faust.

"He's the prototype tight end. You can't expect a 245-pound tight end to block a 270-pound linebacker. Mark does." — Giant guard Billy Ard.

"He looks like a great blacksmith." — Los Angeles coach John Robinson.

He is not fast. But the Giants cared little about that — they wanted a tight end who could block. After a 27-20 victory over Washington last season,

TV's John Madden said of Mark: "He did the greatest blocking of any tight end I've ever seen in a game."

And tough? In one game, five tacklers, totaling 1,265 pounds, had to pile onto Mark after he caught a pass to drag him down.

Mark may not have whirlaway speed, but in 1986 he veered into the open to catch 66 passes for 1,001 yards and 4 TDs. He caught twice as many passes as the second-leading Giant receiver, Tony Galbreath, who caught 33 coming out of the backfield.

For a while the Giant players called him Rambo. He has Sly Stallone's Romanesque nose and muscle-builder's body. Mark asked them to stop. In a rare interview—he dreads talking to strangers—Mark explained why: "Because Rambo exploited the war in Vietnam and I have a lot of respect for people who went over there. People in my family went over there."

Mark grew up in Danvers, Massachusetts. His close friend, Atlanta Falcon end Mike Gann (a Notre Dame teammate), once tried to explain the reclusive Mark.

"Mark doesn't have a false bone in his body. But he's tough to explain. It's tough to put into words what kind of a guy he is. He remains cool in a lot of situations but he opens up to people close to him and rambles on. Sometimes you can't shut him up.

"Mark had been a wild man in high school. Not that he got into trouble...he wasn't like that. He was just a wild-living person. In his freshman year at Notre Dame he had long hair...and he had a big stomach. He was flabby. But after that first year he started to change...he started to get into shape. Now he uses his body as a temple. He works harder than most people to keep in shape."

Mark is Phil Simms's favorite pass-catcher ("He has the most confidence in Mark," says a Giant insider.) But even Phil says Mark confuses him. After a hit during one game, Phil looked woozy. "Are you all right?" Mark asked.

"I thought I was dreaming," Phil said later. "I was thrilled at the thought he would speak to me. The guy must like me."

60 Benson, Brad
Tackle   6-3   270
Born: 11/25/55
NFL Exp.: 9 Yrs.
College: Penn State

A bandage was plastered across the bridge of his nose for much of the season, which distinguished Brad from the rest of the Suburbanites, as Bill Parcells has dubbed his waspish-sounding offensive line of Bart Oates, Billy Ard et al. The tape patch across the nose seemed to be getting larger and larger as the season went on. "They put a lot of stitches in it when it first happened, against Seattle early in the season," he says. "My helmet got jammed down across the nose and it busted open. It keeps busting open. It has got to the point where I'm going to have surgery."

Although he looks like a fighter with that patched beak, Brad insists he and the other members of the offensive line are as suburban as their name. "We're all family men, we all live in the suburbs, with station wagons and dogs and all that business. We get along great together. So do our wives. It's just a wonderful situation, and because of it, I think we play better too."

Brad grew up in Altoona, Pennsylvania, and majored in education at Penn State. The Patriots took him in the 1977 draft but cut him during camp. Brad went back to Altoona and took a fifteen-dollar-a-day substitute teacher's job, his sixth-graders staring up in awe at the giant soon to be a Giant.

Late in that fall of 1977, the Giants, desperate for bodies, asked him to come to Giants Stadium. He made the team, but he did not play until 1978. By 1981 he was a starter. Ray Perkins, then the coach, talked several times about letting Brad go. But the arrival of strength coach Johnny Parker in 1984 may have saved Brad's career. "Lifting those weights," says Parker, "built him into an offensive tackle who can go up against bigger guys with more talent and neutralize them."

Parcells liked something else about Brad. "He sticks his head in where a lot of guys are afraid to go," Parcells says.

Brad is always willing to go where Parcells sends him: he has played left tackle, his usual position, plus both guard positions. Brad has no illusions about himself. "I don't have as much athletic ability as a lot of guys on this team. If I don't get ready to play, I don't play very well."

He got ready to play in the big playoff game in 1986 against Washington's Dexter Manley, who had led the league the year before in sacks. Not once did Manley get through to sack Phil Simms. After the game the other Giants pasted bandages over their noses — the Lunch Pail Guys' way of saluting a job well done.

Defensive lineman Jim Burt likes to play practical jokes on Brad; he lured him into making an illegal turn while driving a car in Costa Mesa, where the Giants were quartered for the Super Bowl. Then Burt told reporters that Brad had bribed a cop to get off being given a summons.

"Look," says Brad, "you can't have thin skin on this team. If someone wounds you, someone else pours salt into the wound." Maybe that's inevitable when suburban man meets the Lunch Pail Guys.

64 Burt, Jim
Nose Tackle   6-1   260
Born: 6/7/59
NFL Exp.: 6 Yrs.
College: Miami

In a locker room filled with tough lunch-pail types, Jim Burt is acknowledged to be the toughest. Cornerback Perry Williams once said of Jim, "The only way I'd fight Jim Burt is with a shotgun." One day Jim asked a player if he could borrow the player's razor. Another Giant overheard. "A razor?" the Giant exclaimed. "For Burt I thought he just pulls out his whiskers."

At times on the field, says Harry Carson, "Jim is foaming at the mouth, he's so ready to crash wildly into a backfield. He's so wrapped up that he might even fight one of his own players. One time he and Leonard Marshall got into it on the field. An official looked at Jim and said, 'Who's playing who?'"

After growing up in Buffalo, playing high-school football near Rich Stadium, home of the Bills, Jim went south to Miami. Despite making several All-Americas, he was not drafted. The Giants signed him as a free agent in 1981. "I knew," he says, "that I wasn't drafted because I was too short. So I wore construction boots to make me look taller. I wore them every day in training camp. The only time I took them off was when I took a shower and then I ran so fast the coaches couldn't see me. It was a paranoid summer."

But he played sporadically, filling in behind Jerome Sally in the middle of the Giant front three. He won the starting job in 1983 but then was felled by an aching back. Injections of a special fluid cleared away the pain in 1984 and 1985. In 1985 he led the down linemen with 90 tackles, and he also had 6½ sacks. In 1986 he again topped the team in total tackles with 120.

But he often played in pain. During the off-season he had to consider if he would ever play again. But Burt didn't look worried. He is a free spirit who leaped into the stands after the Giants beat Washington to win the NFC title, and he celebrated with the joyous fans.

"I didn't know I was going to do that. I didn't plan it. It just happened. And I still don't know how I got over that wall, but I have always been emotional. That's my mentality."

Burt lives with his wife, Colleen, and their one child in Waldwick, New Jersey. If his career were to end, he says, "that would be OK, too. I'm having fun and making the most of this. It's taken me six years, so why not?"

53 Carson, Harry
Linebacker   6-2   240
Born: 11/26/53
NFL Exp.: 11 Yrs.
College: South Carolina State

Bill Parcells makes no bones about his great affection for Harry. "I don't think a day has gone by," Parcells says, "where I didn't talk to him about something. I burden him with a lot of things, and in all honesty I probably shouldn't. Sometimes I ask him to fix things he doesn't even know are broken. But I do it anyway because I know he can take it.

"He's an amazing guy. He said to me, 'Bill, don't worry about the defense. We'll play well. If we don't, I'll take care of it.' I like that. It not only shows me he's confident of what he's doing, but he's willing to put his butt on the line for it. I might be prejudiced, but you're talking about one of the greatest guys ever to play the game."

Harry says he and fellow veteran George Martin, who is nine months older than Harry, still share the same love for the game. "I thoroughly enjoy taking the field every Sunday. There's a point where players get stagnant. If you can't push yourself through that, if you don't continue to enjoy the game, you'd better get out. You can't be effective if you just show up and play. You've got to go through two practices a day in the heat of summer, with meetings at night. You play until December and January, when you get frozen toes and you freeze your buns off. But I love it."

Harry grew up in Florence, South Carolina; in high school he was the senior class president. He was a defensive end in college. The Giants drafted him in the fourth round in 1976, and he won the starting job at middle linebacker midway through his rookie season. He suffered through the losing years of the late 1970s. By 1980, an All-NFC linebacker, he wanted to quit. Ray Perkins begged him to stay. "I didn't want people to recognize me as a player," Harry says of those days. "I didn't want people cheering me when I went into the stadium and cursing me when I went out. But I don't think I ever hit rock bottom. I guess it was personal pride. I was just playing for myself even when the team wasn't doing well."

An eight-time Pro-Bowler, Harry lives in New Jersey. He frequently speaks out for religious and charitable causes. He also owns a master's degree in business. During the season young Giants seek him out for advice and counsel. Bill Parcells has the last word on Harry: "I love Harry Carson. He's a tremendous human being."

44 Carthon, Maurice
Running Back   6-1   225
Born: 4/24/61
NFL Exp.: 2 Yrs.
College: Arkansas State

When Maurice was growing up in Osceola, Arkansas, he and his brother James watched Buffalo Bills games on TV. Everybody else was watching O.J. Simpson. But James told his little brother to watch O.J.'s blocking back, Jim Braxton. "He'd just say, 'Watch Braxton. Look at what he's doing.' " recalls Maurice.

Maurice must have watched carefully. "Maurice is the best blocking back in the NFL," says Joe Morris, the man who followed him through lines for 1,516 yards, a club record, in 1986. "Having Maurice," says offensive lineman Karl Nelson, "is like having an extra lineman in the backfield."

But Maurice, as proud as he is of his blocking, would like to talk to you about his running. As a member of the same team, the Jersey Generals, that starred Herschel Walker, he gained 4.4 yards a try in 1983. He also blew open holes for Walker, who rushed for a pro record 2,411 yards.

"The blocking-back tag came on me since I have been with the Giants," Maurice maintains. "When you don't get the ball often in a game, naturally you get labelled. The sad part is when you are going to contract negotiations, there aren't any stats you can pull out. You also don't get mentioned for the Pro Bowl or the Hall of Fame. It's hard to accept on a winning team — but it would probably be harder to accept on a losing team.

"Anyway, Joe Morris lets me know that he appreciates me. I keep things in the proper perspective. If you know your role is to block and open holes and you're in the Super Bowl, you've got to be satisfied with that. You can't take the personal things that you want to do — like score"

As a blocker, Maurice seldom sees the ball, carrying only 27 times in 1985, 72 times in 1986 (for 260 yards). He was signed as a free agent in 1985, one of the many United States Football League refugees grabbed up by George Young. In three USFL seasons he gained more than 2,000 yards rushing, showing he can run as well as block.

But his blocks set Joe Morris off on those explosive runs that gave the Giants a running attack midway through the 1985 season. "I know he'd rather be carrying the ball for a thousand yards" says Karl Nelson. "But he does a great job at what the team has asked him to do."

But who remembers Jim Braxton?

25 Collins, Mark
Cornerback   5-10   190
Born: 1/16/64
NFL Exp.: 1 Yr.
College: Cal-State Fullerton

The Giants picked Mark on the second round of the 1986 draft — and he quickly proved his value to the Super Bowl-bound Giants. He became friendly with starting cornerback Elvis Patterson. "Mark's a patient person," Elvis says. "He doesn't ever say no. Even if he doesn't think something will work, he would at least try it."

When Patterson pulled a groin muscle in September, Collins had learned enough to step into the lineup to replace his mentor.

"If any of the rookies had something to say," Collins remembers, "we said it. If we had a question, we'd ask. We didn't worry if it was stupid or not. The only stupid question is the one you don't ask."

The pupil soon became confident enough to counsel the teacher. When Patterson returned and then made a mistake in a game, Mark whispered into his ear, "Don't worry about it."

"He's telling *me,"* Patterson said with a grin.

Mark, say scouts, is not fast enough—as Patterson and Perry Williams are—to catch receivers from behind, "but he blankets receivers and tackles hard, never quits. Parcells loves his attitude. He only needs to be more consistent to be a fine cornerback."

A native Californian, Mark still lives in San Bernardino, where he grew up. In high school he was the captain of the football, baseball and basketball teams and all-conference in all three sports.

77 Dorsey, Eric
Defensive End   6-5   280
Born: 8/5/64
NFL Exp.: 1 Yr.
College: Notre Dame

Eric was the Giants' first-round pick in 1986. When strength coach Johnny Parker saw him, he thought Eric might have too much muscle and too little flexibility. For weeks Parker had him doing extra flexibility drills and pronounced him one of the weight room's hardest workers.

Playing behind George Martin and Leonard Marshall, Eric didn't register a sack until the season's seventeenth game. A self-confessed worrier, Eric fretted. The day after his first sack, the other linemen presented him with a brown paper sack, inscribed, "To Eric Dorsey in honor of his first sack in the NFL." Eric proudly hung the sack in his dressing stall.

Of the veterans in the defense, he says, "The sense of being together, like being in a war, is what I think makes us so successful. If I ever went into combat, I'd want to go with these guys. They're some of the toughest people in the country—and they know what they're doing."

Eric grew up in McLean, Virginia, going to school with his cousin, who also starred at Notre Dame, running back Alan Pinkett.

28 Flynn, Tom
Safety   6-0   195
Born: 3/24/62
NFL Exp.: 3 Yrs.
College: Pittsburgh

Tom came out of the University of Pittsburgh in 1984, drafted in the fifth round by the Green Bay Packers. He won the free safety job and picked off 9 passes in that 1984 season, tops in the NFC.

In 1985 opposing passers steered the ball away from Tom, as much as you can against a free safety who roams from side to side. Tom totaled only 1 interception in 1985, but he rang up 89 tackles, tying for the most among the Pack secondary.

In 1986, however, he lost the starting job. The Pack cut him. The Giants signed him late in the 1986 season after safety Terry Kinard went down with an injury. Tom played in the Giants' last two games of the regular season. He blocked a punt in the last game, then returned the ball for a touchdown. That TD had to bring Tom more than the usual sense of satisfaction. He scored it against Green Bay.

30 Galbreath, Tony
Running Back   6-0   228
Born: 1/29/54
NFL Exp.: 11 Yrs.
College: Missouri

Tony often delights the Giants at locker room parties by playing his bass guitar. His role on the Giants has been a specialized one. In 1986 he carried the ball only 16 times for 61 yards. But coming into games on third downs, he caught 33 passes, second on the team. Most of those passes were of the dink variety as Tony circled out of the backfield, the average catch good for a gain of 8 yards.

Tony Dale Galbreath comes from Fulton, Missouri. In 1975 he led Missouri in rushing and pass catching. The Saints picked him on the second round of the 1976 draft. In 1978 he set a club record by latching onto 78 passes. The Vikings got him in 1981 and he came to the Giants in 1984 as part of the trade that sent linebacker Brad Van Pelt away from New York. So far he has caught 464 passes — the most by any running back in NFL history.

61 Godfrey, Chris
Guard   6-3   270
Born: 5/17/58
NFL Exp.: 4 Yrs.
College: Michigan

When Chris was in the fifth grade at St. David's grammar school in Detroit, the tall, skinny boy begged the football coach to let him play. The coach said no, but Chris kept on pleading and made the team. "He wasn't spectacular," the coach remembers. "But he did the job. He was a hard worker."

"That experience," Chris now says, "became the foundation of everything I've ever done in pro football. I keep plugging."

Chris's family moved to Hollywood, Florida, when he was a teenager. There he was an honor-roll student. At Michigan, he played defensive tackle on a Wolverine team that went to three straight Rose Bowls from 1977 to 1979.

"But I had mononucleosis six months after college," says Chris. "And I was rather undersized at the time — I weighed about 230 — to be a defensive lineman in the pros."

NFL drafters passed him by. The Redskins signed him as a free agent, tried him at defensive tackle, but cut him. The Jets signed him and he played for them off and on, still as a defensive lineman, in 1980. A knee injury the following year, 1981, put him on the sideline. He moved to Green Bay, the Packers tried him on the offensive line. He separated a shoulder and was released.

"After the injury I had planned to stay out of football entirely," he says. "I was going to get married and get a real job working in sales in Detroit."

He did marry Daria Chomik, and they now have a daughter. But instead of using his business degree in sales, Chris joined the Michigan Panthers of the United States Football League. In 1984 he was one of almost a dozen USFL survivors rounded up by George Young for the Giants. Limping on a sore ankle, he played little until 1985 when he won the starting job at right guard.

"Chris perseveres," says his college coach, Bo Schembechler. "A solid guy and a good student. He adjusts quickly because he is smart. And you have a tough time breaking his spirit."

54 Headen, Andy
Linebacker   6-5   242
Born: 7/8/60
NFL Exp.: 4 Yrs.
College: Clemson

Now, quick! Who holds the Giant record for the longest return of a recovered fumble? If you said Andy Headen, you win the big cigar. In 1984 Andy picked up a Dallas Cowboy fumble and galloped 81 yards for a touchdown.

Andy is a reserve outside linebacker, filling in for Lawrence Taylor or Carl Banks. When L.T. was hurt in the Washington playoff game, the Giant defense remained like a rock, blanking the Redskins. Andy and Pepper Johnson filled the hole left by L.T.

In the Giants' linebacking set-up, Harry Carson and Gary Reasons usually leave in passing situations, Andy and Byron Hunt coming in. Andy was bothered by injuries for about a month in the middle of the championship season, replaced by Pepper Johnson.

Andy grew up in Ashboro, North Carolina. He went to Clemson as a quarterback but was switched to safety and cornerback. Growing all through college, he ended up as a defensive end; now at 6-5 and 242, he could one day become a down lineman.

48 Hill, Kenny
Safety   6-0   195
Born: 7/25/58
NFL Exp.: 6 Yrs.
College: Yale

The highbrow of the Giants—well, at least the only one with a degree in molecular biophysics from Yale—Kenny was tagged with a five-thousand-dollar fine just before the Super Bowl. Pete Rozelle ordered the fine as a penalty for Kenny's late hit on Jerry Rice in the Giants-49ers playoff game.

Kenny came to a press conference lugging an empty milk carton. On the side of the carton he had written: "Kenny Hill Fine Relief Fund." Kenny said he had placed the carton in the Giant locker room. He needled his rich teammates, people like Lawrence Taylor, as he sought contributions to the fund. But, he said sadly, he had collected exactly two dollars and six cents.

Reporters wanted to know why a cerebral Ivy Leaguer would be fined for an illegal hit. Kenny explained that his hit had been retribution for a crackback block thrown by Rice at Giant linebacker Robbie Jones earlier in the game. But then he dived into the think tank to offer some psychological reasons for the hit.

The game, he said, requires a player to be one person off the field and another person on the field. "You have to make a mental metamorphosis each week," he said, "to go from the generally accepted rules of society and play violently and aggressively for three hours each Sunday. Emotions cause us to act out of character."

Kenny comes from Oak Grove, Louisiana, where he was a flash on tracks and football fields. A running back at Yale, he piled up a 4.8-yard average in his senior season. The Oakland Raiders drafted him on the eighth round in 1984. He played a reserve role as a Raider safety, including an appearance in the Raiders' Super Bowl victory over the Redskins.

Just before the 1984 season, the Giants got him for a seventh-round pick. Almost immediately he became a starter at safety. In 1986 he intercepted three passes. He was asked before the Super Bowl if he would try to intimidate Denver receivers. "Intimidate?" he asked, looking puzzled. "We're real nice gentlemanly guys who compete in gentlemanly sport." And then he went off to raise some more money for that late-hitting five-thousand-dollar fine.

74 Howard, Erik
Nose Tackle   6-4   268
Born: 11/12/64
NFL Exp.: 1 Yr.
College: Washington State

In 1986, his rookie season, Erik elbowed aside the veteran Jerome Sally to become the backup nose tackle behind Jim Burt. He figures to become the future Giant nose tackle.

A Giant scout says of him, "As strong and big as he is, he is extremely quick. He is all the things a nose tackle should be."

Erik often came into games in passing situations when the Giants decided on a four-man pass rush. He has looked to George Martin for help. "If there's a problem," Erik says, "George is the first to clear it up. And when one of us makes a good play, there's George saying, 'Way to go.' "

Erik was born in Massachusetts, but his family moved to San Jose when he was young. He played tackle on offense and defense for a San Jose High School team that won the state championship. At Washington State he won honorable All-American mentions. The Giants drafted him in the second round in 1986 after being impressed with his weight lifting. He bench pressed 585 pounds and lifted 225 in repetition 44 times. He was rated the strongest of all the 1986 rookies tested by the Giants.

57 Hunt, Byron
Linebacker   6-5   242
Born: 12/17/58
NFL Exp.: 6 Yrs.
College: SMU

For much of his career as a Giant, beginning in 1981, Byron shared the outside linebacking with a number of players and filled in for Lawrence Taylor on the other side when L.T. replaced an injured inside backer. But as Carl Banks became a power on the outside in late 1985 and 1986, Byron has put in less playing time.

"I didn't mind not playing when we had a Super Bowl team," he says. "But I know I am good enough to play as a starter — either here or, maybe, somewhere else."

In 1986 Byron excelled on the kickoff and punt return teams. He led both teams in tackles. The Giants also sent him into games on passing situations as one of their five linebackers.

Byron, who grew up in Longview, Texas, earned a political science degree at SMU. In the off-season he goes back to Longview, where he has seven brothers and sisters; his oldest brother, Sam, played as a down lineman for the Patriots. "I think I'm my own best friend," he says. "I've always tried not to look for anybody else for anything. Sometimes you can't do what you have to do, but you have to try. That's something I've always been able to do. My career has been a short run so far. I've got a long way to go."

88 Johnson, Bobby
Wide Receiver   5-11   170
Born: 12/14/61
NFL Exp.: 3 Yrs.
College: Kansas

Bobby is another United States Football League refugee who was corralled by George Young. Bobby never actually played in the now-gone league, but as NFL scouts believed he had signed a USFL contract, nobody drafted him. The Giants signed him as a free agent in 1984. From his first day at preseason camp, Bobby won a starting job. In his first regular-season game of 1984, he caught a 27-yard touchdown pass. For the season he caught 8 for 2 touchdowns.

In the 1986 campaign he caught 31. His fellow wideout, Phil McConkey, described one of his catches. "It happened during our victory over the Broncos in the regular season," Phil reported. "It was a third and twenty. Phil ran an in-cut. He got hit helmet to helmet...and he hung onto the ball.

"I went over to congratulate him. I looked into his eyes. He didn't know where he was. He was woozy and he needed my help to get back to the huddle.

"But two plays later he had to be part of another play—the 46-yard pass to me (that set up the winning field goal in a 19-16 victory). He ran his route and drew his guy with him. If he had to, he could have made the catch. I've seen him go over the middle, catch the ball, do somersaults and land on his head—and do it again. I know teams that have guys who won't go over the middle."

Bobby is the fastest of the Giant wideouts—"sneaky quick," says a scout, "with game-breaking abilities." In 1986 his average gain of 17 yards was the best of the Giant pass-catchers. He caught 5 for touchdowns, also tops on the Giants.

Bobby was born in Shelbyville, Tennessee, but grew up in East St. Louis, Illinois, where he won honors in track as well as football. He went to Independence Junior College in Kansas and played his last two seasons at the University of Kansas. In his senior year he caught 53 passes for 783 yards and won All-Conference honors.

"Catching footballs," he says, "means going into places where people get hurt—but if you think about things like that, you are not a pass receiver. Not in this league."

68 Johnson, Damian
Guard   6-5   290
Born: 12/18/62
NFL Exp.: 2 Yrs.
College: Kansas State

Damian backed up guards Billy Ard and Chris Godfrey on the Suburbanite offensive line during the Giants' drive to the Super Bowl, but he has also played tackle. He is the most weighty Giant, coming to camp above 300 pounds and slimming down to 290 by season's end.

Occasionally the Giants used this version of the Refrigerator as a blocking back. They put Damian in the backfield and sent him charging forward ahead of Joe Morris on short-yardage plays.

"Johnson is a devastating run blocker," says Bill Parcells, "probably better than anyone we have starting. But that's not the entire offensive-line picture. There's pulling and pass protecting, and he's not as far along as the others."

Damian comes from Great Bend, Kansas, where he played football and basketball and squeezed people half to death as a wrestler. He made All-Conference second teams at Kansas State, but his weight scared away scouts. The Giants signed him as a free agent in 1985. He missed all of that season with a knee injury. In 1986 he proved to Parcells, as Bill put it, "that he has a chance to be a starter—maybe soon."

52 Johnson, Pepper
Linebacker   6-3   248
Born: 7/29/64
NFL Exp.: 1 Yr.
College: Ohio State

Giant coaches call him "a bigger and faster Harry Carson who is always around the ball." A rookie in 1986 on a team rich with linebackers, Pepper proved good enough to take playing time away from linebacking subs Andy Headen and Robbie Jones.

"When I came here," he says, "I saw all those good linebackers. I told myself, 'You want to be part of that.' Now I am. I'm having a good time and I'm getting a chance to play. I'm not just a guy sitting in the corner of the locker room."

Once, during a meeting, he fell asleep. Defensive coach Bill Belichick woke him. "I'm sorry, coach," Pepper said, "it was medication that put me to sleep."

From then on he was Medication.

Drafted second by the Giants in 1986, he immediately won a place as a hitter in the Giants' kick-coverage and kicking teams. He arrived for practice one day wearing a red coat, which got him another name: Fire Chief. Millions of TV viewers saw Pepper dance with other linebackers on the field moments after Giant playoff victories—dancing what he calls "my stomp-and-grind routine."

59 Johnston, Brian
Center   6-3   275
Born: 11/26/62
NFL Exp.: 2 Yrs.
College: North Carolina

Brian is Bart Oates's backup as the center on the offensive line. He was the Giants' first choice in the third round of the 1985 draft, but he hurt his back so severely at training camp that he had to be operated on. He spent the entire 1985 season on the NFL's injured reserve list while fellow rookie Oates, a free agent, won the starting job at center.

Brian came back in 1986 to win the backup job on the championship team and earn his Super Bowl ring. He brought the ring back to Baltimore, where he grew up. He played football, basketball and also starred in track and wrestling. At North Carolina he played center on offense and filled in as tackle on defense when people were injured.

"Sure, I would like to start," he says, "and I think I could play on a lot of teams in the league. But here I am playing behind a guy I think is the league's best center, so I can't complain."

51 Jones, Robbie
Linebacker 6-3   230
Born: 12/25/59
NFL Exp.: 3 Yrs.
College: Alabama

Robbie may be another player stuck on the wrong terrain at the wrong time — a linebacker lost in a forest of great linebackers. Like Byron Hunt, Robbie got most of his playing time in 1986 as a tackler on the kickoff and punt-return teams. In 1985 he led the team in kick-coverage tackles with 20, 15 of them solo jobs.

But he played little as a linebacker, filling in late in games for Gary Reasons and Harry Carson, the two inside linebackers. And Pepper Johnson, the rookie, took some reserve-duty time away from Robbie.

Drafted twelfth out of Alabama in 1983, Robert Washington Jones hurt his back and missed the entire 1983 season. Since then he has been strictly a reserve and special teams player — but good enough, says defensive coach Bill Belichick, "to start for many NFL teams."

Robbie, who comes from Demopolis, Alabama, says he would prefer to play for another team if he can't play more often with the Giants. But he knows a happy place when he sees it.

"Other teams look upon the Giants as a happy family," he says. "It's not an uptight atmosphere here. I've heard that coaches on other teams will say to their players, 'You think you'll be here next week if you play like that?' We don't have that kind of tension. My only problem is not playing. But we're winning, and if the machine isn't broke, don't fix it."

43 Kinard, Terry
Safety 6-1   200
Born: 11/24/59
NFL Exp.: 4 Yrs.
College: Clemson

Terry didn't make it all the way to the Super Bowl, dispatched to the sideline when he tore knee ligaments against Washington in game fourteen. The Giants will tell you that Terry was on his way to the Pro Bowl. Although he missed the last three games, he tied Perry Williams for the club lead in interceptions with 4, one of which he brought back 52 yards.

Terry was the Giants' number-one pick in 1983, when he took the free safety job away from Beasley Reece. He was a unanimous pick for the All-NFL 1983 rookie team. In 1984 he led the secondary in tackles with 83 and in 1985 he again was tops with 83 while also totaling 5 interceptions, his most ever.

Terry was born in Germany, where his father was an Air Force sergeant. He grew up in Sumter, South Carolina, an All-State in football and basketball.

"My big job now," he said during the off-season, "is to get my knee back to what it was. Lionel Manuel did it and got to the Super Bowl last season. I am going to do the same thing that Lionel did, because I don't want to miss a second-straight Super Bowl."

5 Landeta, Sean
Punter   6-0   200
Born: 1/6/62
NFL Exp.: 2 Yrs.
College: Towson State

Sensing that veteran Dave Jennings's days as an NFL punter were numbered, Bill Parcells and George Young began a hunt for a pro punter who could outduel Dave at training camp. "We wanted someone who had more than college experience," says Young. "We had been watching Sean at Towson State. We advised his agent to sign him with the Stars of the USFL so he would get experience." Just before the last USFL season in the spring of 1985, Sean okayed a deal to come to the Giants' '85 summer camp—and he did. There he beat out Jennings for the job.

In that 1985 rookie season he averaged 42.9 yards a punt and was picked for the All-NFC second team. In 1986 he led the league with a 44.8 average. In a game against the Redskins, a forty-mile-an-hour wind stopped Redskin punts like a huge hand. Sean booted two long punts into that wind.

Off-seasons, Sean is studying for a degree in communications at Towson State. A bachelor, he also keeps busy dating pretty girls. A pudgy-faced six-footer with sleepy brown eyes and a thin mustache, he denies having any wish to be this generation's Broadway Joe Namath.

"I'm a punter," he says. "I don't think I could live up to that reputation. If I were a quarterback, it would be different. And I don't drink or smoke, but I do like to go out with pretty girls. I'm lucky to live close to Manhattan [he lives in New Jersey] where I can meet all those pretty girls."

One of his dates was Penthouse Pet Toni Larsen. "At a party," he says, "I walked up to her and I tried my best to tell her I was not trying to give her a line, but I did think I had met her before. And it turned out I had and she remembered."

"He's very easy to talk with," Toni says, "very down to earth. Without a doubt he's a 10."

Sean's father died during Sean's first USFL season. "Every week after my first three games with the Stars, I'd give him ten brand-new one hundred dollar bills to do what he wanted with. I saw him on a Thursday. When he died of a heart attack on Friday, he still had the ten one hundred dollar bills in his pocket.

"Now I have my mom, so I baby her. I bought her a mink coat. She wants a two-seat Mercedes so I am going to get her one of those."

How did he become a punter? "I was getting my picture taken with my girlfriend when I was in high school in Baltimore. The football coach came by. He said he'd heard from a phys ed teacher that I punted pretty good in class. He asked me to try out for the team. My girlfriend said I should. I did. You don't kick a football for the first time in your life at sixteen and be drafted into the pros at twenty without a lot of luck and help."

46 Lasker, Greg
Safety   6-0   200
Born: 9/28/64
NFL Exp.: 1 Yr.
College: Arkansas

A grateful rookie talked about a veteran whose job he might one day win.

"Kenny [Hill] was extremely outgoing and helpful to me last season," Greg was saying before the Super Bowl. "I'd talk to him every night at summer camp. That's the way it is supposed to be. When I'm a five- or six-year veteran, I'll do that."

Kenny taught Greg the mental and physical intricacies of playing strong safety. Greg got in enough playing time at strong safety to draw the praise of Giant coaches. "He has the potential to be better than [fellow-rookie] Mark Collins," said one. "He didn't play as much as Collins because safety is more difficult to learn than cornerback. He hits hard on tackles."

He was among the Giant leaders in tackling for the kick-coverge teams. He also served as the nickel back when the Giants used a 3-5-3 defense on passing downs.

The Giants' third pick of the second round of the 1986 draft, Greg grew up in Conway, Arkansas. He majored in finance and banking in college, where he was on many third-team All-Americas. Home is still Conway for part of the year, a New Jersey suburb for the rest of the year.

86 Manuel, Lionel
Wide Receiver   5-11   180
Born: 4/13/62
NFL Exp.: 3 Yrs.
College: Pacific

A music minor in college, Lionel plays the piano, drums and several other musical instruments. He likes music from punk to classical, but the sweetest music he could have heard, he said later, rang in his ears after he caught a 25-yard dart from Phil Simms in the playoff game against the Redskins for the NFC championship.

A Saint tackler had sprained Manuel's knee in the fourth game of the season, and he hadn't played since. "I didn't think about the knee," he said, talking of the first pass he had nabbed since the injury. "But when I caught the ball, I knew I was back. It made all the hard work worth it."

For much of three months he had stretched the sprained knee and lifted weights with the leg. He ran up and down the eighty steps of Giants Stadium five or six times a day.

And he had to worry — would the long layoff make his hands "hard"? "The first time you catch a pass after a long layoff like that," he said after the Washington game, "you just pray that you won't drop it." Lionel held on for a touchdown catch that put the Giants ahead, 10-0, in the game that won the NFC title and sent the Giants to Pasadena.

During Lionel's long layoff, Phil Simms seemed tentative at times as he threw to his moving targets, his confidence not always as strong as it had been in 1985. And why not? His number-one pass-catcher of '85 sat up in the stands with the wives. In '85 Lionel topped the team, catching 49 for 859 yards. "He's definitely their best receiver," said Bronco safety Dennis Smith before the Super Bowl. "He's got great quickness and he's elusive. He is one of the best at getting away from the bump."

"He's got the quickest feet I have ever seen," says Phil McConkey. "The way he can change direction, he's just amazing."

That cutting ability, rather than blazing speed, lets him "float," as he likes to say, to open spaces. In 1986, playing in only four regular-season games, he caught 11 passes for 181 yards. Three of the 11 ended up in the end zone.

Lionel grew up in La Puente, California, where he was a National Football Foundation Hall of Fame Scholar-Athlete at Bassett High. After football, Lionel would like to go into the music or broadcasting fields.

70 Marshall, Leonard
Defensive End   6-3   285
Born: 10/11/61
NFL Exp.: 4 Yrs.
College: LSU

Like their baseball brethren, football players also have slumps. Early in 1986 Leonard Marshall went four weeks without a sack, and this was the guy who led the team in 1985 with 15½ sacks, then a club record.

"Things were very adverse at the beginning of the season and it started eating away at my confidence," says the Giants' big man (in the sense that at 285 he is the heaviest of the Giant starters). "The slump lasted four or five weeks. It made me a little off the edge. I didn't want to deal with the reasons because I didn't have any answers myself."

He did some rationalizing. "I knew Harry Carson went through something like this the year before, and Phil Simms had some of it, too, this season. I just grew out of it. It wasn't one particular game. I just think it was wanting to drive, wanting to be at the ball, wanting to make the big play — and wanting it all too much, so I wasn't relaxed." What helped, some others thought, was what also helped when he got off to a slow start in his rookie season — he lost some pounds.

Leonard grew up in Franklin, Louisiana, playing tackle on both defense and offense for Franklin High. At Louisiana State he led the team in sacks both in his junior and senior seasons.

Drafted second in 1983, Leonard won the starting right end job midway through his rookie season. The Giants' three down linemen try to jam up blockers so that the linebackers can tackle the ball-carrier; on passing downs, their goal is to sack the quarterback. In 1986 Leonard, despite that slow start, had 12 sacks, second to L. T.'s 21½.

Leonard is one of the many Giant defensive players who credit George Martin for help. "In my rookie season, I was a high draft pick and a lot was expected of me," he says. "And then I was overweight and I was expected to step right in and replace Gary Jeter, who was very good. I was confused. George, with his counseling, helped take the pressure off me."

A Pro-Bowler in 1986 for a second straight year, Leonard now knows that not even slumps can stop him.

75 Martin, George
Defensive End   6-4   255
Born: 2/16/53
NFL Exp.: 12 Yrs.
College: Oregon

"George is such a good man," ex-Giant Emery Moorehead once said, "you can't even curse in front of him."

George and his wife Diane often have twenty-five or thirty of the Giants, with their wives, to dinner. He will speak at affairs for charities. Last year he received a Man of the Year Award from Tomorrow's Children's Fund, which helps kids with cancer.

"He's a religious man," Eric Dorsey says, "a man of high moral character. Sometimes when someone cusses in front of him, they'll apologize to George, and he says, 'It's too late now.' It happens all the time."

"He's the grandfather around here [George is nine months older than Harry Carson], one of the wise men," says nose tackle Jerome Sally. "Guys ask him for advice."

"I tell them of the early days," George says, "and what it was like to be so low you had to look up to see the bottom. We were trying to get through the season so we could watch the playoffs on TV and be with your family for Christmas. That was a really bad situation."

"When you're new," says Jerome Sally, "you think you may have to try new things, but George told me, 'Never go away from your best moves.'"

George grew up in Fairfield, California, where he was once named on a list of Outstanding American Teenagers. At Oregon he majored in art education. The Giants drafted him eleventh in 1975.

In 1985 George came in on third downs to rush the passer. But he became a starter once more in 1986. In the Denver regular-season game, he intercepted a short pass by John Elway and ran the ball 78 yards for a touchdown—the Giants' only TD in a 19-16 victory. "That was the biggest play of my career," he says. "Not because it was such a key play in a big game, but because at thirty-three years of age, I was able to run 78 yards."

"In dreams," he says, "you can design the way you want things to go. I can make 10 tackles and have 15 sacks and intercept a pass to win the game. In actuality, there is apprehension. You know your opponents have had the same dreams, too."

80 McConkey, Phil
Wide Receiver   5-10   170
Born: 2/24/57
NFL Exp.: 3 Yrs.
College: Navy

"I've been an underdog all my life."

You'd better believe it about a guy who came back after five years in the sky as a Navy pilot to become an NFL standout. "Everybody told me the odds against me making the NFL were astronomical," he says. "It was just throwing oil on my competitive fire. I used all of it to my advantage."

Phil grew up in Buffalo. As a child he stared down with binoculars from high in Rich Stadium to focus on his heroes—O.J. Simpson, of course, but also on the Bills' two wide receivers, Elbert (Golden Wheels) Dubenion and Glenn Bass. On frigid playgrounds, his friends in warmer places, he tossed footballs high into the air, then dived into snowbanks to catch them, imagining he was Golden Wheels scoring against the Jets.

In his senior year he stood 5-8 and weighed 145 pounds and couldn't understand why no college would offer him a football scholarship. He decided to enter the U.S. Naval Academy, knowing Navy played major teams. He set Navy pass-catching records, but after graduation he had to be a helicopter pilot for five years before he could try to be this generation's Roger Staubach, who won an NFL job after three years away from football in the Navy.

In 1983, still in the Navy, he tried out for the Giants and played in a preseason game against the Jets. "I had number 93, one of those spare receiver numbers. I was so nervous I was shaking. I put that jersey on and I stood in front of the mirror and I couldn't believe it."

He went back for his last year as a helicopter pilot. He tried out again in 1984. Just before the last preseason game, Bill Parcells told him, "Relax, you've made the team." "That night I laid in bed," he says, "and started to cry."

Running back kicks and catching passes, Phil gained 1,001 yards in his rookie season. In 1985 he set a club record for most punt returns — 53; and he galloped for 1,080 yards returning kicks and catching passes.

The Giants traded him to Green Bay at the start of the 1986 season for an eleventh-round draft pick; that was a mistake, the Giants now admit. The Giants got him back when Lionel Manuel went down for the regular season with an injured knee. In 1986 Phil led the team with 32 punt returns and 24 kickoff returns for 724 yards. He caught 16 passes for 272 yards — his third straight season in which he gained 1,000 yards-plus as a returner and receiver.

All season long Phil had waved a towel at Giants Stadium to rouse the fans to roaring. Just before the Super Bowl, Bill Parcells sent him dashing out onto the field, waving a towel to bring the New York fans in the Rose Bowl to their feet. "The idea," said Phil, "was to get the neutral field advantage."

"I'm a very emotional person," he says. "It carries over on the field. I think the fans respond to that. When the fans respond, that provides a boost to the team.

"I'm a marginal player. I have to work my tail off every year to make it. That's okay with me. When you're an underdog, you expect that."

87 Miller, Solomon
Wide Receiver   6-1   185
Born: 12/6/64
NFL Exp.: 1 Yr.
College: Utah State

In 1987 he could be the deep threat the Giants lacked in 1986 after Lionel Manuel hurt his knee and was lost for most of the season. Solomon went so deep when he was in college that the Utah State passers couldn't throw long enough to hit him — he ended up catching only 65 passes in four years. Coaches told him to go deep and drag defenders with him so that the other pass-catchers could operate in the free spaces 20 and 30 yards beyond the line of scrimmage. In 1986, filling in for Stacy Robinson, Solomon caught only 9 passes for 144 yards. But 2 of those catches were big ones — touchdowns in back-to-back games against the Eagles and Seahawks.

Solomon grew up in Los Angeles but now lives most of the year in New Jersey so he can participate in the Giants' off-season conditioning program. At Utah State he majored in sociology and advertising and talks about a career one day in television.

Solomon played on the special teams and impressed the Giants with his hitting ability. "There are not many 185-pound guys who can drill a 250-pound linebacker and knock him 10 yards backward," Phil McConkey says. "Solomon can."

20 Morris, Joe
Running Back   5-7   195
Born: 9/15/60
NFL Exp.: 5 Yrs.
College: Syracuse

A writer once said that Joe Morris was the worst second-round pick by the Giants in their history — and that was a mighty mean back of the hand. During the previous twenty years the Giants had no shortage of bad second-round — and first-round — picks.

Certainly Joe had not lit up the sky above Giants Stadium during his first three seasons, 1982 through 1984. In those three seasons he gained a grand total of 703 yards and scored a measly 5 touchdowns. His longest run had been an unexciting 28 yards.

Then came a ka-boom year in 1985 when he set a club record by gaining 1,336 yards. He broke that record in 1986 by gaining 1,516 yards, an average of 4.4 a carry, his longest 54 yards (his career best is a 65-yard TD jaunt in 1985).

At mid-season of 1986, the Giant pass-catchers were rated so-so at best. NFL people were saying this about the Giant offense:

"Joe Morris is their offense. Stop him and they are dead." — Washington safety Curtis Jordan.

"Joe Morris is their offense." — Dallas coach Tom Landry.

What turned a 3.2 runner of 1983 into a 4.4 runner of 1986? Start with the coming of a mow'em-down blocker, Maurice Carthon. Add the maturing of the offensive line of Oates, Benson, Ard and the arrival of Bavaro; and finally, throw in Parcells's giving Little Joe the starting job midway through the 1984 season.

But don't forget the inner rages that simmer inside Little Joe. ("Joe might be short," Phil Simms says, "but he ain't small.")

"I remember all the negative things that anyone ever said about me," Joe says. "I remember them and I use them. Somebody was always saying, 'You can't do this, you can't do that.' That only added fuel."

His father was an Army career soldier. Joe was born in Fort Bragg, North Carolina. "My father went to Vietnam when I was ten years old. He left me behind as the man of the house. That made me grow up fast. My father was the most influential person in my life, the man I look to in times of crisis. I'm proud of what he did and I want to make him proud of me."

Joe made him proud when he broke rushing records at Syracuse set by Jim Brown and Larry Csonka. When Parcells lost faith in Butch Woolfolk in 1984 and made Joe his starting running back, Joe responded by tying a club record with three rushing TDs against the Redskins. Later that season he had his first 100-yard day.

In 1987 Joe says he wants to polish his pass-catching moves and techniques. In 1986 he caught 21 passes for 233 yards. Veteran back Tony Galbreath was Phil Simms's number-two pass-catcher in 1986. Joe figures to be the guy coming out of the backfield that Simms will look to in the future.

"But I always have to prove something," Joe growls. In 1986 critics noted that he ran better on artificial turf than on grass: almost 5 yards per try on turf, 3.5 on grass. "They say I can't run on grass," smiles Joe. "But I proved them wrong about me before—I'll prove them wrong again."

84 Mowatt, Zeke
Tight End   6-3   240
Born: 3/5/61
NFL Exp.: 3 Yrs.
College: Florida State

Zeke missed the entire 1985 season after a knee injury felled him in the Giants' last preseason game. "I knew there were other players whose careers ended because of the same kind of injury," he says in his reserved way. "But I had a lot of help."

Big help came from trainer John Modelono. Zeke worked every day lifting weights with the leg, flexing the knee with weights strapped to the foot. Back home in Wauchula, Florida, during the off-season, he rode both stationary and rolling bicycles for hundreds of miles.

At 1986 camp, still not 100 percent, he saw Mark Bavaro win the tight end job. "Mark is going to be the greatest to play the position," he says. "He helps me and I try to help him since I've got a couple of years more experience."

Playing behind Bavaro, Zeke caught 10 passes for 119 yards. "I'm 90 percent of what I was," he said at season's end. Zeke, who grew up in Wauchula, came to the Giants in 1983 as a free agent. The unknown beat out regulars Gary Shirk and Tom Mullady. In 1984 he caught 48 passes, tying for the club's best. Then came the knee injury and surgery. In the 1986 playoffs Zeke caught 4 passes in the three games, 2 for TDs. "Zeke," said Bill Parcells early in 1987, "looks like he used to look when he was close to being an All-Pro."

63 Nelson, Karl
Tackle   6-6   285
Born: 6/14/60
NFL Exp.: 3 Yrs.
College: Iowa State

A number-three draft choice in 1983, Karl fractured a foot in training camp and went onto the injured reserve list. Forced to sit out the season, he kept busy lifting weights and built a stronger and harder Karl, going from 270 to 285. Right at the start of the 1984 season, he won the starting right tackle job that he has held ever since.

In that 1984 season he was picked to the NFL's All-Rookie team. In a 1985 game he won New York bragging rights by stopping cold the Jets' quarterback-killer, Mark Gastineau.

Karl lives up to the name of the offensive line, the Suburbanites, by living with his wife, Heidi, in Woodcliff, New Jersey. He grew up in DeKalb, Illinois, where he also starred in basketball and in baseball as a pitcher. At Iowa State he made several All-Americas as well as All-Academic teams. Karl majored in engineering, and he is one of three Giants—Jerome Sally and Raul Allegre are the others—who are engineers.

"I am proud of a lot of things I did in college as a football player," he says. "But if you know how much time is required studying engineering, you can see why I am just as proud of my engineering degree. There were not too many people on the football team, where you have to put in five or six hours a day, who also studied engineering, which will also take six hours of work a day. You can bet I pulled a lot of overnighters."

65 Oates, Bart
Center   6-3   265
Born: 12/16/58
NFL Exp.: 2 Yrs.
College: Brigham Young

When Bill Parcells says that the Suburbanites, his offensive line, all sound like the name of a law firm, he's looking straight at Bart Oates. The names of Ard, Oates, Benson and Godfrey may well sound like a law firm, and now they can boast there is a lawyer in their midst—or soon will be. Bart is studying to be a lawyer.

As the 1985 season began, the Giants were desperate for a center. One prospect, high draft choice Brian Johnston, fractured a foot and was lost for the season. George Young looked at centers in the United States Football League and arrived at two choices—Kent Hull of the Generals and Bart Oates of the Philadelphia-Baltimore Stars. Young and his scouts decided on Bart because he was better at long snaps.

Joining the Giants in mid-season of 1985, Bart immediately became a starter. That season the Giants set all-time club records for rushing. When asked the reason for the running resurgence, Parcells often began by singling out the guy who leads the offensive charge after he snaps the ball to Phil Simms—Bart Oates.

"Playing center calls for a player to do a lot more than block and give the ball to the quarterback," says Bart, who also delivers the long snap for field goals and punts. "Since you can see both sides of the defense, you call out the blocking signals. But that's maybe the bad side. The good side, if you've noticed, is that centers usually have longer careers than most line-men and certainly more than most backs. We may not make as much money per season, but we get a chance to keep on making it over the long term."

Bart was born in Mesa, Arizona, but grew up in Albany, Georgia. His older brother later played in both the NFL and USFL. At Brigham Young he was picked to several second-team All-Americas. And at Brigham Young, the cradle of great college passers, he learned something else that Bill Parcells prizes—protecting the quarterback.

"You make one mistake and Phil gets hurt," Bart says, "and you just could hardly live with yourself."

34 Patterson, Elvis
Cornerback   5-11   190
Born: 10/21/60
NFL Exp.: 3 Yrs.
College: Kansas

The Giants call him "Toast." Ask them why and they say, with a sly look at Elvis: "Because he's been known to get burned by a wide receiver."

"Yeah," says Toast, always willing to talk to a writer, "anytime we lose, I get the blame. If they throw a pass for a touchdown, I'm Toast, so I must have been the one who got burned."

In the 1986 playoffs, both Jerry Rice of the 49ers and Gary Clark of the Redskins beat him on deep patterns. Both dropped what seemed to be sure touchdowns. Elvis will point out to you that the Redskins sent Clark into his area eleven other times—and Clark did not catch a pass against him.

"Playing cornerback," he says, "requires a lot of skill and just as much luck. A wide receiver either will make a big play on you or he won't. But maybe another reason he doesn't catch the ball on you is because of something that happened earlier—a hard hit or something."

Elvis came to the Giants in 1984 as a free agent. He got his chance in 1985 when Mark Haynes, who was later traded, held out and Elvis took over at the left corner. In one of his first starts, Elvis picked off a pass in overtime by the Eagles' Ron Jaworski and returned the ball 29 yards for the winning touchdown. In that 1985 season he led the Giants with 6 interceptions. In 1986 he had 2.

Elvis grew up in Houston and still lives there. But he comes to New Jersey frequently during the off-season to work out at Giants Stadium.

Elvis has been a member of several of the Giant special teams, including the one that defends against field goals. Twice in 1985, once against the Jets in a regular-season game and later in the playoff game against the 49ers, Elvis shot by defenders to block field goals.

"They didn't call me Toast after those blocks," he says, his handsome face flashing a smile. "In those games, I burned someone else and he was Toast."

55 Reasons, Gary
Linebacker   6-4   235
Born: 2/18/62
NFL Exp.: 3 Yrs.
College: Northwestern Louisiana State

Gary won a starter's job midway through his rookie year, 1984, and made nearly all the NFL rookie teams. Standing next to Harry Carson on the inside, Gary became respected by the other Giants for his fast thinking. He calls the Giant defensive signals.

When the Giants go into a 3-5-3 on passing downs, Gary and Carson leave the game. "Everybody's got a job to do," says Gary. "If everybody does his job, the whole defense is going to shine. When people play outside their responsibilities, you have breakdowns.

"For example, if my job is to cover the middle, especially against the running play, I have got to stay inside and let Carl Banks or L.T. take care of their responsibilities, which are on the outside."

Although he did not play often in passing situations, Gary picked off 2 passes in 1986, matching his 2 for 1985 and 2 for 1984. He is, if nothing, consistent. His strong suit physically is tackling. At Northwestern Louisiana State, a division AA school, he set a school record with 172 tackles in a season, including 24 in one game.

Gary was born in Chicago but grew up in Crowly, Texas. At Crowly High he played football, basketball, baseball and found the time to get a 3.45 grade point average. That won him membership in the National Honor Society. At college he majored in business administration and made honor roll with a 3.0 average. He and his wife, Teri, have a son, Nicholas Ryan.

The former Giant coach in their championship days of the 1960s, Allie Sherman, told of his admiration for Reasons and his linebacking mates. "I love those linebackers," Allie said. "They make the whole team go. They even intimidate the other team's defense, the way they get the other team's offense off the field so fast."

"That's what we like to do," says Gary, "Three downs and zip, we're off the field. That's what makes Bill Parcells smile."

66 Roberts, William
Tackle   6-5   280
Born: 8/5/62
NFL Exp.: 3 Yrs.
College: Ohio State

In a warning to the Giant starters that some of them would be replaced for the 1987 season, Bill Parcells singled out Bill Roberts as one of those reserves likely to be a starter—if not in 1987, "soon," as Parcells put it.

Parcells said that Bill would have to compete against Brad Benson for the left tackle job.

"Roberts has to play left tackle," Parcells says, the obvious inference being that right tackle Karl Nelson could not be supplanted. "And that's the quarterback's blind side. One bad mistake a year and you don't have your quarterback. Roberts is a better run blocker than Benson. We don't run the ball as well to the left because Brad is not as good a run blocker as Karl Nelson is on the right. But you want your quarterback safe. That's why Benson is in there."

Drafted number-one in 1984, Roberts, who grew up in Miami, wrestled the starting job from Benson in his rookie season. Then a knee injury finished him for the entire 1985 season. He came back in 1986 to see Benson installed in the job.

"Roberts always had that ability to be a starter," Parcells says. "He has size, speed and athletic ability, superior to anyone we have. But it takes refinement. I'd really like to see him come forward because he has all that talent. But the guy in front of him is a special guy. You have to have an ax to get him out."

And what does William Roberts think? "I won the job once," he says tersely. "I can win it again."

81 Robinson, Stacy
Wide Receiver   5-11   186
Born: 2/19/62
NFL Exp.: 2 Yrs.
College: North Dakota State

Just before the Super Bowl, someone asked Stacy who would win a footrace among the Giant receivers. "It's hard to say," Stacy said. "A lot of people talk about football speed being the same as a flatout race, but it isn't."

"Who would finish last?" someone asked.

"Not me," Stacy said flatly. "Not me."

How fast is Stacy? "He's probably 4.4," says offensive coordinator Ron Erhardt, "but he'd probably say 4.3."

Stacy is well aware that many people talked about Joe Morris runs and Phil Simms passes, but few raved about the Giant pass-catchers. "The problem's been," he said "that we're so good in other areas, they overshadow us."

Stacy was drafted second in 1985, but he broke his hand at training camp and played only after week 12, appearing in the final four games, filling in for Lionel Manuel or Bobby Johnson. When Lionel Manuel was hurt early in the 1986 season, Stacy became a regular at wideout. He missed five games with an ankle injury, but caught 29 passes, fourth best among the Giants, his longest for 49 yards.

Stacy was born in St. Paul, where he was All-State in football while winning state titles at 100 and 200 meters. He led his high school basketball team in scoring for two straight seasons. He went to Prairie View A&M in Texas, a football player and track sprinter. He switched to North Dakota

State where he set school records for pass-receiving yardage. In the Senior Bowl, he was picked as the North's Most Valuable Player.

He knows that fellow receiver Phil McConkey scorns what he calls "pretty boy" trackman pass-catchers who eschew the middle and streak for the safety of sideline patterns. "Hey," he says, "I like to go down the sideline and run away from people for the TD bomb, but if Phil Simms wants me to cut inside, I go inside. I go wherever he's going to throw that ball."

22 Rouson, Lee
Running Back   6-2   225
Born: 10/18/62
NFL Exp.: 2 Yrs.
College: Colorado

When Joe Morris held out during the 1986 preseason, Bill Parcells fingered Lee as his number-one running back. Lee decided to pack on a few more pounds and went from 220 to 225. A year earlier he had added twelve pounds, going from 210 as a college senior to 222. "I found I could carry the extra pounds," he says, "and not lose any speed." (Lee travels the 40 yards in 4.4.) "I'm stronger but I'm not slower."

Joe finally decided to play, and Lee became his backup. Lee was drafted eighth by the Giants in 1985. He gained more than 2,000 yards rushing and more than 800 as a pass receiver at Colorado. But scouts looked at his stats suspiciously because he had both blocked and run at Colorado, and scouts wondered if he could do either at the pro level.

Lee ran back kicks and played on kick-coverage teams for the Giants during 1985 preseason games, then hurt a knee and sat most of the season. In 1986, as a backup, he rushed 54 times for 179 yards and caught 8 passes for 121 yards.

He loves food—Mexican food, southern food, you name it. "In other words," he says, "I eat anything as long as it tastes good."

Lee was president of the student body at his Greensboro, North Carolina, high school, and the winner of a best all-around student-athlete award. He says he never has a bad day. "There may be frustrating days, but I use them to develop myself for what is coming—good days."

17 Rutledge, Jeff
Quarterback   6-1   195
Born: 1/22/57
NFL Exp.: 8 Yrs.
College: Alabama

Jeff threw 30 touchdown passes for the Crimson Tide to break Joe Namath's record. How does the passer who broke a Namath record feel about being a backup?

"That's part of football," says the handsome, dark-haired Jeff. "Only one guy can play. I have proven I can play. [He had three 300-yard plus games as a starter in 1983.] Of course, I must face the fact that I am at the point where I am labeled a backup. Bill Parcells knows I've accepted my role."

That role is holding the ball for extra-point and field-goal kicks. Jeff, who was drafted by the Rams in 1979 and came to the Giants in 1982, plays the lead role when the Giants fake a field goal. Twice in the 1986 season he threw after the Giants faked a kick, one a 13-yard touchdown pass to Harry Carson, another a 23-yarder to Mark Bavaro in the playoffs to set up a Giant TD.

Jeff, of course, wishes Phil Simms well, but he also knows that injuries happen. When asked if he is unhappy being on the sideline, he says, "You must remember, I am always only one play away..." He didn't have to finish the thought.

78 Sally, Jerome
Nose Tackle   6-3   270
Born: 2/24/59
NFL Exp.: 5 Yrs.
College: Missouri

Jerome has served as a backup nose tackle for nearly all of his Giant career. That began in 1982, when he signed as a free agent after the Saints released him as a rookie. Early in his Giant career he filled in for the injured Bill Neill and Jim Burt at nose tackle. Jim Burt took over the starting job in 1984 and Jerome has seen less playing time. In 1986 Erik Howard, the rookie from Washington State, won the backup job behind Burt.

Yet Jerome makes his presence felt when he lines up on defense. In 1985, for example, filling in on three-man or four-man fronts, he had 7½ quarterback sacks, the fourth highest on the Giants.

Jerome was born in Chicago, one of twelve children. Being the twenty-first man on the twenty-one man defensive squad, Jerome has to worry about incoming rookies at 1987 training camp. But he has a career assured away from football: At Missouri he won a B.S. degree in industrial engineering.

11 Simms, Phil
Quarterback   6-3   215
Born: 11/3/56
NFL Exp.: 8 Yrs.
College: Morehead State

"A bunch of quarterbacks say they are blue collar," says Brad Benson, who is blue collar even if he owns a Jaguar dealership. "They say it for the publicity. Phil, he's true blue collar. He's a star but he doesn't think of himself as a star."

Certainly he is a star, the owner — or soon-to-be owner — of all the Giant passing records set by people like Charlie Conerly and Y.A. Tittle and Fran Tarkenton, Hall-of-Fame kind of players. He was the Super Bowl's near-unanimous choice as Most Valuable Player.

But maybe he is blue collar because he remembers hearing the boos when the Giants staggered through losing seasons. And maybe he is down to earth because he can remember being benched in favor of Scott Brunner ("that," says the man who benched him, Bill Parcells, "was a mistake, all right?"). Certainly those bad experiences, he says, did not make him a better quarterback.

"You know what all those bad experiences have done?" he says. "They make you self-doubt everything. If you win a game, you can say, 'I did this and maybe it helped us win the game.' If you lose, you say, 'Maybe if I wouldn't have made such and such a thing, we wouldn't have lost.' The self-doubt creeps into everything and you're in trouble. Now I don't get carried away when people that don't know what they're talking about say something. Because they don't know what they're talking about. The biggest thing to me is myself and a couple of the coaches, Bill Parcells and [offensive coordinator] Ron Erhardt. I know they're happy with me. When the coaches tell me things, I believe it. And that's what means the most to me. Because they're like my dad. I'm trying to please my dad. When you can please your dad, you've done well."

Phil began to please his dad as an athlete at Southern High in Louisville, a quarterback in the fall for the football team, a pitcher for the baseball team in the spring. When Phil was the quarterback at Morehead State, few NFL teams paid much attention to him, the passer for a small school, especially during his senior year when the team switched to a ball-control offense. But Ray Perkins, then the Giant coach and a shrewd judge of quarterback talent, saw he had the makings of an NFL quarterback. The Giants picked him number one in the 1979 draft; he was the first of a string of draft choices made by the George Young regime that would lift the Giants to the Super Bowl.

There were ups and downs for Phil along the way, more downs than ups. Even in 1986, after a loss to Dallas in the opening game, Phil heard the booing. "I was a little down and getting ripped in the papers," he recalls, "and Bill said, 'We think you're great. We know you're great.' Regardless of who you are, you need support sometimes. And that was at the right time and I needed it."

Phil missed most of the 1982 and 1983 seasons because of injuries. He came back in 1984, setting Giant records for pass attempts (533), pass completions (286) and yardage (4,044). In 1986, his championship season, he threw 468 passes, completed 259, for 3,487 yards. "You want lunch pail kind of guys on your team," Bill Parcells says, "the kind who would play a football game after work on a parking lot with no one around. And what you especially want is a lunch pail kind of guy at quarterback. I got that kind of quarterback."

56 Taylor, Lawrence
Linebacker   6-3   243
Born: 2/4/59
NFL Exp.: 6 Yrs.
College: North Carolina

Eyes fixed on L.T. at the Giant preseason camp on the Pace College campus at Pleasantville, New York. A few months earlier the newspapers had broken open the story: L.T., a literal legend not even halfway into his career, had become an "abuser" of drugs, as some papers politely reported. The brutal truth seemed to be that L.T., this hero among heroes, was a drug addict.

L.T. said nothing at camp to anyone. He would not speak to reporters. Earlier, in a written statement, he had said he was being treated for "substance abuse." Parcells, visibly angry when asked about L.T. and drugs, would say only that the biggest giant in the Giant defense was as good as he had ever been.

L.T. proved Bill right as the 1986 Giants streaked to Super Bowl XXI. "I thought in 1984 that he was the best player in the league," said TV commentator John Madden. "I thought he was the most dominant player in football. In 1985 he fell off. Falling off to him was to become a human player. Now he's something between human and superhuman."

"When God created a running back," said Bear assistant coach Johnny Roland "he created Walter Payton. When he created a linebacker, he created Lawrence Taylor."

In 1985 L.T. rang up 13½ sacks, his most ever. He led the Giants in tackles with 104. In 1986 he led the NFL in sacks with 20½, close to a record, and he had 105 tackles.

"He's awesome," said fellow outside linebacker Carl Banks. "He's playing better than ever. They are putting tight ends on him, backs on him, tackles on him, and he's going through them."

L.T. has been awesome since the tenth grade, when he stood 5-10, weighed 180, and made coaches' eyes shine in football and basketball. He grew up in Williamsburg, Virginia. He went to North Carolina where he compiled a record of 192 tackles, 21 sacks, 10 forced fumbles and 3 interceptions. The Giants' number-one pick in 1981, he sacked four quarterbacks in his first camp scrimmage.

In his six seasons with the Giants, he has registered 71½ sacks and 490 solo tackles in regular-season play. He has intercepted 5 passes, one of which he ran back 97 yards, the longest by a linebacker in club history. And he's won just about every conceivable NFL defensive honor, the climax last season's Most Valuable Player award.

So what is a legend really like? Ask his friend, ex-Giant Beasley Reece, what he's like now and Beasley says, "I will make the ultimate statement on Lawrence Taylor. I go to his house [in Upper Saddle River, New Jersey] and there's no beer in the refrigerator. Anybody in the NFL knows how big a statement that is."

Ask L.T. what he is really like and he gives this picture: "I enjoy myself. I do pretty much what I want to do all the time. I go out, I get in my share of ruckuses. I raise hell. I have to be careful where I raise hell because people are always watching.

"Maybe my biggest problem is I'm like a kid in some respects. I still do things I did in college. And I'm in the biggest playground in the world in New York. That can cause problems."

His biggest problem, he conceded in a talk early in 1987, was making too much money. He carried around thousands of dollars in his wallet — and couldn't spend it all. Until he found cocaine. Now, he says, that sickness is behind him.

Despite the frowns on the faces of Giant coaches, L.T. skips the Giants' off-season conditioning work at Giants Stadium. The coaches, he says, "don't play linebacker in the NFL. That's punishing work, especially when you are nearly always double-teamed. Three, four guys on me, that's no fun, not nearly as much fun as it used to be playing linebacker."

How does he stay in shape? Says L.T.: "Hitting a little white ball between 75 and 85 times a day. Every day I play golf. That's all."

The most revealing look at the world of L.T. comes from his wife Linda, mother of their two children:

"Lawrence has always had a role he likes to play. He feels he has to be this big tough guy. We had a party recently and invited a lot of people outside of football. My friends kept coming up to me, saying. 'Your husband is nice!' They were shocked!"

L.T. agrees he isn't just that mean old L.T. he plays as he flattens quarterbacks on the field and growls to the press off the field. "When people see me," he says, "they only see the football side of me. I am not filled with anger and meanness. I have feelings. I'm sometimes mad, I'm sometimes happy, I'm sometimes sad, I'm sometimes lonely. I have every type of emotion."

27 Welch, Herb
Safety 5-11   180
Born: 1/12/61
NFL Exp.: 2 Yrs.
College: UCLA

Herb replaced starter Terry Kinard when Terry's season was ended by an injury in week 14. Herb had to play "centerfield" at the free safety position in both playoff games and the Super Bowl, his rookie season only a year behind him. He shrugged off talk that he and Elvis Patterson were the "weak links" in the Giants' otherwise stout defense.

"We have a lot of inexperience in the secondary and no Pro-Bowlers," he conceded. "But we get the job done and we are as good as we think we are — the best in football."

Was he nervous? At first, sure, he says. But by Super Bowl time, Herb had convinced himself he could do the job.

"I'm a lot less nervous because I know now I can do something about the things I see. I never felt any pressure from the other players' thinking I might cost them a playoff game and the championship. None of the other guys said, 'Uh-oh, we're in trouble now that Herb's back there.' It's all been positive."

Herb grew up twenty minutes from the Rose Bowl. After starring at a California junior college, he attended UCLA, where he got a degree in history. He played both corner and safety, starting in two Rose Bowl games.

The Giants picked him on the twelfth round in 1985. Backing up at safety, in his rookie season, he pulled down 2 interceptions in big games against the Redskins and Cardinals. A special teams player and a fill-in until Kinard was hurt, he intercepted 2 more passes in 1986.

How good is the Giant secondary? It ranked nineteenth against the pass in 1986. But Herb quickly points out that the defense gave up only 16 TD passes, third fewest in the league — proof that someone back there knew what he was doing.

23 Williams, Perry
Cornerback   6-2   200
Born: 5/12/61
NFL Exp.: 3 Yrs.
College: North Carolina State

As long as he can remember, Perry has been a hitter. Perry grew up in Hamlet, North Carolina. He played his first organized game in the seventh grade. "In those days I visualized all kinds of things — making a big tackle, making a big interception, and taking it all the way back. I always wanted to be on defense.

"That was because I liked to hit. I loved it. I stuck my nose in everything. If the ball was going in my direction, I always tried to make the hit."

He made a hit so hard in a 1986 regular-season game against Denver that the man he hit, running back Sammy Winder, wandered around dazed for several plays.

"It was a zone play," Perry remembers. "He came out of the backfield and when he turned up, I gave him a good hit. I don't cheap shot nobody. I like to play hard and clean."

"He took a good shot," Winder says, "I don't think he was trying to hurt me any more than normal football stuff."

Perry won varsity letters at North Carolina State in track as well as football. He won the Atlantic Coast Conference 200-meter championship with a time of 21 seconds flat. He anchored the 400-meter and 800-meter relay teams that won first place in both events at the 1982 Penn Relays. And he was a three-year starter at corner for North Carolina State, where he majored in Humanities and Social Sciences.

The Giants drafted him seventh in 1983, but he broke a bone in his foot and sat out the season on injured reserve. In 1984 he won the starting right corner job, played every game and was picked for an All-Rookie NFL team. In 1986 he tied Terry Kinard for the most interceptions on the team with 4.

Perry still lives in Hamlet during the off-seasons. He knows that the Giant deep four has been criticized for being burned by receivers going deep. "We are an improving group who got thrown together for a bunch of reasons," he says. "None of us had much experience last season except for Kenny Hill [in his sixth season]. The rest of us were rookies or one-, two-, or three-year men. We have got to improve with age."

From Billy Ard to Perry Williams, those are the Giants of 1986 — Bill Parcells's and George Young's Lunch Pail Guys.

They came together for the first time in early July of 1986 at the Pace College campus at Pleasantville, New York. Together, rookies and veterans, they began to get ready for what would be a championship season.

And right from the start, Bill Parcells was worried.

The 1986 Season

```
┌─────────────────────────────────┐
│          — 1986—                │
│             14-2                │
│    1st NFC Eastern Division     │
│                                 │
│   L   Dallas        28-31   A   │
│   W   San Diego     20-7    H   │
│   W   L.A. Raiders  14-9    A   │
│   W   New Orleans   20-17   H   │
│   W   St. Louis     13-6    A   │
│   W   Philadelphia  35-3    H   │
│   L   Seattle       12-17   A   │
│   W   Washington    27-20   H   │
│   W   Dallas        17-14   H   │
│   W   Philadelphia  17-14   A   │
│   W   Minnesota     22-20   A   │
│   W   Denver        19-16   H   │
│   W   San Francisco 21-17   A   │
│   W   Washington    24-14   A   │
│   W   St. Louis     27-7    A   │
│   W   Green Bay     55-24   H   │
│   Playoffs                      │
│   W   San Francisco 49- 3   H   │
│   W   Washington    17- 0   H   │
│   W   Denver        39-20   H   │
└─────────────────────────────────┘
```

Training Camp

The frown on Bill Parcells's stopsign-sized face told it all: This was a worried man.

His best runner, Joe Morris—the breakaway threat the Giants had lacked so long—had left camp, hot words flashing back and forth between Little Joe and George Young over the renegotiation of Joe's contract. Parcells's other starting back, George Adams, chipped a pelvis bone and would be lost for the season. The middle of the Giants' defensive line, Jim Burt, winced with pain after being stricken by back spasms. A slew of draft choices had come to camp and, as Parcells told his assistant coaches, "they didn't have a clue what we were doing." Of the Giants' fourteen top draft choices, six had already been cut.

The Giants' number-one to number-six draft choices were all defensive players, and all six survived the axings.

The number-one choice was 6-5, 280-pound defensive end Eric Dorsey from Notre Dame; number two, cornerback Mark Collins from Fullerton State; number three nose guard Erik Howard from Washington State; number four, linebacker Pepper Johnson from Ohio State; number five, safety Greg Lasker from Arkansas. The sixth choice, defensive end John Washington from Ohio State, would stay with the team as a taxi-squad member, impersonating opposing pass rushers.

"Those six defensive players all look like they will be starters," Young told reporters. "So you have to say it was a solid draft."

But Bill Parcells needed a ball carrier who could pin linebackers in place and give Phil Simms the time he needed to find open receivers. Joe Morris had been paid $157,000 the previous season. His agent talked about how Joe had led the league in scoring touchdowns. The Giant locker room heard talk that Morris was asking for two million dollars over four years.

Morris came back to camp but said he would not go through contact drills. "Why should he?" said a friend. "If he breaks a leg, he won't get a dime more than what his contract now calls for."

Parcells scowled. He told people he might force Morris to run the contact drills as his contract called for.

Morris responded by walking out a second time. He came back after the Giants agreed to pay more than he got in 1985 if he was injured before signing a new contract.

The battle smoke rose over the camp, dark clouds that looked uglier each day as sides began to form—those for Little Joe and those against him. One offensive lineman growled to a reporter, "Do you have any idea what we make? What if we stop blocking for Morris? How much would he be worth then?"

Parcells showed his worry when he began to growl at reporters. He heard that one writer had told Morris he would be traded. "That person," the ex-linebacker snapped, "is going to have a lot of trouble with Bill Parcells."

And there was more rancor, more ugly scenes. Parcells began to act like a man beleaguered. Reporters tried to talk to Lawrence Taylor about his statement earlier in the year that he had been treated for "substance abuse." Taylor glared and refused to talk to the press. The writers went to Parcells, who refused to answer any questions about L.T.'s problem. When one reporter asked about Taylor, Parcells said curtly, "This isn't the six o'clock news." When a reporter persisted, the coach, usually cheerful and relaxed with the press, narrowed his eyes. "The next guy who asks me about Lawrence Taylor" he said, "is going to have trouble getting up."

The anger and tension, Parcells feared, would rot the inside of this team. "All these things going on," he told an assistant, "I am beginning to think we don't have a chance." Would 1986 be another 1983, a year when a playoff team drops to the lower depths?

The Preseason

New York Giants 24
Atlanta Falcons 31

Phil Simms came out firing at his wideouts. He hit Lionel Manuel with a 42-yarder and Bobby Johnson with a bullet good for 35 yards and the Giants led, 14-0, in the second period. The Falcons came back to tie the game, 14-14, at the half.

In the third period, the Falcons ahead, 24-14, Jeff Rutledge replaced Simms. Jeff steered the Giants 85 yards in nine plays, Rutledge pitching to the burly tight end Mark Bavaro for a touchdown that put the Giants within 3, 24-21. But a Rutledge pass was picked off by a Falcon defender, who scooted 49 yards for a TD and a 31-21 lead.

Eric Schubert had been kicking extra points, Ali Haji-Sheikh's leg aching. But Ali kicked a field goal from 40 yards out. That finished the scoring.

Parcells was frowning as he walked off the field. His running attack — he had started Maurice Carthon and Lee Rouson — had seemed to be running in mud. And the field was bone dry.

New York Giants 22
Green Bay Packers 14

During a warmup drill, Ali Haji-Sheikh pulled a groin muscle. He had been hurt during a previous game against Green Bay. "If I was ever traded to the Packers," Ali said, "I'd have to buy an intensive-care wing in a hospital."

That got laughs, but Ali had little to laugh about the rest of 1986. His kicking days for the Giants were numbered.

Jeff Hostetler, fighting Jeff Rutledge for the backup quarterback job, started. The Giants smashed 65 yards in ten plays. From the 11 Jeff threw a brown blur at Mark Bavaro, the tight end catching the ball in the end zone for his second TD catch in two games. Later, after Eric Schubert kicked a field goal, Simms came in and piloted the Giants 39 yards to the Green Bay 5. He threw an arrow to another one of the Giant wide receivers, Phil McConkey, to put the Giants ahead, 17-0.

That was all the offense could muster in the touchdown department. Linebacker Andy Headen tackled passer Glenn Dickey in the end zone for a safety, and Schubert kicked a short field goal. The Packers pushed 61 yards for a second touchdown. The Giants rode home, 22-14 winners.

New York Jets 16
New York Giants 20

On a cloudy, humid day at Giants Stadium, the Lunch Pail Guys won New York City bragging rights. Again Parcells started Lee Rouson and Maurice Carthon at running back, hoping one or the other might explode. Neither would.

Earlier this summer Parcells had hoped that his two starting rushers would be Joe Morris and George Adams. But now Adams limped, his injury soon to be diagnosed as a chipped bone that would put his career in peril. And Morris still bickered with George Young. The Giant players were troubled by Joe's holdout. Harry Carson summed up their feelings: "There is a time to hold out and a time to play, and now is the time to play."

The huge crowd in Giants Stadium stood and roared as Giant rookie Mark Collins snared Pat Leahy's kickoff and streaked 97 yards for a touchdown. Bob Thomas, an ex-Bear brought in to replace Eric Schubert, kicked the extra point for a 7-0 Giant lead.

A little later the Giants scored their first touchdown by rushing in eight quarters. After a 62-yard journey to the 1, Lee Rouson ploughed over for the touchdown and a 14-0 Giant lead. Pat Leahy's three field goals closed the gap at the half to 14-9.

Twice during the third period the Giants broke into Jet territory. But the Jets piled up Giant runners at or near the line of scrimmage. The Giants had to go for 3, Bob Thomas kicking two field goals from 41 and 46 yards out. Midway through the fourth period, the Jets slammed 94 yards in thirteen plays to score on a 1-yard run by Johnny Hector. The Giant defense then shut the door on Ken O'Brien and his offense, but Parcells knew by now that his offense, which had produced only 57 points in three games, was not nearly the tiger he had hoped. He also knew that Joe Morris would sign and be ready to play in the last tuneup game, against the Steelers. But was Morris ready or able to move an offense that seemed to have feet of clay?

Pittsburgh Steelers 3
New York Giants 17

Joe Morris started at running back next to Maurice Carthon, who was in the blocking back slot. Midway through the first period, Joe sliced over from the 1 for a 7-0 Giant lead. The Giant offense could do no more in the half, while the defense shut out the Steelers.

Early in the third period the Giants got the ball on the Steeler 17. Morris rushed to the 13. Stepping into the pocket, Simms saw Mark Bavaro swerve across the middle of the end zone and nailed him with a brown arrow to put the Giants ahead, 13-0. Al Haji-Sheikh, in what would be his last game as a Giant, drove home a short field goal but missed on one from 48 yards, his leg still bothering him. The Giant offense had scored two touchdowns and a field goal, but the two touchdowns had been gifts, the Giants going only 27 yards for the first, 17 for the second.

Next week the season would begin in Dallas. Parcells, feeling better about his defense, had to wonder about his sputtering offense.

Week 1

New York Giants   0   14   7   7   28
Dallas Cowboys   0   17   0   14   31

On a Monday night game, the Giants opened with this offensive lineup:

WR	Stacy Robinson
LT	Brad Benson
LG	Billy Ard
C	Bart Oates
RG	Chris Godfrey
RT	Karl Nelson
TE	Mark Bavaro
QB	Phil Simms
RB	Joe Morris
RB	Maurice Carthon

This was the Giant defense that lined up on the Cowboy 20 after the kickoff:

LE	George Martin
NG	Jim Burt
RE	Leonard Marshall
LOLB	Carl Banks
ILB	Gary Reasons
ILB	Harry Carson
ROLB	Lawrence Taylor
LCB	Elvis Patterson
RCB	Perry Williams
SS	Kenny Hill
FS	Terry Kinard

Preseason forecasters had spoken glowingly of this defense while disparaging the Giant offense, especially the running backs other than Joe Morris and the youthful, inexperienced pass receivers. Bill Parcells had expressed doubts about his offense, but added that he also worried about the defense, especially its secondary. He thought the defense had given up too many points in 1985 to the pass. He inserted George Martin, a veteran pass rusher who had played mostly in passing situations in 1985, into the game on first and second downs to discourage passers from throwing on those downs.

Right away, however, Danny White would prove that Parcells had every reason to worry about his passing defense.

Early in the second period, the game scoreless, the Cowboys pushed that defense back 80 yards in eight plays. The eighth play was the kind that had made Bill Parcells wince all during training, a pass to a fast back circling out of the backfield, in this case a screen to Tony Dorsett, who took off on a 36-yard dash into the end zone for a TD.

The Cowboys scored again on a short plunge by Herschel Walker. Behind 14-0, the Lunch Pail Guys showed the ability to come from behind that they would display all season long.

Starting on their 26, the Giants employed runs by Joe Morris and passes to Bobby Johnson and Mark Bavaro to reach the Cowboy 13 in eight plays. Simms then hit Bobby Johnson for the first Giant TD of the season. A minute and a half later, the Giants stood on the Cowboy 3 after a four-play, 63-yard strike. From the 3 Simms threw to Stacy Robinson for a touchdown that tied the score, 14-14.

The Cowboys punched back. In 25 seconds, with artful time outs, the Cowboys strode to the Giant 35 in three plays. From there Raul Septien kicked a field goal to put the Cowboys ahead at the half, 17-14.

In the third period, the Giants got a break, falling onto a Dallas fumble at the 14. Joe Morris (he had signed a five-year $2.4 million contract) punched across from the 2. Bob Thomas, who seemingly had won the kicking job, kicked the extra point and the Giants jumped ahead, 21-17.

The defense contained the Dallas offense for the third quarter. In the fourth, however, Danny White, who would complete 23 of 39 passes (he was sacked only twice) mixed runs by Herschel Walker and his passes to go 74 yards for a go-ahead touchdown.

Again the Giants came back, taking the kickoff to the 26. In three plays they charged to the Cowboy 44. Simms rifled a pass to Bobby Johnson on the sideline, and he flew by defenders all the way into the end zone. The Giants now led, 28-24.

Herschel Walker had replaced the injured Tony Dorsett, and the Giant defense had its troubles holding him; he gained 64 yards in ten carries. From the Cowboy 28, the Pokes drove to the Giant 10 in five plays. Then White, with less than two minutes to go, gave to Herschel Walker who rumbled up the middle for the winning touchdown, Cowboys 31, Giants 28.

"Our offensive line was so-so," Parcells said after the game, speaking of three sacks of Simms that cost 32 yards. The rushing had gained a net of only 115 yards. "Our pass rush was less than so-so," he added, "and Joe Morris showed he still isn't ready after missing most of the preseason."

On the ride home Parcells gloomed to himself about the defense that had not been able to hold that 28-24 lead in the waning moments of the game.

Key Stats: Rushing: Morris, 20-87; passing: Simms, 22-45-300; receiving: Johnson, 8-115, Bavaro, 7-88, Robinson, 3-48.

STANDINGS								SCORES
AFC East	W	L	T	NFC East	W	L	T	**AFC**
New England	1	0	0	Dallas	1	0	0	Denver 38, L.A. Raiders 36
N.Y. Jets	1	0	0	Washington	1	0	0	Kansas City 24, Cincinnati 14
Buffalo	0	1	0	N.Y. Giants	0	1	0	New England 33, Indianapolis 3
Indianapolis	0	1	0	Philadelphia	0	1	0	N.Y. Jets 28, Buffalo 24
Miami	0	1	0	St. Louis	0	1	0	San Diego 50, Miami 28
AFC Central				NFC Central				Seattle 30, Pittsburgh 0
Houston	1	0	0	Chicago	1	0	0	**NFC**
Cincinnati	0	1	0	Detroit	1	0	0	Atlanta 31, New Orleans 10
Cleveland	0	1	0	Green Bay	0	1	0	Dallas 31, N.Y. Giants 28
Pittsburgh	0	1	0	Minnesota	0	1	0	Detroit 13, Minnesota 10
AFC West				Tampa Bay	0	1	0	L.A. Rams 16, St. Louis 10
Denver	1	0	0	NFC West				San Francisco 31, Tampa Bay 7
Kansas City	1	0	0	Atlanta	1	0	0	Washington 41, Philadelphia 14
San Diego	1	0	0	L.A. Rams	1	0	0	**Interconference**
Seattle	1	0	0	San Francisco	1	0	0	Chicago 41, Cleveland 31
L.A. Raiders	0	1	0	New Orleans	0	1	0	Houston 31, Green Bay 3

Week 2

San Diego Chargers	0	7	0	0	7
New York Giants	3	7	0	10	20

The Chargers came to New Jersey after running up an astonishing 50 points against Miami the previous week. Scouts told Bill Parcells, "You got to blitz Dan Fouts or he'll kill you."

Parcells disagreed. "You can't blitz Fouts," he said, "because he's got too quick a release and too short a drop." The Giants prepared for Fouts by dropping back their linebackers to assist on double coverage of the three Charger receivers, Charlie Joiner, Kellen Winslow and Gary Anderson.

That blanket coverage worked. The Giants snared 5 of Fouts's passes, the most by a Giant defense since 1963. "It seemed wherever I wanted to throw the ball," Fouts said, "the Giants were already there."

A new kicker, Joe Cooper, had replaced Bob Thomas, who had missed a 36-yarder against Dallas. Cooper put the Giants ahead, 3-0, with a kick from the 21. An interception set up a Giant touchdown, Joe Morris going over from the 1. Dan Fouts finally hit one of his targets, running back Gary Anderson, who eluded Giant defenders for a 29-yard touchdown that made the score at the half 10-7, Giants ahead.

That was still the score as the fourth period began. The Chargers reached the Giant 31. Fouts sent his receivers deep and threw. Charlie Joiner cut at the 15, and leaped for the ball. It bounced off his fingers. Safety Kenny Hill lunged for the looping ball, grabbed it and weaved to the Giant 35.

Three drives into the line by Joe Morris moved the ball to the Charger 48. Simms gave again to Morris, who circled around right end and sped to the 31. A minute later, after a holding penalty had set back the Giants to the 35, the Giants looked at a second and fourteen. Simms went to the pass. He hit Stacy Robinson for 12, Tony Galbreath for 11. On third and ten from the 12, he sent Lionel Manuel cutting into the right side of the end zone. Simms put a line drive into Lionel's chest and the Giants, after Cooper's kick, led 17-7.

A little later, safety Terry Kinard intercepted another Fouts pass (Terry had two of the day's five interceptions, and strong safety Kenny Hill also had two). From the San Diego 48, the Giants pounded to the 3, the big play a 28-yard pass from Simms to Stacy Robinson. At the 3 the Chargers held. Cooper kicked his second field goal, and the Giants had a 20-7 victory. The 70,000-odd fans streamed down the aisles of Giants Stadium under a bright blue sky, the Giants now 1-1.

Terry Kinard was named the NFC's defensive player of the week. Besides intercepting those two passes, Terry had recovered a fumble to set up a Giant touchdown, broken up 3 passes and made 6 tackles.

Parcells expressed his delight that the defense, which he had come to suspect during the last few weeks, had slammed a lid on the explosive Charger offense. He told his assistants that he thought the defense was at least "capable." He had lots of reasons to suspect his offense, the biggest reason one that he would explain the following week in Los Angeles.

Key Stats: Passing: Simms, 18-37-1-300, Fouts, 19-43-5-224; rushing: Morris, 30-83, Carthon, 8-23, San Diego, 13-41; receiving: Bavaro, 5-89, Robinson, 4-69, Manuel, 3-71, Morris, 3-35.

WEEK 2

STANDINGS								SCORES
AFC East	W	L	T	NFC East	W	L	T	AFC
New England	2	0	0	Dallas	2	0	0	Cincinnati 36, Buffalo 33 (OT)
Miami	1	1	0	Washington	2	0	0	Cleveland 23, Houston 20
N.Y. Jets	1	1	0	N.Y. Giants	1	1	0	Denver 21, Pittsburgh 10
Buffalo	0	2	0	Philadelphia	0	2	0	Miami 30, Indianapolis 10
Indianapolis	0	2	0	St. Louis	0	2	0	New England 20, N.Y. Jets 6
AFC Central				NFC Central				Seattle 23, Kansas City 17
Cincinnati	1	1	0	Chicago	2	0	0	NFC
Cleveland	1	1	0	Detroit	1	1	0	Atlanta 33, St. Louis 13
Houston	1	1	0	Minnesota	1	1	0	Chicago 13, Philadelphia 10 (OT)
Pittsburgh	0	2	0	Green Bay	0	2	0	Dallas 31, Detroit 7
AFC West				Tampa Bay	0	2	0	L.A. Rams 16, San Francisco 13
Denver	2	0	0	NFC West				Minnesota 23, Tampa Bay 10
Seattle	2	0	0	Atlanta	2	0	0	New Orleans 24, Green Bay 10
Kansas City	1	1	0	L.A. Rams	2	0	0	Interconference
San Diego	1	1	0	New Orleans	1	1	0	N.Y. Giants 20, San Diego 7
L.A. Raiders	0	2	0	San Francisco	1	1	0	Washington 10, L.A. Raiders 6

Week 3

New York Giants	0	0	7	7	14
Los Angeles Raiders	6	0	0	3	9

"We need a big fullback," Bill Parcells was telling West Coast writers on the eve of the game. "Heck, we just need running backs. We have only four on the roster [Joe Morris, Maurice Carthon, Lee Rouson and Tony Galbreath]." Asked about their quality, he said, "After Joe Morris, there's a pretty steep dropoff."

Parcells was also unhappy with his field goal and kickoff man, Joe Cooper, who did not kick long enough — nor, in this, his last game, straight enough, missing a 39-yarder against the Raiders. And the missing of field goals had to stick like a bone in his throat after the 3-point loss to Dallas in which Bob Thomas missed from the 36. Parcells may have been reminded of missed field goals by his kickers when the Raiders got off to the early lead, 6-0, with a pair of first-quarter field goals by Chris Bahr.

The score was still 6-0 as the third period began. From the 50 the Giants flashed to the 18 in three plays. At the 18 Simms sent Lionel Manuel on a favorite pattern, crossing over the middle of the end zone, and put the ball into his hands for a touchdown. Cooper kicked the point-after and the Giants led, 7-6.

Parcells knew that Raider quarterback Jim Plunkett could put his team on the scoreboard from any place on the field. Parcells wanted another touchdown for 8 points of breathing room. That touchdown was set up in a way that could not have been more satisfying to him.

The Giants stood at their 37. Joe Morris sped around right end and flashed into the open. He streaked 52 yards, the kind of breakaway run the Giants hoped to get from him. He finally was pushed out of bounds at the 11. Simms again sent his favorite TD target, Lionel Manuel, angling across the end zone and hit him with a low clothesliner. The Giants, after Cooper's kick, led, 14-6.

Midway through the final period, the Raiders took almost seven minutes to grind from their 13 to the Giant 16. On third down, Plunkett missed tight end Jack Christiansen at the 2. The Raiders took the field goal to cut the lead to 5, 14-9.

The Giants used four minutes before giving up the ball to the Raiders at their 20. There was about a minute and a half to go. The Giants dropped back into a prevent. Plunkett hit three receivers on short patterns, then heaved a prayer pass that Terry Kinard batted away at the Giant 5. The Giants sped to the airport for what Bill Parcells enjoys most about football — "the ride home after a win." It was an especially satisfying ride for the defense — it had held running back Marcus Allen to 40 yards, ending his NFL record of eleven straight 100-yard games.

Key Stats: Passing: Simms, 18-30-239, Plunkett, 21-41-281; receiving: Bavaro,

6-100, Manuel, 6-81, Galbreath, 4-13, Robinson, 2-39; rushing: Morris, 18-110, Allen, 15-40, Los Angeles, 21-58.

WEEK 3

STANDINGS								SCORES
AFC East	W	L	T	NFC East	W	L	T	AFC
New England	2	1	0	Washington	3	0	0	Cincinnati 30, Cleveland 15
N.Y. Jets	2	1	0	Dallas	2	1	0	Kansas City 27, Houston 13
Buffalo	1	2	0	N.Y. Giants	1	2	0	N.Y. Jets 51, Miami 45 (OT)
Miami	1	2	0	Philadelphia	1	2	0	Seattle 38, New England 31
Indianapolis	0	3	0	St. Louis	0	3	0	NFC
AFC Central				NFC Central				Atlanta 37, Dallas 35
Cincinnati	2	1	0	Chicago	3	0	0	Chicago 25, Green Bay 12
Cleveland	1	2	0	Minnesota	2	1	0	San Francisco 26, New Orleans 17
Houston	1	2	0	Detroit	1	2	0	Tampa Bay 24, Detroit 20
Pittsburgh	0	3	0	Tampa Bay	1	2	0	Interconference
AFC West				Green Bay	0	3	0	Buffalo 17, St. Louis 10
Denver	3	0	0	NFC West				Denver 33, Philadelphia 7
Seattle	3	0	0	Atlanta	3	0	0	L.A. Rams 24, Indianapolis 7
Kansas City	2	1	0	L.A. Rams	3	0	0	Minnesota 31, Pittsburgh 7
San Diego	1	2	0	San Francisco	2	1	0	N.Y. Giants 14, L.A. Raiders 9
L.A. Raiders	0	3	0	New Orleans	1	2	0	Washington 30, San Diego 27

Week 4

New Orleans Saints	14	3	0	0	17
New York Giants	0	10	3	7	20

The Giants had their third field goal kicker in four games, their sixth in their last nineteen. They signed Raul Allegre, a former Colt. "I can't remember a single team, college or pro," said Parcells, "that I was ever associated with, having this kind of turnover of kickers."

Again the Giants showed the kind of bounce-back strength that Parcells, despite his worries about his running attack, had come to prize in these Giants. And what had to be especially satisfying to Parcells: They came back to win without Joe Morris, who missed the game because of an allergic attack.

The Meadowlands crowd of 67,555 was still settling into seats when the Saints struck for a touchdown, a 63-yard bomb from Dave Wilson to wideout Eric Martin. A little later the Saints ended a 48-yard drive with a 1-yard plunge for a second touchdown and a 14-0 lead. That jumped to 17-0 in the second period on a 27-yard field goal.

The Giants closed the gap later in the period. After a drive by the Giants from their 27 bogged down at the Saint 14, Raul Allegre kicked his first field goal ever for the Giants, a 29-yard kick that left the Giants two touchdowns behind, 17-3. Late in the period the Giants rolled from their 24 to the Saint 19. Simms hit Mark Bavaro cutting into the end zone. At the half the Saints led, 17-10.

Allegre kicked a second field goal from 28 yards away to close the gap to 4, 17-13. That was still the score about midway through the fourth period when the Giants recovered a fumble at their 28. That turnover stopped a Saint drive for a touchdown, one that could have iced the game for New Orleans.

Simms went back to pass, then dashed out of the pocket and ran for 18 yards to the Giant 46. He went back again and saw Mark Bavaro cut to the left sideline. Simms drilled a strike into big Mark's midsection, and the blacksmith-strong tight end fought to the Saint 28 for a 26-yard gain.

Two plays lost 2 yards. On third and twelve, Simms went back into the shotgun. He took the snap and looked left, then right. Stacy Robinson swerved toward the right sideline. Simms gunned the ball to him for a 17-yard gain and a first down at the 13.

Rouson broke through to the 4. The Giants brought in an extra tight end, Zeke Mowatt, as the Saints bunched up for the assault they expected up the middle by a rusher. Simms went back with the ball, then unleashed a short dart to Zeke as he crossed the middle of the end zone. Allegre's kick put the Giants ahead for the first time, 20-17.

The Giants defense, meanwhile, had put clamps on the Saint offense after those first two touchdowns. The Saint rushers would gain only 65 yards. And Wilson, after that 63-yard bomb, would complete 11 of 19 — but for only 83 yards. Indeed, the Giant defense had become more than just "capable."

The Giants, 20-17 winners, had won three of their first four. They went to St. Louis reading newspapers that told them a win against the Cardinals would be the best start of a Giant team in almost twenty years.

Key Stats: Rushing: Rouson, 24-71, St. Louis, 25-65; passing: Simms, 24-41-286; receiving: Bavaro, 7-110, Robinson, 4-66, Mowatt, 4-48.

STANDINGS

SCORES

AFC East	W	L	T	NFC East	W	L	T	AFC
N.Y. Jets	3	1	0	Washington	4	0	0	Denver 27, New England 20
New England	2	2	0	Dallas	3	1	0	Kansas City 20, Buffalo 17
Buffalo	1	3	0	N.Y. Giants	3	1	0	L.A. Raiders 17, San Diego 13
Miami	1	3	0	Philadelphia	1	3	0	Pittsburgh 22, Houston 16 (OT)
Indianapolis	0	4	0	St. Louis	0	4	0	N.Y. Jets 26, Indianapolis 7
AFC Central				NFC Central				NFC
Cincinnati	2	2	0	Chicago	4	0	0	Atlanta 23, Tampa Bay 20 (OT)
Cleveland	2	2	0	Minnesota	3	1	0	Dallas 31, St. Louis 7
Houston	1	3	0	Detroit	1	3	0	Minnesota 42, Green Bay 7
Pittsburgh	1	3	0	Tampa Bay	1	3	0	N.Y. Giants 20, New Orleans 17
AFC West				Green Bay	0	4	0	Philadelphia 34, L.A. Rams 20
Denver	4	0	0	NFC West				Interconference
Kansas City	3	1	0	Atlanta	4	0	0	Chicago 44, Cincinnati 7
Seattle	3	1	0	L.A. Rams	3	1	0	Cleveland 24, Detroit 21
L.A. Raiders	1	3	0	San Francisco	3	1	0	San Francisco 31, Miami 16
San Diego	1	3	0	New Orleans	1	3	0	Washington 19, Seattle 14

Week 5

New York Giants   0   6   7   0   **13**
St. Louis Cardinals 3   0   3   0   **6**

Rarely, if ever, had Bill Parcells felt so down after a victory. Later he called this game the "low point" of the championship season.

The Giants gained only 61 yards on the ground, 53 of those in 17 carries (a 3.1 average) by Joe Morris. Phil Simms completed only 8 of 24 passes for 104 yards. The Cardinals gained 83 yards rushing, 206 by passing — and lost their fifteenth of seventeen games, sunk by an official's call.

The Cardinals led, 3-0, in the second period. Two field goals by Raul Allegre — one from 44 yards, the other from 31 — moved the Giants ahead, 6-3, at the half.

That was still the score when the Giants — or, perhaps more accurately, an official — scored the only touchdown of the day for either team.

The Giants had picked off a Neil Lomax pass at the New York 45. Three rushes and a 10-yard pass from Simms to Mark Bavaro put the ball at the 33.

Since most else had failed to produce a TD, the Giants dipped into their bag of tricks. Simms handed off to Joe Morris, who gave the ball on an end-around play to Bob Johnson. Bob took the handoff from Little Joe, stopped and looked downfield. He lofted a high pass to Stacy Robinson waiting in the end zone.

Also waiting was Cardinal defender Lionel Washington. "He [Stacy] was trying to get through me to get to the ball," Washington said later. "We both went for the ball. Then I turned around and there was a flag on the ground. I couldn't believe the call."

The Giants were happy to take it, right or wrong. From the 1, where the interference call placed the ball, Joe Morris jumped into the end zone. Allegre's point-after put the Giants ahead, 13-3.

A little later in the third period, the Cards' John Lee drove home a 47-yard field goal. The Cardinals could not get closer the rest of the way against a Giant defense that limited the Cardinal rushing to 2.6 yards a crack. (The Giants got only 2.4.) And Sean Landeta's punts, which averaged 47.9, kept the Cardinals outside striking range. The Giants left St. Louis with an ill-deserved victory, but their 4-1 record placed them only a game behind the first-place Redskins in the NFC East.

Parcells sat in the front of the plane, his boyish face glum. "We were getting mutilated at running back," he said later. "Joe Morris still was weak from that allergic reaction. Lee Rouson was hurt, Maurice Carthon broke this thumb, and Tony Galbreath was old. We didn't do anything on offense against the Cardinals. We were just out there running around, not even running, just trotting."

"Practice that next week," one Giant offensive player said, "was lively." He was not smiling when he said it.

Key Stats: Passing: Simms, 8-24-104; rushing: Morris 17-53, Johnson 2-55, Galbreath 3-30; receiving: Bavaro 2-16.

WEEK 5
STANDINGS   SCORES

AFC East	W	L	T	NFC East	W	L	T	AFC
N.Y. Jets	4	1	0	Washington	5	0	0	Cleveland 27, Pittsburgh 24
New England	3	2	0	N.Y. Giants	4	1	0	L.A. Raiders 24, Kansas City 17
Buffalo	1	4	0	Dallas	3	2	0	New England 34, Miami 7
Miami	1	4	0	Philadelphia	2	3	0	N.Y. Jets 14, Buffalo 13
Indianapolis	0	5	0	St. Louis	0	5	0	Seattle 33, San Diego 7
AFC Central				NFC Central				NFC
Cincinnati	3	2	0	Chicago	5	0	0	Chicago 23, Minnesota 0
Cleveland	3	2	0	Minnesota	3	2	0	L.A. Rams 26, Tampa Bay 20 (OT)
Houston	1	4	0	Detroit	2	3	0	N.Y. Giants 13, St. Louis 6
Pittsburgh	1	4	0	Tampa Bay	1	4	0	Philadelphia 16, Atlanta 0
AFC West				Green Bay	0	5	0	Washington 14, New Orleans 6
Denver	5	0	0	NFC West				Interconference
Seattle	4	1	0	Atlanta	4	1	0	Cincinnati 34, Green Bay 28
Kansas City	3	2	0	L.A. Rams	4	1	0	Denver 29, Dallas 14
L.A. Raiders	2	3	0	San Francisco	4	1	0	Detroit 24, Houston 13
San Diego	1	4	0	New Orleans	1	4	0	San Francisco 35, Indianapolis 14

Philadelphia Eagles 0   3   0   0   3
New York Giants   0 14 14   7   35

The Giants came into this game with the big back that Bill Parcells had been seeking—Cardinal veteran Ottis Anderson, one of the league's all-time top rushers. His effect on the Giant rushers was akin to Parcells giving all of them a hotfoot.

Opposing an Eagle team coached by defensive genius Buddy Ryan, the Giant runners shot through the Eagles for 178 yards, by far their biggest production of the season.

Joe Morris got the Giants started early in the second period of a scoreless game. He skirted the end and sped 30 yards for the Giants' first touchdown. The Giants still led, 14-3, in the third period. The Giants took the kickoff and drove from their 20 to the Eagle 10. Simms stepped back and hit rookie Solomon Miller, filling in for Lionel Manuel (who had been injured in the Saints game and thought lost for the season), right between the numerals. The Giants, after Allegre's kick, led 21-3.

Next came what would become a favorite "gotcha" trick play of the Lunch Pail Guys—the fake field goal.

The Giants stood at the Eagle 13, fourth down and 12 yards to go. Allegre came in with Jeff Rutledge, his presumed holder. But Jeff was about to make his dramatic debut as an actor. Rutledge knelt as if to catch the snap, then jumped up after Allegre, acting a second banana role, swept his foot through a ball that wasn't there.

It was in Jeff's hands. Harry Carson, the canny old linebacker, had been sent in as a tight end. He turned in the end zone and caught Jeff's pass for the first offensive touchdown of his career and a 28-3 Giant lead.

In the fourth period the Giants drove 76 yards in nine plays. Simms looped a short pass to Lee Rouson, who rumbled 37 yards into the end zone for the final touchdown.

In their dressing room the Giants would learn that Dallas had beaten the previously unbeaten Redskins. The Redskins and Giants, each with a 5-1 record, were tied for first in the NFC East. Bill Parcells had another reason to smile: the stat sheets. His defense had limited the Eagles to 59 yards on the ground, 98 in the air. And that defense had given an advance showing of how Lawrence Taylor & Co. would terrorize (and kayo) NFL quarterbacks by sacking the Eagle passers 6 times. Simms had gained 214 yards; his rushers picked up 178 to come close to topping Phil. The Giants had a balanced attack for the first time since the seventies and the heyday of Ron Johnson.

Key Stats: Passing: Simms, 20-29-214; rushing: Morris, 19-69, Carthon, 7-43; receiving: Bavaro, 3-22, Robinson, 3-41, Mowatt, 3-41.

STANDINGS							SCORES
AFC East	W	L	T	NFC East	W	L	T	AFC
AFC East	W	L	T	NFC East	W	L	T
N.Y. Jets	5	1	0	N.Y. Giants	5	1	0
New England	3	3	0	Washington	5	1	0
Miami	2	4	0	Dallas	4	2	0
Buffalo	1	5	0	Philadelphia	2	4	0
Indianapolis	0	6	0	St. Louis	1	5	0
AFC Central				NFC Central			
Cincinnati	4	2	0	Chicago	6	0	0
Cleveland	4	2	0	Minnesota	4	2	0
Houston	1	5	0	Detroit	3	3	0
Pittsburgh	1	5	0	Tampa Bay	1	5	0
AFC West				Green Bay	0	6	0
Denver	6	0	0	NFC West			
Seattle	4	2	0	Atlanta	5	1	0
Kansas City	3	3	0	L.A. Rams	4	2	0
L.A. Raiders	3	3	0	San Francisco	4	2	0
San Diego	1	5	0	New Orleans	2	4	0

SCORES

AFC
Cincinnati 24, Pittsburgh 22
Cleveland 20, Kansas City 7
Denver 31, San Diego 14
L.A. Raiders 14, Seattle 10
Miami 27, Buffalo 14
N.Y. Jets 31, New England 24
NFC
Atlanta 26, L.A. Rams 14
Dallas 30, Washington 6
Detroit 21, Green Bay 14
Minnesota 27, San Francisco 24 (OT)
N.Y. Giants 35, Philadelphia 3
St. Louis 30, Tampa Bay 19
Interconference
Chicago 20, Houston 7
New Orleans 17, Indianapolis 14

Week 7

New York Giants 0 9 0 3 12
Seattle Seahawks 7 0 3 7 17

The Giants flew west for their first indoor game at the Kingdome. The hothouse atmosphere may have put the Giants' offensive line to sleep. The Seahawk rushers had sacked only 6 quarterbacks in nine games, but they sacked Phil Simms 7 times.

"I thought I could step up into the pocket like I usually do," Simms said later. "They caught me every time."

A hassled Phil threw 4 interceptions, completing only 14 of 25. Joe Morris had his best day, gaining 116 yards, averaging almost 5 yards a try. The Giant defense buried Curt Warner, one of the AFC's leading ground gainers; he gained only 56 yards in 19 tries. The Seahawks' runners netted only 72. But 2 of those interceptions cost the Giants their second defeat.

The Hawks scored first with a 16-yard pass. The Giants replied early in the second period by unreeling a 57-yard drive that ended as Simms tossed a 32-yarder to Solomon Miller, his second TD in two weeks as Lionel Manuel's replacement. Rutledge fumbled the snap on the point-after, but the Giants went ahead late in the period, 9-7, when Raul Allegre kicked a 23-yard field goal.

Seattle jumped ahead, 10-9, kicking a field goal midway through the third period. Early in the fourth period Simms threw to Maurice Carthon as Mo came out of the backfield. But a Seattle linebacker got in the way, grabbed the ball, and bulled to the Giant 19. Three plays later Curt Warner shot over from the 1 and the Seahawks led, 17-9.

The Giants moved 76 yards in 12 plays, reaching the Seattle 14. A third-down pass, Simms to Solomon Miller, flew wide. Allegre kicked a 31-yard field goal to narrow the gap to 5, 17-12.

With a little more than two minutes to go, the Giants got the ball at their 34. Simms saw Phil McConkey alone over the middle and hit him right in the hands. Phil raced to the Seattle 35. A minute later the Giants stood at the 26, fourth down and fourteen yards to go. Standing in the shotgun formation, Simms took the snap, looked left and right as Seattle hands and arms shot at his face. He saw Bobby Johnson veer toward the left sideline. Phil threw. Cornerback Dave Brown stepped in front of Bobby at the 10 and pulled the ball down—this fourth interception a Giant-killer.

Washington had won, defeating St. Louis. The Giants flew home knowing they had slipped into a second-place tie with Dallas. They had some six hours in the sky to dwell upon the 17-12 loss, their second in seven games, that could easily have been a victory.

They would never have to think such thoughts again this season.

Key Stats: Rushing: Morris, 24-116, Giants, 38-162; receiving: Bobby Johnson, 3-49, McConkey, 3-49, Miller, 3-46; passing: Simms, 14-25-190; punting: Landeta, 3-44.3.

WEEK 7

STANDINGS								SCORES
AFC East	W	L	T	NFC East	W	L	T	AFC
N.Y. Jets	6	1	0	Washington	6	1	0	Buffalo 24, Indianapolis 13
New England	4	3	0	Dallas	5	2	0	Cincinnati 31, Houston 28
Buffalo	2	5	0	N.Y. Giants	5	2	0	Kansas City 42, San Diego 41
Miami	2	5	0	Philadelphia	2	5	0	L.A. Raiders 30, Miami 28
Indianapolis	0	7	0	St. Louis	1	6	0	New England 34, Pittsburgh 0
AFC Central				NFC Central				N.Y. Jets 22, Denver 10
Cincinnati	5	2	0	Chicago	6	0	0	NFC
Cleveland	4	3	0	Minnesota	5	2	0	Dallas 17, Philadelphia 14
Houston	1	6	0	Detroit	3	4	0	L.A. Rams 14, Detroit 10
Pittsburgh	1	6	0	Green Bay	1	6	0	Minnesota 23, Chicago 7
AFC West				Tampa Bay	1	6	0	New Orleans 38, Tampa Bay 7
Denver	6	1	0	NFC West				San Francisco 10, Atlanta 10 (OT)
Seattle	5	2	0	Atlanta	5	1	1	Washington 28, St. Louis 21
Kansas City	4	3	0	L.A. Rams	5	2	0	Interconference
L.A. Raiders	4	3	0	San Francisco	4	2	1	Green Bay 17, Cleveland 14
San Diego	1	6	0	New Orleans	3	4	0	Seattle 17, N.Y. Giants 12

Washington Redskins	0	3	14	3	20
New York Giants	3	10	7	7	27

The Giants were playing for a first-place tie in this Monday night game at Giants Stadium, while the Mets were playing for their lives in the sudden-death seventh game of the World Series at Shea Stadium some twenty-odd miles away. The crowd roared when there was no action on the gridiron, startling the players. Spectators had their ears on, Walkman radios relaying how the Mets were rallying to beat Boston for the world championship.

The Giants were not amused. "If they wanted to see the Mets play," Brad Benson growled, "they should have gone to the ballgame."

The Giants leaped ahead, 10-0, after Raul Allegre kicked a field goal and Joe Morris climaxed an 80-yard roll by slicing over from the 11. Two more field goals by each side made the halftime score 13-3.

Early in the third period, the Giants seemed on their way to a laugher. They built their lead to 20-3 when Phil Simms hit Bobby Johnson for a 30-yard TD strike.

But the Redskins went on a warpath for 17 unanswered points. The Giants had stopped the Redskins running cold (Washington rushers netted only 32 yards in 18 tries). But passer Jay Schroeder connected more often than he missed, completing 22 passes for 420 yards. He took the Redskins 77 yards for a touchdown, then hit wideout Gary Clark on a 42-yard bomb for a second. Another march, this one of 74 yards, stalled at the Giant 12; Washington kicked a field goal from the 29 and the score was tied, 20-20.

There was slightly more than two minutes to play, the Giants with the ball at their 44, first down and twenty yards to go. Joe Morris showed he might be worth all that money. He burst through the right side, cut to the left with one of his zigzagging maneuvers that baffled tacklers, and sped 34 yards to the Redskin 22.

Simms stayed with a hot hand. He sent Little Joe left and then right, the two jabs bringing the ball to the 13. Again Phil gave to Joe, who turned right end and flashed into the end zone for what would prove to be the winning touchdown. The roaring that now filled Giants Stadium had nothing to do with what had happened at Shea. The Giants had squirmed their way into a first-place tie with Washington and Dallas. And once more the Giants had won with almost equal dashes of passing and running (Joe Morris, with 181 yards, had piled up his highest total of the season).

Key Stats: Rushing: Giants, 37-202, Morris, 31-181, Rogers, 16-30; passing: Simms, 20-30-219, Schroeder, 22-40-420; receiving: Bobby Johnson, 3-53, Morris, 5-59, Galbreath, 5-54, Bavaro, 5-41.

WEEK 8

STANDINGS

AFC East	W	L	T
N.Y. Jets	7	1	0
New England	5	3	0
Miami	3	5	0
Buffalo	2	6	0
Indianapolis	0	8	0
AFC Central			
Cincinnati	5	3	0
Cleveland	5	3	0
Pittsburgh	2	6	0
Houston	1	7	0
AFC West			
Denver	7	1	0
Kansas City	5	3	0
L.A. Raiders	5	3	0
Seattle	5	3	0
San Diego	1	7	0

NFC East	W	L	T
Dallas	6	2	0
N.Y. Giants	6	2	0
Washington	6	2	0
Philadelphia	3	5	0
St. Louis	1	7	0
NFC Central			
Chicago	7	1	0
Minnesota	5	3	0
Detroit	3	5	0
Green Bay	1	7	0
Tampa Bay	1	7	0
NFC West			
L.A. Rams	6	2	0
Atlanta	5	2	1
San Francisco	5	2	1
New Orleans	3	5	0

SCORES

AFC

Denver 20, Seattle 13
L.A. Raiders 28, Houston 17
Miami 17, Indianapolis 13
New England 23, Buffalo 3
Pittsburgh 30, Cincinnati 9

NFC

Chicago 13, Detroit 7
Dallas 37, St. Louis 6
L.A. Rams 14, Atlanta 7
N.Y. Giants 27, Washington 20
San Francisco 31, Green Bay 17

Interconference

Cleveland 23, Minnesota 20
Kansas City 27, Tampa Bay 20
N.Y. Jets 28, New Orleans 23
Philadelphia 23, San Diego 7

Week 9

Dallas Cowboys	0	7	0	7	14
New York Giants	3	7	0	7	17

The Giants had lost three straight games to the Cowboys by a total of 11 points. "You try to put the past behind you," Harry Carson said before the game. "But some things are hard to put out of your mind. This game is something special."

Raul Allegre put the Giants ahead, 3-0, late in the first period with a 25-yard field goal. Steve Pelluer, replacing Danny White, who was injured early in the game, tossed an 11-yarder to wide receiver Mike Renfro, and Dallas vaulted ahead early in the second period, 7-3. Midway through that period the Giants slogged 69 yards in 13 plays, Simms calling most often on Joe Morris. Now the Giants — after an 8-yard dash up the middle by Joe Morris — led, 10-7.

The Giants still led 10-7 as the fourth period began on a cloudy, cool November day at East Rutherford. The Cowboys had to punt from the Giant 44. As Mike Saxon took the snap, he saw Lawrence Taylor blow by blockers and veer directly at him. Saxon hurried the punt, catching the ball too high on his foot. The ball soared straight up in the air, as if climbing a haystack, then came down the other side to fall dead at the Giant 38 — a punt of 6 yards.

Two plays later the Cowboys were caught interfering on a pass thrown by Phil Simms to Phil McConkey. That put the ball at the Dallas 29. Simms gave to Little Joe, who banged off right tackle, then burst into the open, scooting 22 yards to the Dallas 7. One play later he broke through left guard for 6 yards and his second touchdown of the day. The Giants led, 17-7.

The Cowboys promptly rampaged 90 yards in eight plays, Tony Dorsett speeding for 23 yards and a touchdown that brought the Cowboys within field goal range, 17-14.

Back once more came the Cowboys. They rode to the Giant 36. Steve Pelluer lobbed a pass to Dorsett, who weaved behind a screen to the Giant 6. But Dallas tackle Phil Pozderac had been caught holding George Martin, and the ball went back 40 yards to the Giant 46.

George Martin would make Phil Pozderac's ride home even gloomier. With 40 seconds to go, Dallas reached the Giant 27. As Pelluer called the signals, Martin suddenly jumped up, waving his arms. Pozderac reacted, jumping off the line. Pelluer threw a pass that was caught at the Giant 11, but that, too, was called back because of the penalty against Pozderac. The frustrated Cowboys finally tried a 63-yard field goal, but Rafael Septien's boot fell short, and the Giants came away with a 17-14 squeaker.

"Joe Morris is their offense," Dallas coach Tom Landry said, perhaps still fuming over those two costly penalties. But as strange as it seemed, the truth was that the Giant running attack, a popgun weapon for so long while the passing had been a cannon, had suddenly roared louder than the passing attack. The Giants had gained 245 yards on the ground, 181 by Morris, while Phil Simms had gained only 47 yards through the air, his lowest ever as a Giant. He completed a measly 6 of 18, only 2 in the second half. The mainstay of the Giant offense for two seasons, Phil Simms had suddenly become a shaky reed.

Key Stats: Rushing: Morris, 29-181, Dallas, 24-102; passing: Simms, 6-18-47; receiving: Bavaro, 3-47.

WEEK 9
STANDINGS

AFC East	W	L	T		NFC East	W	L	T
N.Y. Jets	8	1	0		N.Y. Giants	7	2	0
New England	6	3	0		Washington	7	2	0
Miami	4	5	0		Dallas	6	3	0
Buffalo	2	7	0		Philadelphia	3	6	0
Indianapolis	0	9	0		St. Louis	2	7	0
AFC Central					NFC Central			
Cincinnati	6	3	0		Chicago	7	2	0
Cleveland	6	3	0		Minnesota	5	4	0
Pittsburgh	3	6	0		Detroit	3	6	0
Houston	1	8	0		Tampa Bay	2	7	0
AFC West					Green Bay	1	8	0
Denver	8	1	0		NFC West			
Kansas City	6	3	0		L.A. Rams	7	2	0
L.A. Raiders	5	4	0		Atlanta	5	3	1
Seattle	5	4	0		San Francisco	5	3	1
San Diego	1	8	0		New Orleans	4	5	0

SCORES

AFC
Cleveland 24, Indianapolis 9
Denver 21, L.A. Raiders 10
Kansas City 24, San Diego 23
Miami 28, Houston 7
N.Y. Jets 38, Seattle 7
NFC
L.A. Rams 20, Chicago 17
New Orleans 23, San Francisco 10
N.Y. Giants 17, Dallas 14
St. Louis 13, Philadelphia 10
Washington 44, Minnesota 38 (OT)
Interconference
Cincinnati 24, Detroit 7
New England 25, Atlanta 17
Pittsburgh 27, Green Bay 3
Tampa Bay 34, Buffalo 28

Week 10

New York Giants   0   10   7   0   17
Philadelphia Eagles 0   0   0 14   14

Phil Simms's slump stretched into a second week. He went 8 for 18. He passed for 130 yards, what he had been often gaining in two periods. After the Eagles intercepted two of his passes, he seemed tentative, throwing short, and his longest gain of the day would be 36 yards.

But Joe Morris again was the mouse that roared. He gained 111 yards in 27 tries and scored both Giant touchdowns. In truth, however, all 17 Giant points were set up by the Giant defense, which had 2 interceptions and 7 sacks, 3 by Lawrence Taylor.

In the second period of a scoreless game, a partially blocked Eagle punt fell dead on the Eagle 48, a 4-yarder. On five plays, the two big ones a 12-yard pass from Simms to back Tony Galbreath and a 15-yard toss to tight end Mark Bavaro, the Giants pushed to the 18. Little Joe then raced up the middle for the touchdown. Allegre's point-after moved the Giants ahead, 7-0.

Near the end of the period, cornerback Elvis Patterson intercepted a pass by Ron Jaworski at the Eagle 30. The offense could get only to the 7. Allegre kicked a field goal from the 22, and at the half the Giants led, 10-0.

Linebacker Gary Reasons took in another Jaworski pass early in the third period, bringing the ball from the Eagle 36 to the 18. Simms tossed a short pass to Bavaro, who struggled to the 8. Joe Morris slammed to the 3, and then drove into the end zone. Allegre converted, and the Giants had a seemingly cushy 17-0 lead.

They still led, 17-0, as Randall Cunningham replaced Jaworski in the fourth period. He struck quickly, hitting wideout Mike Quick with a 75-yard touchdown bomb. The Giants tried to protect the lead with cautious running plays, but after four minutes of possession, they had to punt the ball back to the Eagles, Landeta kicking to the Eagle 13.

Undaunted, Cunningham—he would complete 10 of 21 for 152 yards—slung a succession of passes that carried the Eagles 87 yards in twelve plays. Cunningham lunged over from the 1 for the TD, and the Giant lead had shrunk to three, 17-14.

But there were only forty-nine seconds to play. Tony Galbreath fell on the squibbed on-side kick at the Eagle 43, and Simms knelt for two plays that ran out the clock.

The Giants' running attack, for the second week in a row, had gained more yards (153) than the Giants' passing (130). Joe Morris had rung up a fourth-straight 100-yard-plus day, but the passing had become more suspect. The Giant offense went back to the Meadowlands knowing it would hear more than a word or two during the week from Bill Parcells.

Key Stats: Rushing: Morris, 27-111, Eagles, 18-78; passing: Simms, 8-18-130, Eagles, 18-36-202; receiving: Bavaro, 4-76.

WEEK 10
STANDINGS | SCORES

AFC East	W	L	T	NFC East	W	L	T	AFC
N.Y. Jets	9	1	0	N.Y. Giants	8	2	0	Buffalo 16, Pittsburgh 12
New England	7	3	0	Washington	8	2	0	Cleveland 26, Miami 16
Miami	4	6	0	Dallas	6	4	0	Houston 32, Cincinnati 28
Buffalo	3	7	0	Philadelphia	3	7	0	Kansas City 27, Seattle 7
Indianapolis	0	10	0	St. Louis	2	8	0	New England 30, Indianapolis 21
AFC Central				NFC Central				San Diego 9, Denver 3
Cleveland	7	3	0	Chicago	8	2	0	NFC
Cincinnati	6	4	0	Minnesota	6	4	0	Chicago 23, Tampa Bay 3
Pittsburgh	3	7	0	Detroit	3	7	0	Minnesota 24, Detroit 10
Houston	2	8	0	Tampa Bay	2	8	0	New Orleans 6, L.A. Rams 0
AFC West				Green Bay	1	9	0	N.Y. Giants 17, Philadelphia 14
Denver	8	2	0	NFC West				San Francisco 43, St. Louis 17
Kansas City	7	3	0	L.A. Rams	7	3	0	Washington 16, Green Bay 7
L.A. Raiders	6	4	0	San Francisco	6	3	1	Interconference
Seattle	5	5	0	Atlanta	5	4	1	L.A. Raiders 17, Dallas 13
San Diego	2	8	0	New Orleans	5	5	0	N.Y. Jets 28, Atlanta 14

| New York Giants | 3 | 6 | 3 | 10 | 22 |
| Minnesota Vikings | 3 | 3 | 7 | 7 | 20 |

The Play. It won this game against the Vikings. The Play, if you believe that one play can turn a self-doubting quarterback into one of Super-Bowl caliber, could be said to have made Phil Simms into a championship quarterback.

In the first half the defenses of both teams turned stubborn inside their 30-yard lines. A Giant drive stopped at the 26 and Allegre kicked a 41-yard field goal. A Viking drive was stopped at the 24 and Minnesota went for a 39-yarder to tie the game, 3-3. A Giant drive stopped at the 22 and Allegre kicked a 37-yarder to put the Giants ahead, 6-3. The Giants jammed up a Viking thrust at the 29 and the Vikings kicked a 44-yarder to tie the game, 6-6. Near the end of the second period, another Giant drive, after going 71 yards, could not push past the 9. Allegre kicked a 24-yarder to put the Giants ahead at the half, 9-6.

Early in the third period, Tommy Kramer steered the Vikes 79 yards, tossing a pass from the 8 to nail fullback Allen Rice in the end zone for the game's first touchdown and a 13-9 Minnesota lead.

As in Seattle, playing indoors seemed to mesmerize the Giant offense. But a break — a pass interference penalty — may have jolted them awake. The penalty moved the ball from the Vikes' 46 to the 15. Even with that break, the Giants couldn't score a touchdown. A rush by Maurice Carthon and two pass attempts by Phil Simms lost 5 yards. Allegre then kicked his fourth field goal from 37 yards out, and the lead was down to one, 13-12, as the fourth period began.

Still seeking their first TD of the game, the Giants pushed to the Viking 47. On an end-around play, Simms gave the ball to Joe Morris, who gave to end-arounding Bobby Johnson. The rangy Bobby streaked 22 yards down the left sideline to the Viking 25. Then Phil danced back and shot a pass to Johnson as he cut across the middle. Bobby ran away from Viking defenders to score and put the Giants ahead, after Allegre's kick, 19-13.

The Vikes took the kickoff and churned upfield to the Giant 33. Wideout Anthony Carter grabbed a pass in the end zone and the Vikings had jumped back out in front, 20-19.

The Giants had to punt, but so did the Vikings. There were two minutes remaining as the Giants took the ball on their 41. The Giants pushed to the Viking 43. Then, on a third and eight, Simms went back to pass. The Vikings' defensive end Doug Martin roared by a blocker and sacked Phil for a 9-yard loss.

Fourth down, seventeen yards to go, the ball on the Giant 48, a minute and twelve seconds to play.

Simms and Parcells huddled at the sideline. The Giants had no choice:

Pass for the first down. At the snap, wideout Bobby Johnson sped down the right sideline, then turned in just 5 yards past the first-down marker. The ball arrowed toward his outstretched hands, hit those hands, and Bobby went down at the Viking 30.

The Play — that 22-yard pass — had given life to a seemingly breathless corpse. Down by 1, the Giants needed only 3 to win. Three rushes by Joe Morris drained time out of the clock and moved the Giants to the Viking 15. Allegre trotted in, along with Jeff Rutledge, the Metrodome hushed. Bart Oates snapped the ball, Rutledge set it down at the 33. Allegre's foot swept through the ball. It arched squarely between the uprights for a 22-20 Giant victory — one that will rank among the most dramatic in Giant history.

The defense had given up 255 yards passing, 109 (and a 4.4 average) rushing — not one of its best performances. But, oh that offense! True, the running had slumped — 90 yards in 25 tries. But Simms had rocketed the ball 38 times and completed 25 for 310 yards (although his longest was only 25 yards). And by winning, the Giants stayed locked with the Redskins for first place in the NFC East.

Key Stats: **Rushing: Morris, 18-49; passing: Simms, 25-38-310; receiving:** Johnson 4-79, Bavaro 4-81, Anderson 4-19.

WEEK 11

STANDINGS

SCORES

AFC East	W	L	T	NFC East	W	L	T	
N.Y. Jets	10	1	0	N.Y. Giants	9	2	0	**AFC**
New England	8	3	0	Washington	9	2	0	Cincinnati 34, Seattle 7
Miami	5	6	0	Dallas	7	4	0	Denver 38, Kansas City 17
Buffalo	3	8	0	Philadelphia	3	8	0	L.A. Raiders 27, Cleveland 14
Indianapolis	0	11	0	St. Louis	2	9	0	Miami 34, Buffalo 24
AFC Central				NFC Central				N.Y. Jets 31, Indianapolis 16
Cincinnati	7	4	0	Chicago	9	2	0	Pittsburgh 21, Houston 10
Cleveland	7	4	0	Minnesota	6	5	0	**NFC**
Pittsburgh	4	7	0	Detroit	4	7	0	Chicago 13, Atlanta 10
Houston	2	9	0	Green Bay	2	9	0	Detroit 13, Philadelphia 11
AFC West				Tampa Bay	2	9	0	Green Bay 31, Tampa Bay 7
Denver	9	2	0	NFC West				New Orleans 16, St. Louis 7
Kansas City	7	4	0	L.A. Rams	7	4	0	N.Y. Giants 22, Minnesota 20
L.A. Raiders	7	4	0	San Francisco	6	4	1	Washington 14, San Francisco 6
Seattle	5	6	0	New Orleans	6	5	0	**Interconference**
San Diego	2	9	0	Atlanta	5	5	1	Dallas 24, San Diego 21
								New England 30, L.A. Rams 28

| Denver Broncos | 3 | 3 | 3 | 7 | 16 |
| New York Giants | 0 | 10 | 3 | 6 | 19 |

This was the eighth game in ten victories that the Giants won by 7 or fewer points. Said George Martin, one of the heroes of this game: "I've been here long enough to remember when we used to lose games like that. Benson and I can remember when we were never good enough to play close games with anyone."

This one stayed close because the Giant offense did a balanced job — Simms gained 148 yards, the rushers 143. It stayed close because the defense, though burned often by John Elway's passes (29 of 47 for 336 yards), would yield to him only 1 touchdown (while holding his rushers to 80 yards). And it stayed close enough for the Giants to win in the last few seconds, for a second straight week, because of an early Giant touchdown — by the defense.

The Broncos led, 6-3, after 2 field goals by Rich Karlis and 1 by Raul Allegre. Early in the second period the Broncos drove to the Giant 22. There the defense would produce one of its most electrifying moments of the 1986 season.

John Elway backpedaled to pass, pursued by George Martin. Elway tried to loop a pass over George to one of the Bronco backs curving toward the sideline. George leaped and grabbed the ball with one hand. He raced for the goal line three quarters of the field away.

A posse of Broncos pursued George. Elway dived at him, but big George shrugged him off. George saw another Bronco angling toward him. George knew that L.T. chugged right behind him. He thought about lateraling the ball to L.T., then chopping down the Bronco.

"I thought better of lateraling," George said later, "because of the prize." The prize was a thousand-dollar jackpot for the first Giant defender to score a touchdown. George crashed into the end zone with his seventh career TD, a record for a down lineman, and the Giants, after Allegre's PAT, led 10-6.

That touchdown would be the Giants' only TD of the afternoon. Early in the third period, Allegre kicked his second field goal, from 45 yards out, and the Giants led, 13-6.

The Broncos moved into field goal position as Elway, mixing his scrambling runs and passes to wideout Steve Watson and tight end Clarence Kay, reached the Giant 28. The barefooted Karlis kicked his third field goal, and the Giant lead was reduced to seven, 16-9.

The Broncos got that seven with only two minutes left in the game. They moved 73 yards in nine plays, the big one a 27-yard pass up the middle from Elway to Watson. Sammy Winder blasted over from 4 yards out and the game, after Karlis' PAT, was tied, 16-16, and apparently headed for overtime.

Karlis kicked off. Phil McConkey took the ball at the 7 and burst straight up the field to the 29. Now it was all up to Phil Simms and his offense that had yet to cross a goal line.

And almost immediately that offense seemed to have flopped again. On second down, left guard Keith Bishop smashed through a Giant blocker to dump Phil for an 11-yard loss, the third Bronco sack of the day.

Phil faced third and twenty-one from his 18. He took the ball in the shotgun formation. He looked for the same guy he had looked for a week earlier when it was fourth and seventeen against the Vikings. Bobby Johnson crossed the middle behind the linebackers. Phil threw a do-or-die pass. Bobby caught the ball at his waist and sprinted to the Giant 42, a 24-yard gain and a first down.

There was only about a minute to play, the ball near midfield. A holding penalty against Karl Nelson set the Giants back to their 39, second down and thirteen to go. The Giants needed another big play — and fast.

They got it from Simms. He sent Phil McConkey flying up the left sideline, then arched a long pass that Phil snared near the Bronco 15, a 46-yard strike that brought the Giants within range of what they needed to win — field goal.

The Giants ran twice into the line to scrub time off the clock. Then Allegre came in and, just as he done the week before against the Vikings, kicked a last-second field goal, this one from 34 yards out, and the Giants came away with another tight one, a 19-16 triumph. Their quarterback had proved to himself, for a second straight week, that when his team needed the big play in the two-minute drill, he could give them that big play.

Washington also won — and big. The Redskins trampled the Cowboys, 41-14. The Giants and Skins were still locked together at the top of the NFC East. Their showdown was coming two weeks hence.

As the Giants looked toward that showdown, they could reflect on the discomforting fact that they seldom won big: They had won five in a row — the last four by a total of 11 points.

Key Stats: Passing: Simms, 11-20-148, Elway, 29-47-336; rushing: Morris, 23-106, Denver, 22-80; receiving: Morris, 2-16, McConkey, 2-54, Willhite, 5-42, Winder, 6-32.

WEEK 12
STANDINGS

SCORES

AFC East	W	L	T	NFC East	W	L	T	AFC
N.Y. Jets	10	2	0	N.Y. Giants	10	2	0	Cleveland 37, Pittsburgh 31 (OT)
New England	9	3	0	Washington	10	2	0	Houston 31, Indianapolis 17
Miami	6	6	0	Dallas	7	5	0	L.A. Raiders 37, San Diego 31
Buffalo	3	9	0	Philadelphia	3	9	0	Miami 45, N.Y. Jets 3
Indianapolis	0	12	0	St. Louis	3	9	0	New England 22, Buffalo 19
AFC Central				NFC Central				NFC
Cincinnati	8	4	0	Chicago	10	2	0	Chicago 12, Green Bay 10
Cleveland	8	4	0	Minnesota	6	6	0	Detroit 38, Tampa Bay 17
Pittsburgh	4	8	0	Detroit	5	7	0	L.A. Rams 26, New Orleans 13
Houston	3	9	0	Green Bay	2	10	0	San Francisco 20, Atlanta 0
AFC West				Tampa Bay	2	10	0	Washington 41, Dallas 14
Denver	9	3	0	NFC West				Interconference
L.A. Raiders	8	4	0	L.A. Rams	8	4	0	Cincinnati 24, Minnesota 20
Kansas City	7	5	0	San Francisco	7	4	1	N.Y. Giants 19, Denver 16
Seattle	6	6	0	New Orleans	6	6	0	St. Louis 23, Kansas City 14
San Diego	2	10	0	Atlanta	5	6	1	Seattle 24, Philadelphia 20

Week 13

New York Giants	0	0	21	0	21
San Francisco 49ers	3	14	0	0	17

At the half Bill Parcells had every reason to stare at the stat sheet with horror in his eyes. This is what the stats showed:

↙The Giants had given up two touchdowns and a field goal without any kind of a reply.

↙The Giants had gained a total of two yards rushing, all of them by Joe Morris, who had carried six times for an average gain of 0.3 yards.

↙Phil Simms had thrown 22 passes, completing 14 for 175 yards, but not one for a score.

↙Joe Montana, meanwhile, had completed 17 of 24 attempts for 145 yards. He had engineered drives of 69, 72 and 77 yards for the 49ers' field goal and 2 touchdowns.

This looked like a blowaway, a first for the 1986 Giants.

Once more, the Lunch Pail Guys proved to Parcells that they were come-from-behind guys. The defense came out for the second half and held Montana to 15 completions in 28 attempts. It held the 49er rushers to 32 yards in 9 tries. It did not allow another 49er point.

And during a nine-minute frenzy of scoring, Phil Simms threw 3 lightning-bolt TDs at the 49ers that left the 60,000 spectators at Candlestick Park stunned.

The Giants took a punt early in the third period and moved to the San Francisco 49. Phil sent Mark Bavaro deep and hit him near the 30, Mark plunging on to the 21. Moments later, from the 17, Simms hit Joe Morris in the end zone, and the Giants were on the scoreboard: San Francisco 17, Giants 7.

The 49ers had to punt against a Giant defense that had steam coming out of its ears. The Giants took the ball at their 29. A screen pass to Ottis Anderson gained 12 yards. Joe Morris cracked through right tackle for 17 and a first down at the San Francisco 34.

Again Simms sent a receiver deep. Stacy Robinson forged ahead of a 49ers defender on a post pattern and caught the ball going into the end zone—a 34-yard toss that brought the Giants within 3, 17-14.

Joe Montana went three downs and the 49ers had to punt against the defense that suddenly had no holes in it. The Giants took over once more at their 29. Simms's arm flashed twice, once flinging a pass to Maurice Carthon for 7 yards, then to Phil McConkey for 12, and the ball sat on the 50. Again Stacy Robinson went deep, and he shot ahead of defender Don Griffin. Stacy turned and pulled in Phil's spiral, crashing to the ground at the 1. Ottis Anderson ploughed over, and the Giants, after Allegre's third straight PAT, led, 21-17.

One measure of the swiftness of those three TD strikes: a total of 15 plays had scored the 3 touchdowns.

Montana brought the 49ers back to the Giant front door late in the game, reaching the Giant 17. On third and four, Carl Banks dropped running back Wendell Tyler for a 4-yard loss, and a pass to Roger Craig was batted down by linebacker Andy Headen.

The Giants flew home with their sixth straight triumph—the cumulative margin of victory 22 points. Washington squeaked by St. Louis, 20-17, and the two teams, at 11-2, prepared for the showdown that would decide the winner of NFC East.

In the back of the plane, offensive guard Brad Benson wore a worried look on his square face. The NFL's sack leader was the Redskins' Dexter Manley—and it would be Brad's job, all alone, to keep Dexter out of the face of Phil Simms.

Key Stats: Passing: Simms, 27-38-388, Joe Montana, 32-52-251; rushing: Morris, 13-14, San Francisco, 27-116; receiving: Bavaro, 7-98, Robinson, 5-116, Morris, 4-42, McConkey, 2-46, Roger Craig, 12-75, Jerry Rice, 9-86.

WEEK 13
STANDINGS

AFC East	W	L	T	NFC East	W	L	T	SCORES
								AFC
New England	10	3	0	N.Y. Giants	11	2	0	Buffalo 17, Kansas City 14
N.Y. Jets	10	3	0	Washington	11	2	0	Cleveland 13, Houston 10 (OT)
Miami	6	7	0	Dallas	7	6	0	Denver 34, Cincinnati 28
Buffalo	4	9	0	Philadelphia	4	9	0	San Diego 17, Indianapolis 3
Indianapolis	0	13	0	St. Louis	3	10	0	**NFC**
AFC Central				NFC Central				Green Bay 44, Detroit 40
Cleveland	9	4	0	Chicago	11	2	0	Minnesota 45, Tampa Bay 13
Cincinnati	8	5	0	Minnesota	7	6	0	N.Y. Giants 21, San Francisco 17
Pittsburgh	4	9	0	Detroit	5	8	0	Washington 20, St. Louis 17
Houston	3	10	0	Green Bay	3	10	0	**Interconference**
AFC West				Tampa Bay	2	11	0	Atlanta 20, Miami 14
Denver	10	3	0	NFC West				Chicago 13, Pittsburgh 10 (OT)
L.A. Raiders	8	5	0	L.A. Rams	9	4	0	L.A. Rams 17, N.Y. Jets 3
Kansas City	7	6	0	San Francisco	7	5	1	New England 21, New Orleans 20
Seattle	7	6	0	Atlanta	6	6	1	Philadelphia 33, L.A. Raiders 27 (OT)
San Diego	3	10	0	New Orleans	6	7	0	Seattle 31, Dallas 14

Week 14

New York Giants	0	14	10	0	24
Washington Redskins	0	7	0	7	14

"I probably have three ulcers sitting around waiting to play him today," offensive tackle Brad Benson was saying a few hours before the game in Washington. "Everywhere I turned this week, I saw a picture of him. You have to stop his momentum to beat the Redskins. When he gets going, it really fires up the rest of the Redskins."

Benson had to stop Dexter Manley, at that point the NFL leader in sacks, so that Phil Simms would have time to fire the artillery of the Giant passing attack. Brad did the job so well that Simms threw for 265 yards and was sacked only once, never by Manley. Washington coach Joe Gibbs said after the game: "I don't feel like we got good pressure on their quarterback and I think they did on ours."

The Giants pressured the Redskin quarterback, brawny Jay Schroeder, so severely that he might have come out of the game thinking he had been in a wrestling match. The Giants sacked him 4 times (3 by Lawrence Taylor) and hounded him so persistently that he threw 6 interceptions.

For keeping Dexter Manley out of Phil Simms's throat, Brad Benson was awarded the NFC Offensive Player of the Week award—the first time in history that a lineman had won the award. And how did Dexter feel about being held to only 3 tackles and no sacks? "I feel," he said, "like I've just sucked a bunch of raw eggs."

As important as the duel between Manley and Benson was, some players thought the pivotal play was a pass completed by Phil Simms late in the first half that seemed to swing the tide of the game toward the Giant side.

After a scoreless first period, the Giants drove 77 yards in ten plays, the big play a sideline pass to Bobby Johnson good for 19 yards. (Joe Morris was not a major factor in the game, carrying 22 times for only 62 yards, his biggest gain for 11, and the Giant rushers could total only 74 yards.) From the 9, Phil Simms saw tight end Mark Bavaro cut across the middle of the end zone. Phil threw a streamliner pass that Mark's big hands hooked onto. The Giants had drawn first blood in this showdown duel for the NFC East championship.

Raul Allegre's kick put the Giants ahead, 7-0. A little later Schroeder took the snap at the Washington 20, stepped into his pocket and watched wideout Gary Clark break clear near the 40. Schroeder nailed him with a dart that Clark grabbed at the Washington 48. He streaked to the Giant 26, where Elvis Patterson finally hauled him down.

A minute later, Kelvin Bryant plunged over from the 4, the Redskins kicked the extra point, and with only a minute and 50 seconds to play, it seemed that the half would end in a 7-7 tie.

It wouldn't. After the kickoff, the Giants moved from their 19 to their 40. There Simms looked at a third and seven, with only 53 seconds to play. The Redskins geared up to sack Simms as he called signals from the shotgun. But the Redskin pass rushers were stonewalled by Brad Benson and Co., Parcells's Suburbanites. Phil had time to see Stacy Robinson go deep, then turn in near the Washington 30. When Stacy turned, the ball was hissing toward his hands — a 34-yard stab that put the Giants within field goal range.

Phil went for the jugular. He sent Stacy Robinson veering to the right side and hit him at the Washington 7. On the next play he rifled the ball into Bobby Johnson's hands in the end zone, and after the kick, the Giants went to intermission ahead, 14-7.

"Simms had us confused after that long pass to Robinson," Washington safety Curtis Jordan said after the game. "After he threw that long one, our coverage was upset and he was able to complete his next two to get the touchdown. But the pivotal play was that third and seven to Robinson."

Early in the third period the Giants went 76 yards, their longest gain in the thirteen-play drive a 22-yarder from Simms to Mark Bavaro. But the Giants, hurt by a penalty inside the Washington 10, could not get by the 4 and had to settle for a 21-yard field goal.

Behind 17-7, the Redskins took the kickoff to their 22. Jay Schroeder came out of the huddle ready to throw. The Giants poured in on him. He threw hastily. Linebacker Harry Carson stepped in front of a Redskin receiver at the 34, snatched the ball and ran it to the Washington 14. Simms then put the ball into the hands of Phil McConkey as Phil angled into the left corner of the end zone.

Behind now, 24-7, Schroeder had to pass, especially since his running attack had been of no use to him, the Giants holding Redskin rushers to 73 yards in 17 carries. As the fourth period started, 3 completions moved the Redskins into Giant territory. Schroeder went back one more time, harried by L.T. and Leonard Marshall. He threw over their grasping hands. Linebacker Byron Hunt tipped the ball and it came down into the arms of Marshall. A little later another Schroeder pass was picked off by Andy Headen. An 80-yard Washington drive, with about three minutes to play, ended with a 22-yard TD pass, Schroeder to Kelvin Bryant, for a touchdown. But all that last TD did was to make the 24-14 game seem closer than it really was.

L.T. had led the assault on Schroeder with 3 sacks and at least 3 knockdowns. L.T. was on his way to catching Dexter Manley and becoming the NFL's sack champion.

The Giants had won first place in the NFC East. And they had won by what was, for them, a wide margin, their 14-point victory the biggest since their victory over the Eagles, 35-3, eight weeks earlier.

Key Stats: Passing: Simms, 15-19-265, Schroeder, 28-51-309; receiving: Bavaro, 5-111, Galbreath, 2-22, Johnson, 3-60, McConkey, 2-24; Giant interceptions: Lasker, Welch, Williams, Carson, Marshall, Headen, 1 each; rushing: Washington, 17-73.

WEEK 14
STANDINGS

AFC East	W	L	T
New England	10	4	0
N.Y. Jets	10	4	0
Miami	7	7	0
Buffalo	4	10	0
Indianapolis	1	13	0
AFC Central			
Cleveland	10	4	0
Cincinnati	9	5	0
Pittsburgh	5	9	0
Houston	3	11	0
AFC West			
Denver	10	4	0
Kansas City	8	6	0
L.A. Raiders	8	6	0
Seattle	8	6	0
San Diego	4	10	0

NFC East	W	L	T
N.Y. Giants	12	2	0
Washington	11	3	0
Dallas	7	7	0
Philadelphia	4	9	1
St. Louis	3	10	1
NFC Central			
Chicago	12	2	0
Minnesota	8	6	0
Detroit	5	9	0
Green Bay	3	11	0
Tampa Bay	2	12	0
NFC West			
L.A. Rams	10	4	0
San Francisco	8	5	1
Atlanta	6	7	1
New Orleans	6	8	0

SCORES

AFC
Cincinnati 31, New England 7
Cleveland 21, Buffalo 17
Kansas City 37, Denver 10
San Diego 27, Houston 0
Seattle 37, L.A. Raiders 0

NFC
Chicago 48, Tampa Bay 14
L.A. Rams 29, Dallas 10
Minnesota 32, Green Bay 6
N.Y. Giants 24, Washington 14
St. Louis 10, Philadelphia 10 (OT)

Interconference
Pittsburgh 27, Detroit 17
Indianapolis 28, Atlanta 23
Miami 31, New Orleans 27
San Francisco 24, N.Y. Jets 10

St. Louis Cardinals	0	0	0	7	7
New York Giants	7	10	3	7	27

This was a game the Giants didn't have to win. The Giants had clinched their first division title since 1963 a day earlier when the Redskins lost to the Broncos. But this victory gave the Giants the home-field advantage for the playoffs — an advantage that most NFC teams in the past ten years had employed to vault to the Super Bowl.

This game, moreover, seemed to be the one when the 1986 Giants put everything together — artful passing, breakaways bursts by Joe Morris and a suffocating defense. The time for the close ones was now behind the Giants. No more would there be last-second field goals to win nail-biting 3 point victories. From here on in, during the final five games of the journey to the championship, all the Giant wins would be resounding ones. And those wins would be climaxed by what had become a Giant ritual during this eight-game winning streak — the dousing of Bill Parcells with a barrel of Gatorade.

Joe Morris ran wild against the Cardinals, gaining 179 yards and scoring 3 touchdowns. He took off on nonscoring spins of 49 and 54 yards. He ended the day with 1,401 yards for the season, breaking his club record of 1,336.

Phil Simms completed only 5 of 21. But he seemed to have regained his trust in his receivers. He threw no completions to halfback Tony Galbreath, who would end the season as his second-leading receiver. Instead, passes went to his wide receivers, Stacy Robinson, Phil McConkey and Bobby Johnson, and 2 to his tight end, Mark Bavaro.

The Giant defense swarmed over Cardinal runners, yielding only 84 yards in 20 tries. Early in the game Harry Carson dumped Neil Lomax (he would be sacked 9 times) at the 1. A Cardinal punt gave the Giants the ball on the Cardinal 25. Seven plays later, Joe Morris sliced through right tackle for his first TD.

He got his second in the second period. From the 20 he exploded out of the line of scrimmage to race 54 yards, caught from behind at the Cardinal 26. Five plays later he slanted off right tackle for 3 yards and touchdown number two.

Raul Allegre kicked a field goal near the end of the period to give the Giants a 17-0 halftime lead. Allegre kicked another field goal in the third period for a 20-0 Giant lead. Joe Morris lost a fumble at the Giant 26, but even from this short distance, the Cardinals were lucky to score against the Giant defense. On a sweep, halfback Stump Mitchell was trapped near the sideline at the 15 by Giant defenders. He saw wideout Roy Green alone in the end zone and flipped the ball to him for the TD. Later TV's John Madden said of the Giant defense, "I thought I had seen great defenses, but these Giants are playing the best defense I have ever seen."

Ahead 20-7, the Giants picked up a Cardinal fumble at the Giant 48. On a third and eight from the 50, Simms gave to Little Joe, who shot through right tackle and zipped to the 1, where he was tripped from behind by cornerback Lionel Washington. On the next play Joe tumbled over the right side for his third touchdown and the wrapper on the 27-7 triumph.

Relishing the pleasure of a no-sweat win, Bill Parcells said, "I believe we're destined to do something great."

Key Stats: Rushing: Morris, 28-179, Cardinals, 20-84, Giants, 47-251; passing: Simms, 5-21-82, Lomax, 20-27-153; receiving: Bavaro, 2-42.

WEEK 15

STANDINGS								SCORES
AFC East	W	L	T	**NFC East**	W	L	T	**AFC**
New England	10	5	0	N.Y. Giants	13	2	0	Cleveland 34, Cincinnati 3
N.Y. Jets	10	5	0	Washington	11	4	0	Indianapolis 24, Buffalo 14
Miami	8	7	0	Dallas	7	8	0	Kansas City 20, L.A. Raiders 17
Buffalo	4	11	0	Philadelphia	5	9	1	Pittsburgh 45, N.Y. Jets 24
Indianapolis	2	13	0	St. Louis	3	11	1	Seattle 34, San Diego 24
AFC Central				**NFC Central**				**NFC**
Cleveland	11	4	0	Chicago	13	2	0	Chicago 16, Detroit 13
Cincinnati	9	6	0	Minnesota	8	7	0	Green Bay 21, Tampa Bay 7
Pittsburgh	6	9	0	Detroit	5	10	0	New Orleans 16, Atlanta 10
Houston	4	11	0	Green Bay	4	11	0	N.Y. Giants 27, St. Louis 7
AFC West				Tampa Bay	2	13	0	Philadelphia 23, Dallas 21
Denver	11	4	0	**NFC West**				**Interconference**
Kansas City	9	6	0	L.A. Rams	10	5	0	Denver 31, Washington 30
Seattle	9	6	0	San Francisco	9	5	1	Houston 16, Minnesota 10
L.A. Raiders	8	7	0	New Orleans	7	8	0	Miami 37, L.A. Rams 31 (OT)
San Diego	4	11	0	Atlanta	6	8	1	San Francisco 29, New England 24

Week 16

Green Bay Packers	0	17	7	0	24
New York Giants	21	3	14	17	55

The game meaningless, the Giants still put on a show for the capacity crowd at Giants Stadium. On a cold, cloudy day, the Giants scored more points than in any game since 1972. The 79 points scored by both teams were the third highest in Giants' history. And both sides of the team had outstanding days—Phil Simms passed for 245 yards, Joe Morris rushed for 115 and his fourteenth TD of the season. The defense did relax in the second and third periods—it allowed 119 yards rushing, 199 passing—but it clamped down in the fourth period to blank a Packer team that seemed to be making a dramatic comeback.

The Giants jumped out to a 24-0 lead. The offense got the first, a 24-yard pass from Simms to Mark Bavaro. The defense got the second when safety Tom Flynn picked up the bounding ball after the Giants blocked a punt and weaved 36 yards for the TD. Late in the first period Joe Morris went over from the 3 for a 21-0 lead. Midway through the second period, Raul Allegre kicked a 46-yarder to put the Giants ahead, 24-0.

The Packers fought back. They stormed 76 yards in six plays to score on a 13-yard pass from Randy Wright to Eddie Lee Ivery. Two minutes later, safety Ken Still picked off a pass by Simms and shot 58 yards for the Pack's second TD, the score now 24-14.

Just before the half, Al Del Greco hit a 34-yard field goal and the Giants' fat lead of 24 had shrunk to 7, 24-17. At halftime Bill Parcells had to feel a sense of *deja vu*. Was this another one of those nail-biting squeakers?

Simms told him not to worry. On the Giants' first possession of the third period, the offense went 80 yards in 12 plays, Simms passing to Bavaro for the TD. Score: Giants 31, Pack 14.

Still battling, the Pack struck right back, Wright hitting Ken Davis in the end zone. Again, after the extra point, the Giant lead was down to one touchdown, 31-24.

But the defense had enough. It shut down Wright and his rushers the rest of the way. Simms hit Zeke Mowatt with a 22-yard pass, Zeke making a circus catch in the end zone for a 38-24 lead.

By now Parcells was inserting his second stringers, the playoffs ahead. Lee Rouson ended a 60-yard drive by sweeping right end for the Giants' sixth touchdown. A few minutes later, after the Giants' Perry Williams snagged a Wright pass at the Pack 46, the Giants' rushers — Rouson and Ottis Anderson — teamed on drives to reach the Packer 21. Jeff Rutledge, now the quarterback, gave to Rouson, who sprinted around left end and charged into the end zone and a 52-24 lead. With about five minutes to play, Allegre finished off the scoring spree with a 26-yard field goal.

The field goal angered the Pack players, who thought Parcells was piling on points. Bill shrugged. "It was first and one at their 8," he said. "If I go for the first down, it's embarrassing, and if I kick the field goal, it's embarrassing. I can't win there."

The only blemish on the day, for the defense, was L.T.'s failure to get a sack. He finished the season with 20½ sacks, 1½ shy of the NFL record set by Mark Gastineau of the Jets. "I wanted the record," L.T. said. "But they really knocked the stuffing out of me a few times."

The Giants would have two weeks off to prepare for the playoffs. Their opponents — although the Giants could not know it at the time — were three opponents they had beaten during the season: Washington (twice), San Francisco and Denver. The Giants had won all four games by a total of 24 points — and no margin had been wider than 7 points.

San Francisco...Washington...Denver...Each had come close to beating the Giants during the season.

But somewhere after mid-season, maybe in Minnesota facing a fourth and seventeen, this Giants team had become a super Giants team — as it would soon prove.

Key Stats: Passing: Simms 18-25-245; receiving: Bavaro, 5-59, Johnson, 2-44, Robinson, 3-39; rushing: Giants, 45-226, Morris, 22-115.

WEEK 16

STANDINGS								SCORES
AFC East	**W**	**L**	**T**	**NFC East**	**W**	**L**	**T**	
New England	11	5	0	N.Y. Giants	14	2	0	**AFC**
N.Y. Jets	10	6	0	Washington	12	4	0	Cincinnati 52, N.Y. Jets 21
Miami	8	8	0	Dallas	7	9	0	Cleveland 47, San Diego 17
Buffalo	4	12	0	Philadelphia	5	10	1	Houston 16, Buffalo 7
Indianapolis	3	13	0	St. Louis	4	11	1	Indianapolis 30, L.A. Raiders 24
AFC Central				**NFC Central**				Kansas City 24, Pittsburgh 19
Cleveland	12	4	0	Chicago	14	2	0	New England 34, Miami 27
Cincinnati	10	6	0	Minnesota	9	7	0	Seattle 41, Denver 16
Pittsburgh	6	10	0	Detroit	5	11	0	**NFC**
Houston	5	11	0	Green Bay	4	12	0	Atlanta 20, Detroit 6
AFC West				Tampa Bay	2	14	0	Chicago 24, Dallas 10
Denver	11	5	0	**NFC West**				Minnesota 33, New Orleans 17
Kansas City	10	6	0	San Francisco	10	5	1	N.Y. Giants 55, Green Bay 24
Seattle	10	6	0	L.A. Rams	10	6	1	St. Louis 21, Tampa Bay 17
L.A. Raiders	8	8	0	Atlanta	7	8	1	San Francisco 24, L.A. Rams 14
San Diego	4	12	0	New Orleans	7	9	0	Washington 21, Philadelphia 14

Giants' 1986 Season Statistics

Overall Defense		
Points Allowed Per Game	14.8	League Rank 2nd
Yards Allowed Per Game	297.3	League Rank 2nd
Yards Allowed Per Play	4.78	League Rank 8th
First Downs Allowed per Game	17.8	League Rank 6th

Offense		
Passing		
Passing Yards Per Game	195.8	League Rank 17th
Completion Percentage	55.1%	League Rank 15th
Times Sacked	46	League Rank 18th
Passes Had Intercepted	22	League Rank 17th tied
Touchdowns	22	League Rank 9th tied

Rushing		
Yards Per Game	140.3	League Rank 6th
Yards Per Play	4.02	League Rank 11th
Touchdowns	18	League Rank 7th tied

Passing Defense		
Yards Allowed Per Game	217.1	League Rank 19th
Yards Allowed Per Pass Play	5.38	League Rank 4th
Sacks	59	League Rank 4th
Passes Intercepted	24	League Rank 7th tied

Rushing Defense		
Yards Allowed Per Game....... 80.3	League Rank 1st
Yards Allowed Per Play........ 3.67	League Rank 6th

Special Teams	
Field Goal Percentage.......... 70.3% ...	League Rank 15th
Punting Average.............. 44.8	League Rank 1st
Punt Return Average.......... 7.0	League Rank 24th
Kickoff Return Average........ 17.4	League Rank 27th tied

Giants' 1986 Individual Statistics

Rushing	No	Yds	Avg	Long	TD
Morris	341	1516	4.4	54	14
Carthon	72	260	3.6	12	0
Rouson	54	179	3.3	21t	2
Anderson.................	24	81	3.4	16	1
Simms	43	72	1.7	18	1
Galbreath	16	61	3.8	10	0
B. Johnson...............	2	28	14.0	22	0
Manuel...................	1	25	25.0	25	0
Rutledge	3	19	6.3	18	0
Miller	1	3	3.0	3	0
Hostetler	1	1	1.0	1	0

Passing	Att	Comp	Pct	Yards	Avg	TD	%TD	Int	%Int	Long	Rating
Simms.....	468	259	55.3	3487	7.45	21	4.5	22	4.7	49	74.6
Rutledge ..	3	1	33.3	13	4.33	1	33.3	0	0.0	13t	87.5
Galbreath..	1	0	0.0	0	0.00	0	0.0	0	0.0	0	39.6

Receiving	No	Yds	Avg	Long	TD
Bavaro	66	1001	15.2	41	4
Galbreath	33	268	8.1	19	0
B. Johnson	31	534	17.2	44t	5
Robinson	29	494	17.0	49	2
Morris	21	233	11.1	23	1
McConkey	16	279	17.4	46	1
Carthon	16	67	4.2	10	0
Manuel	11	181	16.5	35	3
Mowatt	10	119	11.9	30	2
Miller	9	144	16.0	32t	2
Anderson	9	46	5.1	12	0
Rouson	8	121	15.1	37t	1
Carson	1	13	13.0	13t	1

Interceptions	No	Yds	Avg	Long	TD
Kinard	4	52	13.0	25	0
Williams	4	31	7.8	15	0
Hill	3	25	8.3	23	0
Reasons	2	28	14.0	18	0
Patterson	2	26	13.0	26	0
Welch	2	22	11.0	16	0
Martin	1	78	78.0	78t	1
Carson	1	20	20.0	20	0
P. Johnson	1	13	13.0	13	0
Headen	1	1	1.0	1	0
Collins	1	0	0.0	0	0
Flynn	1	0	0.0	0	0
Lasker	1	0	0.0	0	0
Marshall	1	0	0.0	0	0

Punting		No	Yds	Avg	Long	Blk
Landeta		79	3539	44.8	61	0

Punt Returns	No	FC	Yds	Avg	Long	TD
McConkey	32	12	253	7.9	22	0
Collins	3	1	11	3.7	6	0
Galbreath	3	1	1	0.3	1	0
Manuel	3	6	22	7.3	12	0

Kickoff Returns	No	Yds	Avg	Long	TD
McConkey	24	471	19.6	27	0
Collins	11	204	18.5	26	0
Miller	7	111	15.9	23	0
Hill	5	61	12.2	30	0
Rouson	2	21	10.5	12	0
Lasker	1	0	0.0	0	0

Field Goals	1-19	20-29	30-39	40-49	50+	Total
Allegre	0-0	10-11	8-8	6-11	0-2	24-32
Cooper	0-0	2-2	0-1	0-1	0-0	2-4
Thomas	0-0	0-0	0-1	0-0	0-0	0-1

The Playoffs

San Francisco 49ers	3	0	0	0	3
New York Giants	7	21	21	0	49

Some of the 76,000 fans were still looking for their seats when 49er flanker Jerry Rice took off from the line of scrimmage, slanting toward the inside. Giant cornerback Elvis Patterson cut with him, but Rice swerved and gained a full step on Patterson.

Joe Montana's arm swept downward. The football streaked on a brown arc toward Rice's straining arms. The broomstick-thin pass receiver greeted the ball with outstretched fingers at about the 35, pulled it toward his chest and saw only turf between himself and the goal line.

He crossed the 30, knees pumping high, Patterson running a fading second. But Rice stumbled. One knee hit the arm that carried the ball. The ball popped loose, tumbling ahead of Rice's reaching arms in a scene that must have seemed nightmarish to Rice.

The ball bounded crazily toward the goal line, Rice in pursuit of the ball, a blue cloak of Giants chasing Rice and the ball.

Rice dived. The ball twisted away, spinning into the end zone. A blue jersey crashed on top of it. Giant safety Kenny Hill jumped up, clutching the ball. The crowd roared with a mixture of delight, surprise and relief.

That fumble was the good news for the 49ers on this afternoon that turned even more nightmarish for them, more astonishing for the Giants. For never again would the 49ers come as close to scoring a touchdown. "Never in my wildest nightmares could I have envisioned this," 49er tackle Keith Fahnhorst said after the game. "Shattered, we were simply shattered," 49er coach Bill Walsh said. "They played a perfect game. They destroyed our offense, shattered our blocking angles. We were dealt with."

Free safety Ronnie Lott sat on a stool in the quiet 49er dressing room and muttered, "The only time I was ever whipped this bad was when I was a little kid playing in the backyard. But in organized football — never!"

The Giants offensive line had been embarrassed by the 21-17 victory over the 49ers on December 1. The Giants had gained only 13 yards rushing. Strong safety Carlton Williamson had come close to the line to glue himself to Joe Morris. The linemen and linebackers drove on an angle into the Giants' strong side.

The 49ers decided to change tactics for this playoff game. They moved Williamson back into pass coverage and put Ronnie Lott up near the line to rove against the run.

Giant coaches suspected that the 49ers would not use Williamson to stop the rush. At practice during the week they showed Phil Simms a 49er defense that had Lott moved up to play the run and Williamson dropped back to defend against the pass.

Simms looked confused. Frowning, he told the coaches, "You should have it the other way around." After the game, aware the coaches had guessed correctly, he told a reporter, "Just goes to show you how much I know."

The Giants practiced with two tight ends. The idea was to check the 49ers from overloading on the strong side and jamming up Giant runners. "They didn't know which way we were going," guard Billy Ard said after the game. "So that made it tough for them to pull tricks."

The Giants were wound up, ready to explode onto the Meadowlands gridiron even before the sun rose on January 4. "I woke up at three a.m.," Ard said. "In the next room in our hotel I could hear one of our guys banging the walls. Harry Carson was already up. Lots of guys were, even the sound sleepers. We wanted it bad. Thirteen yards last time, that's an embarrassment."

The embarrassment would vanish within minutes after Rice's fumble of what seemed like a sure touchdown pass.

After the recovery, the Giants started on their 20. In nine plays they moved to the 49ers' 24. From there Simms threw to Mark Bavaro for what would be the first of 7 touchdowns. After Raul Allegre's kick, the Giants led, 7-0.

In the December game, Joe Montana had driven Giant defenders to distraction with timed passes, usually on a dropback consuming less than two seconds, to receivers hooking toward the sideline. To put pressure on Montana in this game, the Giants—rather than blitzing Lawrence Taylor as the 49ers expected—stunted and blitzed their inside people. That surprise attack threw a monkey wrench into the middle of the 49ers' passing machinery. "We had brought in two tight ends and worked them all week to contain the pass rushing of Taylor," Walsh confessed later. "And then they didn't blitz him much and we were stuck looking at new formations."

Cool Joe, though, moved the 49er machine 45 yards to the Giant 26. A third-down pass fell wide. Ron Wersching kicked what would be the 49ers only score of the day. Giants 7, 49ers 3.

The smiles on the 49er side, breaking out for the first time since that Rice fumble, soon would disappear.

Midway through the second period, the ball on the 49ers' 45, Joe Morris shot up the middle, a 45-yard bolt into the end zone that put the Giants ahead, 14-3. Now the touchdowns began to pile up at a rate almost too brisk to count.

The Giants got to the 49ers' 28, fourth down. Bill Parcells sent in his field goal team — but three regulars were smuggled onto the field in the midst of the special team, one of them tight end Mark Bavaro.

The Giants lined up in field-goal formation, quarterback Jeff Rutledge kneeling in front of Allegre.

"Switch," Rutledge shouted, Allegre darted wide to the left. Rutledge stood up, alone in the backfield waiting for the pass from center in shotgun formation.

49er defensive back Tom Holmoe ran wide to cover Allegre. He didn't see Bavaro, who shot by him as the ball was snapped to Rutledge. Gripping the ball, Rutledge looked for Tony Galbreath or Maurice Carthon, both of whom had been smuggled into the game with Bavaro. He couldn't find them open. He looked for his third option, Bavaro, and saw him all alone. Rutledge lofted a short pass to the burly tight end, who was dragged down near the 5. The Giant crowd was still roaring over this Parcells hocus-pocus as Simms drilled Bobby Johnson in the end zone and the Giants led, 21-7.

Just 22 seconds later they had what now seemed like the clinching touchdown — and Montana had been knocked out of the game. Stepping back to pass near his 15, Montana looked downfield for Jerry Rice. Coming straight at him was some 255 pounds of nose tackle — Jim Burt. Burt steamrollered into Montana. Burt's right forearm struck Montana in the chest as Montana came over the top with his throw. Burt rammed into Montana, lifting the passer into the air so that he was almost horizontal to the ground. Montana landed on his back, his helmet hitting the hard turf.

The ball, its force broken by Burt's jolting blow to Montana, wobbled weakly well short of the cutting Rice. Lawrence Taylor, dropping back near the right sideline, saw the ball sinking. He grabbed the ball at his beltline and sped down the sideline. He crossed into the end zone before a 49er could cut him off.

Montana lay curled on the ground. "I didn't mean to hit him like that," Burt said after the game. "I couldn't stop my momentum and he had thrown off his back foot and was leaning toward me. I never want to hurt anybody. This puts a damper on the game for me."

Within the hour Montana was being carried by ambulance to a Manhattan hospital, where doctors treated him for a concussion.

Ahead now 28-3, the Giants began the second half with a 75-yard drive that ended with a 28-yard touchdown strike from Simms to Phil McConkey. Seven minutes later the Giants drove 51 yards to score on a 29-yard pass from Simms to Zeke Mowatt. The Giants ended the 49ers' agony in the closing seconds of the third period, Morris plunging over from the 2 for the game's final score.

Ahead now 49-3, the Giants ran out the last 15 minutes with time-wasting sweeps to the left and right by Morris, Rouson and Carthon.

Jack Kemp had stepped into the 49er huddle to replace Montana. In the third period he let loose a stream of passes, usually backpedaling away from

Giant blitzers, and he completed only 7 of 22. By the fourth period the 49ers had called in the dogs, knowing the hunt was over for another Vince Lombardi Trophy. Walsh told Kemp what Parcells had told Simms: run out the clock. Walsh could have added, "So we can get out of here as soon as possible."

Talking to writers in the locker room, Bill Parcells could not contain his astonishment: "No one expected a game like this in the NFL, especially in the playoffs. It was just one of those things, when everything went right, no matter what we did. We made no mistakes. Everything we tried worked, just like on a blackboard."

Only two games in playoff history had ended in more lopsided scores: The Bears' 73-0 wrecking of the Redskins in 1940, and the Raiders' 56-7 thumping of Houston in 1969.

Other numbers told just how overwhelming was the Giant victory: 29 yards rushing for San Francisco, 217 for the Giants, 4 turnovers by San Francisco each costing a touchdown, no turnovers by the Giants. "You make mistakes in a game," said 49er guard Randy Cross, "but every one we made today resulted in points."

Would the score have been different if Rice had not fumbled that sure touchdown pass? Said Lawrence Taylor: "If they score on that one, they lose 49-10."

A day earlier the Redskins had shocked the champion Bears. Washington came from 13-7 behind at the half to score 20 points in the last half while blanking the Bears to win, 27-13.

In 1940 the Giants had to beat the Redskins three times in a row to win the eastern division title and go to the playoff final. They won the first two, but lost the third—and stayed home.

Could this year's Lawrence Taylor and Phil Simms's club do what Mel Hein's and Tuffy Leemans's 1940 team could not do—beat Washington a third straight time?

GAME STATISTICS
GIANTS

Rushing	Att	Net Yards	Avg	Long Gain	TD
Morris	24	159	6.6	45	2
Carthon	6	17	2.8	8	0
Rouson	8	28	3.5	5	0
Simms	1	15	15.0	15	0
Manuel	1	-5	-5.0	-5	0
Anderson	4	2	0.5	2	0
TOTALS	44	216	4.9	45	2

Passing	Att	Comp	Yards	TKD	YDS	TD	LG	Had Int
Simms	19	9	136	1	9	4	29	0
Rutledge	1	1	23	0	0	0	23	0
TOTALS	20	10	159	1	9	4	29	0

Pass Receiving	No	Yards	Lg	TD
Carthon	1	7	7	0
Rouson	2	22	18	0
Bavaro	2	47	24	1
Morris	1	2	2	0
Galbreath	1	9	9	0
Johnson, B.	1	15	15	1
McConkey	1	28	28	1
Mowatt	1	29	29	1
TOTALS	10	159	29	4

Interceptions	No	Yards	Lg	TD
Welch	1	0	0	0
Patterson *	0	16	16	0
Taylor	1	34	34	1
Johnson, T.	1	27	27	0
*(lateral from Welch)				
TOTALS	3	77	34	1

Punting	No	Yds	Avg	Tb	In 20	Lg
Landeta	7	307	43.9	1	1	55
TOTALS	7	307	43.9	1	1	55

Punt Returns	No	FC	Yards	Lg	TD
McConkey	7	1	57	15	0
TOTALS	7	1	57	15	0

Kickoff Returns	No	Yards	Lg	TD
Hill	1	15	15	0
Rouson	1	17	17	0
TOTALS	2	32	17	0

GAME STATISTICS
49ers

Rushing	Att	Net Yards	Avg	Long Gain	TD
Craig	5	17	3.4	5	0
Cribbs	12	14	0.3	7	0
Rathman	3	8	2.7	5	0
TOTALS	20	29	1.5	7	0

Passing	Att	Comp	Yards	TKD	YDS	TD	LG	Had Int
Montana	15	8	98	0	0	0	24	2
Kemp	22	7	64	1	7	0	30	1
TOTALS	37	15	162	1	7	0	30	3

Pass Receiving	No	Yards	Lg	TD
Craig	4	22	9	0
Rice	3	48	24	0
Margerum	1	12	12	0
Francis	3	26	20	0
Cribbs	1	2	2	0
Clark	3	52	30	0
TOTALS	15	162	30	0

Interceptions	No	Yards	Lg	TD
NONE				
TOTALS	0	0	0	0

Punting	No	Yds	Avg	Tb	In 20	Lg
Runager	10	400	40.0	0	3	49
TOTALS	10	400	40.0	0	3	49

Punt Returns	No	FC	Yards	Lg	TD
Griffin	2	3	11	7	0
TOTALS	2	3	11	7	0

Kickoff Returns	No	Yards	Lg	TD
Cribbs	3	71	29	0
Craig	4	48	16	0
TOTALS	7	119	29	0

| Washington Redskins | 0 | 0 | 0 | 0 | 0 |
| New York Giants | 10 | 7 | 0 | 0 | 17 |

Bill Parcells came into the locker room under Giants Stadium after his fifth trip onto the field. He had made his first one at 7:15 this January 11 morning. For the past three hours — there was only an hour to go before the four p.m. game time — he had called the weather bureau at Newark airport for readings on the wind. Now, his square face reddened by a wind that had reached gusts of 30 miles an hour, he turned to an assistant and said, "That's the toughest wind I've seen since I've been here."

Giant punter Sean Landeta went out to take a look. An hour before the game he and field goal kicker Raul Allegre met with Parcells and the other coaches.

"The wind is going to be a force," Landeta said. "You know what kind of a force Lawrence Taylor is. The wind is going to be even greater."

Parcells nodded. He had made up his mind. He went over to his captain, Harry Carson, who would be the Giant envoy at the meeting before the game when the referee tossed the coin. "If we win the toss," Parcells told Carson, "take the wind." If the Giants won the toss, they would choose to kick off and give up the ball for the first series. Then they could choose to play with their backs to the wind during the first and fourth periods.

Most NFL coaches agree that it is sometimes a good ploy to kick off and begin the game with your defense, especially if in return you can have a strong wind at your back for the opening and closing periods. First of all, the wind will help your passing game as you try to take an early lead or, later on, to come from behind. Second, a defensive team is usually more ready, temperamentally, to begin a game than the offense — the defenses have cranked themselves up, almost manic in their eagerness to blow people away. Offensive players are often jittery before they feel a first hit — and thus, early in a game, are more likely than later to fumble, bobble a handoff or drop a pass.

This Giant team, both the offense and the defense, was "plain antsy like I've never seen us all season long," Harry Carson said. "I'm intense already," running back Lee Rouson said. "Everyone is. David Jordan told me how nervous he was — and he can't even play."

"Our intensity level all season has been high," said rookie nose tackle Erik Howard. "For the 49ers game last week, it was up 50 percent. This week it's more — it keeps going up and up."

"You can sense the anxiety," said guard Billy Ard. "Fuses are shorter. There have been pushing and shoving matches in practice."

Tackle Brad Benson felt the tension. All week long he had watched TV sportscasters speculating whether he could once more stop Dexter Manley, the Redskins' pass rusher and the NFL's number-one sacker in 1985, from savaging Phil Simms. "Sure it started working on me," the bewhiskered

Brad said. "I'd wake up in the morning and have a cup of coffee, and there he was on 'The Morning Program' ".

The Giants had worked through a schedule exactly the same as their regular-season schedule: off Monday and Tuesday, full practice Wednesday and Thursday, a light practice Friday and a walk-through of plays on Saturday.

While the Giants went through their period of angst, the team had become a political football. Giant fans had called for a ticker-tape parade up Broadway to hail the Giants after the Super Bowl, a parade like the ticker-tape celebration honoring the Mets after their 1986 World Series triumph. Mayor Ed Koch angrily said no, calling the Giants a carpetbagging team that had left New York in 1976 for the New Jersey gold. But American Express, its new building rising in downtown Manhattan, offered to pay up to $750,000 for a parade.

The Giants stayed silent for a while. But on the eve of the Washington game, Mara Tech gave the back of its hand to Ed Koch. The Giants announced that they would not go back to Manhattan for a parade even if asked. In a terse statement the Giants said that a Super Bowl celebration, win or lose, would be held in New Jersey. And with a tip of their helmets to a loyal New Jersey governor, the Giants told why:

"The only logical place for a Giants celebration is here at Giants Stadium in the New Jersey Sports Complex. We appreciate the many offers of our loyal [New Jersey] mayors. We are grateful also to our friends and fans who would like a New York City parade. Last year, when we returned from Chicago after our playoff loss to the Bears, Gov. Tom Kean, without any fanfare, was waiting to greet us and cheer us as we got off the plane. Giants Stadium is our home and the perfect spot for a celebration."

Mayor Koch, of course, had not greeted the Giants after the loss to the Bears.

Down in Washington, meanwhile, Redskin coach Joe Gibbs had been glancing anxiously at the newspaper forecasts calling for strong winds on the day of the game. "Wind is one of the biggest factors in a football game," Gibbs said. "It changes things more than anything else because of the passing and kicking game."

The Giants came out onto the field for their pregame warmups, looking up at a stadium more than half-packed. Thousands more streamed in, and by game time some 76,663 people, most ever to see a Giant game, filled the double tiers. They huddled under overcoats and blankets, the temperature in the twenties but the wind making the air feel an icy twelve degrees.

As Sean Landeta boomed his pregame punts, he took the time to watch Redskin punter Steve Cox. He knew that Cox always punted well into strong winds. Cox used a low drop, releasing the ball as close to his foot as possible. But, to his surprise, Sean saw Cox's kicks blow back toward him.

"I was trying to kick low and get a roll," Cox said later, "but the ball kept coming back."

Landeta knew well what the whipping wind could do to a punter. He still recalled, wincing when he talked about it, last year's 21-0 playoff defeat to the Bears, when he missed a wind-blown drop and the Bears recovered the flub for a touchdown.

The two teams left the field, then came out again—the crowd booming now—for the pregame introductions and the coin toss, the Giants in blue and scarlet, the Redskins in white jerseys striped with burgundy. At the Redskin bench, Gibbs told his seven captains: If you win the toss, get the wind at your back. "I was hoping, praying, we'd win it," he said later.

The seven Redskins met the lone Giant captain in the middle of the field. Referee Pat Haggerty clutched his favorite game coin—an oversized silver nickel with an Indian on one side (heads), a buffalo on the other (tails). He'd found it in an antique shop.

Most of the Redskins captains wanted to call heads. But one, Charles Mann, said he had a hunch that tails would come up. The Redskins decided to ride on Mann's hunch.

Haggerty flipped the coin. As it rose in the air, a Redskin captain, Russ Grimm, called "tails!"

The coin struck the turf, bounced upward and came down showing an Indian.

Heads—the Giants had won the toss. On the sideline Parcells's face broke into a tight grin as he saw Haggerty motion with his foot to indicate that the Giants would kick off. Carson turned, his back to the wind, showing which goal the Giants chose to defend.

Giant offensive lineman Chris Godfrey stared, surprise showing in his eyes, at the other Giant linemen. He had expected that the Giants would take the kickoff if Carson won the coin toss. "The Redskins," he said later, "have a powerful offense and if they score first..."

Allegre kicked the ball into the end zone. The Redskins could gain only 4 yards on three plays. On fourth down Cox came in to kick. The punt swayed high into the air, obviously short, and rolled dead 23 yards away on the Washington 47.

In six plays the Giants punched their way to the Redskins 32, the big play a 25-yard pass by Phil Simms over the middle to Phil McConkey. At the 32 the Redskins held on third down and Raul Allegre faced a 47-yard field goal.

The wind billowed his jersey as he lined up behind holder Jeff Rutledge. He booted the ball and it took off like a drive off a golf tee, streaking between the goal posts—his longest ever as a Giant. The Giants had taken a 3-point step toward Pasadena.

The Redskins pulled down another kickoff, then lost 9 yards trying to make 10. Standing on his own 11, Cox skyrocketed another tremulous punt that seemed to go straight up and straight down. It went 27 yards to the Redskins 38.

"It was frustrating," Cox said, "because you can't do anything about it. The ball just comes back to you when you kick."

The Giants made their way to the 26. On third and ten, Simms saw wideout Stacy Robinson all alone, threw—and missed him.

A flag was thrown. The Giants had been holding. The Giants expected Washington to decline the penalty and force Allegre, on fourth down, to try another long field goal—this one from the 43. But Joe Gibbs signaled that he wanted his defense to take the penalty. That put the Giants back to the 36, but it was still third down, now twenty yards to go.

In the huddle Simms called for a pass. "In those situations," Simms said later, "nobody talks in the huddle. You just try to make the play."

Taking the snap from center Bart Oates, Simms saw Lionel Manuel, playing in only his second game after being out twelve weeks with a bad knee, cut across the middle. Simms threw a high rifle shot that Manuel leaped for and plucked down at the 11. That 25-yard gain gave the Giants a first down.

The Giants pushed to the 5. A penalty moved them back to the 11. Simms scrambled out of the pocket. He saw Manuel move laterally across the end zone and lose safety Todd Bowles in the crowd. Simms drilled the ball into the numerals of Manuel and the Giants led, 9-0. Allegre kicked the extra point for a 10-0 lead.

"We took a gamble on taking that penalty," Gibbs said after the game. "It didn't pay off."

"I would have refused the penalty and made them try to kick from past the 40," a Redskin safetyman said, "but I only work here."

The Redskins took the kickoff and pushed to their 37. On third down and three, the Redskins decided to go for the quick score. The Redskins' best wideout, Gary Clark, took off on a long post pattern, streaking by cornerback Elvis Patterson. At the Giant 30, three steps ahead of Patterson and flying, Clark turned for a ball thrown well over 50 yards into the wind by Schroeder.

Clark saw the football tunnel through the wind and arch downward toward him. "I was looking to score before I even caught it," Clark said later. "When you do that, most of the time you'll drop it."

He dropped this one. For the second week in a row, a dropped pass had saved the Giants 7 points. "That was the big play of the game," Gibbs insisted later. "A play like that could've made our day, but we blew it."

Subsequent events, most observers thought, disproved that optimistic view. If the Redskins had scored that touchdown, the final score would have been 17-7.

The Redskins looked forward to the second period when the wind would be at their backs. Landeta, punting for the first time into the wind as the period began, rammed the punt 46 yards, the ball downed by Andy Headen at the Redskin 4.

What was Sean's secret? "I made sure I dropped the ball properly. I tried to kick the ball out of my hand. That's what I didn't do in Chicago last year and the wind blew the ball two or three feet off course."

From the 4 the Redskins leapfrogged 62 yards in six plays, most of the yards gained on passes to Art Monk and Kelvin Bryant. By now the Redskins realized they could not run against the Giants. The Giants had four men up on the line—the three down linemen plus either one of their outside linebackers, Carl Banks or L.T.

On fourth down, the wind still blowing at their backs, the Redskins lined up for a field goal, the ball to be placed down at their own 49. Schroeder knelt to hold what would have been a 51-yard attempt.

As center Jeff Bostic snapped the ball, a gust of wind swirled between him and Schroeder. The wind flattened the snapped ball and it bounced along the turf, skidding by Schroeder. Carl Banks fell on the ball at the Redskin 49. As more than one would-be wag said the next day, another Redskin effort had gone with the wind.

The Giants now had to throw into the wind. On second and fifteen, Simms threw to Mark Bavaro, who went to the Redskin 17. Two plays later the Giants reached the 9. Simms called for a handoff. "It was a busted play," he said later with that country boy grin of his. "I turned the wrong way."

Simms took off around the weak side where there were only Redskins, also running the wrong way. "If I wasn't so startled," Simms said, "I might have scored."

He hesitated at the 2 as safety Ken Coffey charged toward him. Coffey bowled him over a foot from the goal line. On the next play Joe Morris slugged through, and the Giants, after another Allegre point-after, led 17-0.

Now it was defense time. "They got ahead and played their usual self," said Redskin tackle Dean Hamel, "they got real stingy."

In the second half the Redskins knew they had to pass. They attempted 36—2 ended up in sacks—and only 1 running play.

One Redskin ran like the fox pursued. That was Schroeder. To keep Schroeder safe from Taylor, who had hounded him mercilessly in their previous game, Washington doubled-teamed L.T. They put 262-pound reserve guard Raleigh McKenzie in the backfield, lining up on Taylor's side. McKenzie and a lineman both blocked L.T. on pass plays.

L.T. moved with both blockers, usually to the outside. That opened up lanes for other Giants to pour through. Taylor banged a thigh against a Giant helmet early in the second half and had to leave the game, but he was not even missed, the Giants still crashing through to flush Schroeder out of the pocket, where he is at his best.

"He was scared," said end Leonard Marshall, who dumped him once for 19 yards. "A lot of his passes weren't even close to anyone and he lost his cool."

Schroeder would complete 20 of 50, his average gain a little more than a measly 3 yards. Sometimes, fleeing 15 or 20 yards to escape the rushers, he had to complete a 20-yard pass to get even with the line of scrimmage.

The Giants stuck to the ground in the second half, running down the clock, throwing only one pass. With 1:56 to go, Schroeder threw a desperation fourth-down pass that flew wild. The Redskins slouched off the field.

The crowd now knew that the Giants had won the championship of the NFC. The stadium's roaring rose to a crescendo and then seemed to burst, like the grand finale of a fireworks display. Torn newspapers, confetti and toilet paper came down onto the field like a blizzard. The paper covered the sidelines, swirling like snow. Harry Carson dumped the obligatory barrel of Gatorade onto Bill Parcells as Parcells pretended not to see him coming.

But Parcells had a secret weapon: He turned and shot a water pistol at the players.

A minute later the game ended. In the press box the writers tapped out leads that told how a coin toss had decided the game because of the stiff winds. But did the Giants win because of the wind?

The wind unquestionably had played a devilish role all day long—but it blew in both faces. "We got the ball for thirty minutes with the wind and thirty minutes against it, the same as them," said veteran Washington safetyman Curtis Jordan. "We scored zero both ways." The Giants had scored 7 with the wind in their faces—enough to win. Added Jordan: "They turn the ball over on their 37 [on a fumble by Joe Morris] at the end of the first half and we have the wind. What do we get out of it? Zero."

So much for the wind. In what had been in effect two blowouts, the Giants had vaulted to the championship of the National Football Conference. At game's end they learned what most of the nation knew: Denver had come from behind in the last five minutes with a 98-yard march to tie Cleveland, 20-20, and then win in overtime with a field goal.

The Giants had beaten the Broncos earlier, 19-16, at Yankee Stadium on that tipped interception by George Martin and a last-second field goal by Allegre. "We were lucky to beat them," George Martin said after hearing that the Broncos would be the foe two weeks hence in Super Bowl XXI.

Wellington Mara had been in the stands when a Giant team last played in an NFL championship game twenty-three years earlier. Mara had seen the Giants win four championships—in 1928, 1934, 1938 and 1956.

Thirty years ago—that last championship season. Only two Giant players—George Martin and Harry Carson—had been alive when that championship was won. Wellington showed some of the Giants the NFL championship ring on his finger.

He said he hoped to wear another—the Giants' first Super Bowl ring.

"Getting ready to win that ring," Parcells said, "starts tomorrow."

GAME STATISTICS
GIANTS

Rushing	Att	Net Yards	Avg	Long Gain	TD
Morris	29	87	3.0	22	1
Carthon	7	28	4.0	10	0
Simms	7	-2	-0.3	8	0
Galbreath	1	-1	-1.0	-1	0
Rouson	1	2	2.0	2	0
Anderson	1	3	3.0	3	0
TOTALS	46	117	2.5	22	1

Passing	Att	Comp	Yards	TKD YDS	TD	LG	Had Int
Simms	14	7	90	1 8	1	30	0
TOTALS	14	7	90	1 8	1	30	0

Pass Receiving	No	Yards	Lg	TD
Carthon	3	18	8	0
Manuel	2	36	25	1
Bavaro	2	36	30	0
TOTALS	7	90	30	1

Interceptions	No	Yards	Lg	TD
Reasons	1	15	15	0
TOTALS	1	15	15	0

Punting	No	Yds	Avg	Tb	In 20	Lg
Landeta	6	254	42.3	0	1	46
TOTALS	6	254	42.3	0	1	46

Punt Returns	No	FC	Yards	Lg	TD
McConkey	5	0	27	8	0
TOTALS	5	0	27	8	0

Kickoff Returns	No	Yards	Lg	TD
NONE				
TOTALS	0	0	0	0

GAME STATISTICS
REDSKINS

Rushing	Att	Net Yards	Avg	Long Gain	TD
Rogers	9	15	1.7	4	0
Bryant	6	25	4.2	9	0
Schroeder	1	0	0.0	0	0
TOTALS	16	40	2.5	9	0

Passing	Att	Comp	Yards	TKD YDS	TD	LG	Had Int
Schroeder	50	20	195	4 45	0	48	1
TOTALS	50	20	195	4 45	0	48	1

Pass Receiving			No	Yards	Lg	TD
Monk			8	126	48	0
Bryant			7	45	24	0
Warren			3	9	10	0
Didier			1	7	7	0
Griffin			1	8	8	0
TOTALS			20	195	48	0

Interceptions			No	Yards	Lg	TD
NONE						
TOTALS			0	0	0	0

Punting	No	Yds	Avg	Tb	In 20	Lg
Cox	9	320	35.6	0	1	46
TOTALS	9	320	35.6	0	1	46

Punt Returns		No	FC	Yards	Lg	TD
Yarber		3	0	19	10	0
TOTALS		3	0	19	10	0

Kickoff Returns			No	Yards	Lg	TD
Orr			1	10	10	0
Branch			1	5	5	0
TOTALS			2	15	15	0

Super Bowl XXI: Getting Ready

The Lunch Pail Guys gathered around Bill Parcells at midfield in Giants Stadium. Four days earlier they had taken apart Washington to win the NFC championship and the trip to Pasadena for Super Bowl XXI. It was Super Bowl XXI that Bill Parcells wanted to put in proper perspective. "Fellas," he barked in his drill sergeant's bellow, "nobody's goin' to remember who lost this game ten years from now..."

Eight years after the coming of George Young, three years after finishing 3-12-1, one year after being blown out of the playoffs, 21-0, by the Bears, and four days after their second destruction of a playoff opponent, the two destroyed by a combined score of 66-3, the Giants stood at the doorway of the Super Bowl.

"But the big thing is not going to the Super Bowl," Harry Carson told the Giants. "The big thing is to win it."

The Giants would play the Broncos, the team they had beaten, 19-16, on a last-minute field goal and George Martin's interception of a John Elway pass. After that game, Parcells saw center Bart Oates smiling. "What are you smiling about?" Parcells growled at his offensive lineman. "They shut you out, didn't they?"

Why had the offense been shut out? Bart tried to explain. "The Denver defense kept shifting around as soon as I stood over the ball," he said. "That can cause an offense to be tentative. When you see them shift, it can make you hesitate and that can make you tentative in your blocking. I think that's what happened to us last time. The big thing is to recognize the defense, fire out and be aggressive. We have to run straight ahead, right at them."

It was on a Thursday that Parcells had reminded the Giants that only one Super Bowl team would be remembered ten years hence. On Friday, Brad Benson said, "Coach Parcells kind of got on us. He said, 'I expected a low-key practice, but this won't do. You've got to pick it up.' "

"He ran our tails off," Jeff Rutledge said, "But that's good. We needed it." "Simon Legree found his whip," Kenny Hill said. "Oh, God, that was a tough one."

Parcells began the week and a half of preparation for Super Bowl XXI by meeting with the offense. "He has to start with us," Phil Simms said,

A Story of Glory   187

"because the offense didn't score a touchdown against the Broncos last time."

Billy Ard laughed when he heard that. "Not so," he said. "He had to start with us because that was the way he started to get us ready for the 49ers and we won. He did it against the Redskins and we won. He's superstitious. I can hear him now. 'You guys got no touchdowns against those guys. You guys got hammered along the line. Are you going to let them do that to you again?' "

At the defensive meetings, the Giants agreed their biggest problem would be to pressure John Elway. After holding the Bronco rushers to 80 yards in that 19-16 victory, they were sure they could stonewall them again. But they had not lassoed Elway, who threw for 336 yards against them, completing 29 in 47 tries. "He throws better out of the pocket than he does in it," said defensive coordinator Bill Belichik. "He will get his passing yardage, you have just got to hold it to a minimum."

"Denver is a big-play team," said cornerback Mark Collins. "If we don't let them have the big play for a touchdown, we will win."

A day before the Giants departed for California, the front office gave a party for former Giants who would go to the Super Bowl as guests of Mara Tech. One veteran was Kyle Rote, who was asked about this defense compared to the famed umbrella defense of the 1950s.

"You can't compare the two," he said. "Everything's different. Size and speed, schedule and the money. Everything. But you can say that the Giants defense in those years was the best of its time, and that this Giant defense is the best of its time."

Other old Giants were surprised by the poise of this team. "I was in the locker room after last Sunday's game against the Redskins," said former tackle Rosey Brown, now a Hall-of-Famer. "They just walked in after winning the NFC championship like it was after practice."

And the man who once was the inspiration for the Yankee Stadium chant — *Dee-fense! Dee-fense! Dee-fense!* — had this to say about Lawrence Taylor: "Lawrence Taylor," said Sam Huff, "is the best defensive player I have ever seen."

"They know how to win," said one-time defensive tackle Rosey Grier. "And they believe in themselves. And they seem to have that extra amount of love for each other."

"Yes," said former Giant running back Chuck Mercein, "you see guys rooting for the guys who don't play regularly."

"But there was a difference between this year's Giants and last year's Giants," said L.T. "We didn't really believe in ourselves after the playoffs last year," he said. "If we did, we could have won in Chicago. This year we believe there is no one who can beat us."

For at least two Giants, these playoffs meant a cut in their pay rate. For each regular-season game, Lawrence Taylor got one-sixteenth of his salary, or $53,125. Phil Simms earned, per game, $40,625. In the NFC championship game, each had earned $18,000. And even if the Giants won the Super Bowl, Taylor and Simms would earn "only" $36,000 — $18,000 if they lost — considerably short of their regular season pay rate. (Each earned, per game, more than the entire Giant team of 1925 made in a season.)

On the morning of January 18, a Sunday, the week before the Super Bowl, the Giants gathered in their locker room at Giants Stadium. They waited to board a bus to Newark Airport as a snowstorm swirled outside. They had to wait because Bart Oates's car had been stopped by a flat tire, delaying him. When Bart arrived, the Giants boarded buses and, escorted by the wailing sirens of police cars, rode to the airport.

They boarded a United DC-10, its pilot picked by Parcells because he had flown the Giants to California on their last trip, and the Giants had won. There was nothing superstitious about Tuna, as the Giants call Parcells; he was just not meddling with fate.

The huge plane took off into a white fog. Players glanced anxiously out of the windows, looking into blankness. "If something happens to us," shouted the old helicopter pilot, Phil McConkey, "will they call off the Super Bowl or call the Redskins to replace us?" The question was answered by weak grins.

Later, the plane fastened against a china-blue sky, the Giants watched a movie, *Tough Guys*, with Burt Lancaster and Kirk Douglas. Most players had changed from suits, required for boarding, to sweat pants and shirts. "Phil Simms, who can sleep anywhere," Phil McConkey later reported, "dozed off for a while."

All the 1986 Giants were aboard, including six on the injured-reserve list who could not play. They included running back George Adams, who had missed the entire season with a chipped pelvic bone, and safety Terry Kinard, hurt in the season's twelfth game, against Washington. Parcells told all six they would stand on the sideline at this, their first Super Bowl. He knew that NFL regulations said injured-reserve players were not allowed on the field but, typically, he was taking care of his Lunch Pail guys. "I arranged with my security guy, Ricky Sandoval," he later told the *Times*'s Dave Anderson, "to let our assistant coaches on the field without credentials. Then I gave the coaches' credentials to the injured-reserve guys."

"This is one big family," McConkey later wrote in a newspaper column. "That's been one of the keys — our togetherness. It sounds corny, but it's true."

Some four hours after takeoff, the DC-10 swooped down onto the runway at Long Beach Airport. The players stepped out into sunny, sixty-three degree, spring-like weather. Some 150 Giants fans cheered and waved banners. Even the California cops, holding back onlookers, asked for autographs.

A bus whisked the Giants to the South Coast Plaza Hotel. To protect his players from the press and fans, Parcells told a security man to usher the team into the hotel through a rear door.

"It's a funny kind of feeling," Harry Carson, ever the candid one, said. "I kind of felt like the President being ushered into a building, or like Michael Jackson, avoiding the crowds."

About a half hour after their arrival, Giant players began to drift downstairs into the hotel lobby. A huge cigar sticking out of his mouth, Lawrence Taylor signed autographs. Raul Allegre picked up tickets for his family.

Other Giants phoned home to tell of their arrival. The Giant wives and other family members would be coming west on Thursday in another chartered jet. Lisa Benson told Brad that the police in Tuxedo, New York, where they live, had promised they would shovel out her driveway if the snow continued to pile up, so that she would get to the plane on time.

"Those police won't get their names in the paper," Brad said to a friend. "But they're nice people."

The next day, Monday, the Giants practiced at Rams Park in nearby Anaheim. The Giants went through a full-pads drill. Once more the offensive line, the Suburbanites, heard how they had failed to score a touchdown against those guys the last time out. Were they going to be pushed around again?

Tuesday was part work day, part media day, a time for the Giants to talk to reporters. Early in the morning, buses carried the Giant players to LeBard Stadium, home of the Orange Coast College Oranges, where more than 2,000 reporters, photographers, radio and TV people gathered on the field and in the stands. Hundreds clustered around people like Phil Simms and Lawrence Taylor. Smaller numbers encircled other starters, while some of the reserve players, people like Solomon Miller or John Washington, had only each other to talk to.

Reporters asked Phil Simms about John Elway, the Bronco quarterback.

"Elway's pretty," Phil said. "But if you look at me and John Elway over the past three years, I've been the more productive quarterback. But nobody cares. I mean, I've had three productive years. Not many guys have done much more than me.

"Elway deserves all the attention he gets. When you think of the Broncos, you think of John Elway. When you think of the Giants, you don't think of me. You think of Lawrence Taylor. Hey, I like Elway. I hope he has a horrible game, though."

Other reporters sought angles on players that they hoped no one else had thought of. One asked Brad Benson, "Are you crazy?"

"No, I'm sorry, I'm not," Brad replied. Later he said, "I think she was disappointed."

That afternoon, after practice, he, Bart Oates, Brian Johnston and Chris Godfrey boarded a small boat and bounced out to sea to fish. Jim Burt went along—but decided to nap below deck. He came up once to cast a line— and caught a napping sea gull.

The Broncos talked to the press that afternoon at the same park. They fed the press the stuff that makes headlines—if only for an afternoon. Receiver Vance Johnson said that whenever he wanted to score a touchdown, he'd just go to number 34's side.

Number 34 on the Giants was Elvis Patterson, whom the Giants called Toast because wide receivers had burned him more than once this season. "When Elvis heard," Phil McConkey said later, "he just smiled."

The Giant pass receivers were being put under the magnifying glass by the media, some writers asserting that this department was the Giants' weak link. The always brash Phil McConkey talked about the charge in one of his *New York Post* columns:

"We started to take the brunt of the criticism about mid-season...Our running game was going so well...that the emphasis shifted away from us...That's when we heard aboul Phil Simms being inconsistent and about how we didn't have any receivers...I called my friend [Green Bay wideout] James Lofton, maybe the greatest receiver of all time.

"I remember saying, 'We get all this heat because we don't have a great burner who can run down and score five TDs a game on a bomb.'

"Lofton told me, 'Let me tell you what's much more important than having a guy like that. It's having a guy who can go across the middle on a run-cut, catch the ball, get his jock knocked off and do it again. You guys have five guys who will do that.'

"He was right, of course. So what kind of guy do you want on your team? Do you want a pretty boy trackman who can run a go on the outside and occasionally break a big play, or do you want guys with courage who will do those things for your team?"

"We've been underrated all year," said wideout Bobby Johnson, "It's just a case that we don't have a speed merchant, a guy who can run a 4.3 or 4.4. But we get the job done."

But now, for the Super Bowl, the Giants had Lionel Manuel zigzagging through his patterns, almost recovered from a knee injury that kept him on the sideline most of the season. "Lionel's great strength is the precise patterns he runs—he's our best pattern guy," said Ron Erhardt, the offensive coordinator. "Lionel can make the cut without losing any speed. Bobby Johnson is the 'feel guy,' a guy who knows nice patterns and knows how to get open. Phil McConkey is more of a deliberate guy."

The next day the press again interviewed the Giants. Later Brad Benson wrote in the *New York Times*:

"I think some of the press is having trouble with us because we don't have a lot of characters. We have a lot of family men. I think the team has just assumed Bill Parcells's personality. We're just a basic, fundamental football team with a goal, guys who like their home towns and where they live."

That Wednesday Parcells sent his reserve defensive players at the offense in pads and sweat pants. He wanted rookies Eric Dorsey and John Washington to simulate the lightning-fast Denver pass rush.

"You guys can't go three days without hard work," he shouted. "Let's go harder! C'mon, John Washington, all you have to do on this trip is to give these guys [the offense] a look. I want it harder than that."

Tension began to build within the players, within the dressing room, within hotel rooms. Phil McConkey said he couldn't sleep well. "They want to take from us something we want, something we deserve," growled Jim Burt, the toughest guy on a team of tough guys. "We're 16-2, the best team in football. Our reward is sixty minutes away. We can't be denied. We've got to slam our fist on it and claim it as our own."

"The pressure is increasing tremendously with each passing day," Kenny Hill said. "But that is a burden we expect because we impose pressure on ourselves. This team, we tend to be a little overly reverent of our opposition."

One man dominated their thoughts — Elway. "Elway's the key," said Lawrence Taylor. "And if you take away the key, you can't open the door."

Kenny Hill agreed that Elway was on the mind of the defense. "As much as you press guys have brought him up this week, we have been giving him as much thought. When you're a defensive back, you read your quarterback's eyes and stance, where they are. You watch those things and they tip you off about what they might do.

"But Elway has such a strong arm, he'll catch you looking for those things, and then he throws his arm back and lets it go. His arm's so strong — it's a cannon — and right to the end of a play, he can make you look bad."

The offense had been making its adjustments after Ron Erhardt had stared for hours at films of the previous Denver game — the one in which the offense scored no touchdowns. He had seen what center Bart Oates had described as the tentativeness of the New York blocking, caused by Denver defenders shifting just before the snap.

"We've changed a few things," Erhardt said, "so that we'll recognize where they will be."

On Thursday night the Giant plane, carrying wives, children, other family members and Giant office personnel, touched down at Long Beach Airport. It had been a harrowing flight, the plane called back from the Newark runway for de-icing after sitting on the ground for nearly four hours.

The Giant players rode to the hotel to greet wives, mothers and other relatives and friends. But they went back alone to their hotel. Unlike the Broncos, who would share hotel rooms with their wives, the Giants would live Super Bowl week like monks.

"Sure I'll miss him," one Giant wife said. "But you'll see on Sunday, those Broncos players will be tired."

On Friday afternoon, the Super Bowl little more than forty-eight hours away, Parcells shifted the team to a North Hollywood hotel where there would be no clamoring fans and reporters. Friday would be the last full practice. Phil Simms hit 6 different pass receivers with 6 straight passes. "Phil had this strange sort of glow," Bart Oates said. "It was like he was in a perfect biorhythm stage or something."

Lawrence Taylor shouted, "I'm ready, Bill!" then went all out in a one-hundred-minute practice session. Even Parcells was awed. "Hey, this is too much," said a grinning Tuna. "Save something for the game."

On Saturday Parcells said the players would walk around the Rose Bowl. But several players, as superstitious as Tuna, reminded him that twice before this season the team had practiced the day before on an away field on which they played the next day—once in Dallas, once in Seattle. The Giants lost both games.

Parcells said he wasn't concerned: The hoodoo didn't apply here. For the Super Bowl the Giants were officially the home team. And this wouldn't really be a practice, he said, "just a chance to stretch their legs for a couple of hours."

The buses arrived to take the Giants to the Rose Bowl. Parcells hesitated, then sent the buses away. He was not tempting the gods, home team or no home team.

The offensive and defensive units went off into separate conference rooms to study films. Parcells sensed their mood. "You can tell they're ready. The bus rides yesterday were quiet. Usually during the week they're laughing, scratching, talking. They should be irritable. They'll be tight for the game. So will the Broncos. Only thirty-six countries will be watching or something like that. It's the only football game that's being played in the entire world."

By noon on Sunday, the Giant players began to drift into the Rose Bowl. "We were like caged animals," wideout Stacy Robinson said. "Everybody wanted to bust the door down."

They angrily turned down requests for interviews or autographs. Mark Bavaro ran into a wall evading a tourist with a camera. "It's over! The talk is over!" shouted Raul Allegre. "There's nothing but the game," guard Chris Godfrey repeated over and over: "We will concentrate on nothing but the game!"

The hours ticked toward the three p.m. starting time. Jim Burt began to chant, his words ricocheting like rocks against the concrete walls. "Let us out! Let us out!"

"It was like no other locker room I've ever seen," Phil McConkey said.

As usual, Parcells first sent out the players who would not be introduced. He told Phil McConkey, this team's crowd-rouser, to lead the players out, waving a towel. "You get out there," he said to Phil, "and stir up those fans before the defense is introduced."

Phil came out, leading the long scarlet and blue line, towel whipping in the bright sunshine. Patches of scarlet and blue, embedded like islands in the sea of 100,000 faces, rose, roaring.

The Giant players formed two long lines. Then, one by one, their names barked across the humid air, came the Giant defense...Jim Burt...George Martin...Leonard Marshall...Carl Banks...Gary Reasons...Harry Carson...Lawrence Taylor (oh, what a roar for him and Harry Carson, too)...Elvis Patterson...Perry Williams...Kenny Hill...Herb Welch...

Each defensive player ran onto the field and through the chute formed by the two lines of Giant players. Teammates slapped hands, pounded backs, yelled words of promise and hope and encouragement...at this moment, starters and nonstarters, defense and offense, stars and nonstars, at this moment were one...one...ONE...

Minutes later the two teams lined up, the Giants to kick off (having lost the coin toss), the Broncos to receive. After twenty-five years a Giant team was going into combat for a championship, and as Sinatra's words would tell them, right now, New York, *it's up to you, New York...New York...*

Super Bowl XXII:
Getting Ready

Bill Parcells stared out at the field. There was a minute left to play, the Giants ahead of Denver, 39-20, and millions knew that the Giants had won their fifth NFL championship, their first in thirty years, and their first Super Bowl ever.

Harry Carson stalked the sideline, a wide grin on his face. Almost every pair of eyes in this huge bowl was fixed on him. In the TV booth, John Madden sketched the route that Carson would trace as he dumped another barrel of Gatorade on Parcells.

Super Bowl victory was his, but Tuna's mind had gone back to 1964. He saw himself standing on the sideline at a game in Hastings, Nebraska. It was his first college game as a coach—the linebacker coach of Hastings College. His defense, with a minute to go, was on its way to blanking the Colorado School of Mines. It was funny, he had to concede to himself, the way a defensive coach never forgets a shutout.

Splash! Down it came, the greenish fluid cascading over his shoulders. He bent sideways, with a wince and a grin, as the icy Gatorade chilled his face and ruined another expensive sweater (a check, sent regularly to Tuna from Gatorade, would pay for the sweater and a lot of other things).

A minute later the Giants spilled out onto the field. Two big Giants carried Parcells to midfield. He shook hands with Denver coach Dan Reeves. Set on his feet, Parcells, his grin as wide as an ocean, walked toward the awards ceremony. In the past the thrill of victory vanished by the time he got to the locker room, replaced by the worry: What had to be fixed after the game? What had to be readied for next week?

There would be no next week—the season was done, the championship won. He had run the good race and now came the laurel wreath. "I think I know what real euphoria is," he said later. "It's absolutely wonderful. I don't know if you can ever duplicate this feeling."

In the locker room Phil Simms rubbed his hands through wet hair, then said in that good old boy, easy way of his: "In my wildest dreams I couldn't have hoped it would work out this way." He had set playoff records with 22 completions in 25 tries for 268 yards and 3 touchdowns. "In years to come," said the game's Most Valuable Player, "I can say I won the Super

Bowl. We won the Super Bowl — the Giants won the Super Bowl. They can't take that away from us."

He was asked about the game and its tactics. "I knew we were going to start out aggressive," he said. "I didn't want to run, run, get to third and ten and have them ask me to get 10 yards. And then when you get only 8, they wonder why we're not in the game in the first quarter. I wanted the chance to be a factor in the game.

"I threw the ball in practice all week as well as I could have. Before the game I told several of the players that I could put it in there when and where I wanted."

The big play? To Simms, it was the 63-yard drive that ended when he hit Mark Bavaro from the 11 for the touchdown that put the Giants ahead for good, 16-10. After that play, Simms said, "Things seemed to shift. I knew then that we could move the ball on those guys."

But most observers thought it was one play — during that drive — that was the pivotal play. That was the plunge by Jeff Rutledge for a yard and a first down after the Giants had lined up for a punt. It was then, said those observers, that the Giants, behind 10-9, swung the tide toward them.

Parcells, however, held out for the flea-flicker play, Simms to Joe Morris and back to Simms, who threw to Phil McConkey for a first down on the 1, a 44-yard gain. Morris then went over for a 26-10 lead.

"When we hit the flea-flicker," Bill Parcells said, "we really had a tremendous volume of momentum. We were dominating the third quarter pretty well. Once we hit that one and got the touchdown, I knew we would be hard to beat."

Joe Morris still talked about that flea-flicker play three days later in Hawaii, where he had gone for the Pro Bowl. "That flea-flicker will always stick in my mind. We've practiced that play since week one . . . When coach came to me on Friday and said we'd see it in the game, I thought he was crying wolf. I never thought I'd see it.

"But we worked it perfect. I flexed my knees and flipped the ball back to Phil. In practice I always get hit hard on that play, but nobody hit me. I was able to turn and watch Phil make the pass. Then I turned and saw McConkey make the catch."

In the loser's locker room, Dan Reeves said he thought the turning point came when the Broncos, after arriving at the Giant 1 with first down and goal to go, saw three running plays stopped in their tracks.

"Was there anything I would do over?" he asked, repeating a reporter's question. "With first and goal, I've got forty plays in my mind I could have used."

Would one of those plays have been a pass instead of one of the three running plays that failed? He still wasn't sure. "When you have an inadequate running game," he said, speaking candidly about a rushing offense that gained only 52 yards, "it hurts you most inside the plus territory" — the opponents' side of the field. On the other hand, he conceded, "trying to find a pass to use against the Giants is tough down there." His receivers, he was saying, had much less room to work themselves open.

At the awards ceremony under the glare of TV lights, Wellington Mara stood with Pete Rozelle to accept the Vince Lombardi Trophy. Symbol of the NFL championship, that trophy was named for the former Giant assistant coach who had attended Fordham with Mara some fifty years earlier. Wellington had watched Giant teams win the NFL championship in 1927, 1934, 1938 and 1956. No, he said, he could not put this Super Bowl victory over any of the others.

Reporters asked Parcells what he had told the Giants before the game. "I told them," he said, "that because it's a Super Bowl, don't tell me that you're automatically gonna play hard. I've seen Super Bowl teams that didn't."

"He's right," guard Billy Ard later told a friend. "The Patriots [who lost, 46-10, to the Bears in the previous Super Bowl] took a dive. Some of those guys had to quit. The Bears are a great team, but they weren't 40 points better."

And what, Tuna asked, did he tell the Giants when they came in at halftime down, 10-9? "I told them they were running around too wild and doing some stupid things like throwing a flag that put the Broncos in place for the first touchdown. Hey, I said, you're gonna give the game away. I don't mind getting beat, but let's not give the game away after getting this far."

That night the Giants celebrated with a party for the players, coaches, wives and family and office personnel. Among the guests were old Giants like Y.A. Tittle and Charlie Conerly. Chuckin' Charlie began to talk to Tuna and Tuna saw that Charlie's eyes were moist. "Charlie was so happy, he was crying," Parcells recalled later. "That really impressed me. Charlie was saying, 'I don't know how they can criticize Phil Simms, he's great.'"

Wellington Mara overheard that conversation and told Charlie, "You and Y.A. had great games for us. But maybe never in a game as big as this one was. I wouldn't trade Simms for any quarterback in the league. For our team in our environment, he's the perfect quarterback. He's tough, although maybe strong is a better word. He's strong mentally, physically and spiritually."

Tuna would have put it more simply: "He's a lunch pail guy."

Reporters thought many of the Giants seemed subdued. "That's how Bill Parcells has made this team," said Kenny Hill. "When I won with the Raiders, it was wild. We didn't care about rules. We still brought our champagne to the clubhouse. But this team is essentially emotionless."

Some were not subdued. Jim Burt always liked to savor the deliciousness of victory with fans, even jumping into the stands to celebrate with them. He didn't sleep, mingling with Giant fans as he wandered around the hotel. "We're the world champions," he said to someone, knowing that the pain in his back, which needed surgery, might be telling him he had played his last game. "We deserve to be champions because we worked so hard." And then he added with a boyish grin, "And besides that, we blew those guys out."

Reality hit many of the Giants the next morning. "I jolted awake," Harry Carson said. "Out of a sound sleep, I opened my eyes and looked around and I thought, 'I must be dreaming. Darn, I hope it's real.' Now it's sinking in."

When Leonard Marshall awoke, he streaked off to get a newspaper. "I wanted to make sure it really happened." Phil McConkey said he still felt stunned.

Back in New York, Mayor Ed Koch was having second thoughts about his flip decision that New York would not stage a ticker-tape parade for this Giant team that had moved to Jersey — Koch called it Joisey. He wanted part of the publicity.

"The Giants can have two parades," said Koch, who had been told by the Giants that they would have a celebration of their own in New Jersey, thank you. "One can be a practice parade in the Meadowlands, a walk around the stadium," Koch said, smirking, "and the second a ticker-tape parade down Broadway."

The Giants said there would be just one celebration. It would be held at the Meadowlands, where it belonged, and all Giant fans could come. The celebration's theme would be: "California, Here We Come" — the rallying cry for the 1987 season that would end in San Diego at Super Bowl XXII.

But right now it was "California, Here We Go" for the Giants. They boarded two planes, one for the wives and team personnel, the other for the players and coaches. The two planes winged their way back to New Jersey. The planes touched down in freezing weather. The players hurried into buses to take them to their cars at the Meadowlands and then home.

At noon the next day, in stinging thirteen-degree cold, some 25,000 Giant fans stood and roared as the loudspeakers blared, "We Are the Champions!" Red and blue balloons soared into the air.

One by one the Giant players were introduced. Then Joe Morris, Harry Carson, L.T. and the other Giants who were in California, on their way to the Pro Bowl, were seen on the stadium's video screen. L.T. and the rest said they wished they could also have attended this victory party.

A New York City official came and was booed. New Jersey Governor Tom Kean, with words as gracious as Koch's had been insulting, had said earlier that this party was a way to "unite the region." Wellington Mara tried to close the gap that Koch had widened. He called the team the New York-New Jersey Giants (although the NFL refers to the team as the New York Giants).

Whatever, they play in New Jersey. Parcells came up to speak and spoke of Giants Stadium in the Meadowlands. "These players have a special name for this place," he said, the words booming across the huge bowl. "When we come out of that tunnel on every Sunday, we refer to this as our house. And you are our family."

The roaring told him that he, too, was now family. Tuna held up the silvery Vince Lombardi Trophy and said, "I have a little something to show you."

The Giants had gone west and come home Number One.

Phil Simms stepped up to speak and the roaring for the Super Bowl's MVP swelled for more than a minute. When Phil could speak, he said, "I hope some time in the near future"—a wide grin spread over his fair face—"we can all be together and do this again."

Do this again!

Of course, the Giants had to do this again. Later, Parcells told how:

"Keep getting good players, collecting them and not paying any attention to those things about having too many good players because they will be unhappy about not playing enough. There's not one unhappy guy on the New York Giants today."

And then he added: "I won't rest until we win it again."

And so the race was won and another race began—the race to San Diego and Super Bowl XXII.

The Giants of 1987
Once more, *It's Up to You, New York,*
New York...

Bill Parcells gripped the steering wheel of the fishing boat. He had taken the wheel of the boat, owned by a friend, after a long afternoon fishing in the Manasquan Inlet off the Jersey shore. Now, staring into the gray dusk, he looked toward shore, straining to find the boat's pier. And it was then, looming in front of him, that he saw the rocks.

Bill's bulky arms swung the wheel. The stern of the boat slid wide of the rocks. It had been a frustrating day — a frustrating week, actually, for Parcells — but frustration, as he would say the next day, is easier to live with than destruction. This boat would sail another day.

The next morning, Monday, April 27, 1987, Bill walked into the weight room at Giants Stadium a little after seven in the morning. He heard grunts, turned and saw 280-pound William Roberts, the tackle he hopes will replace Brad Benson, pumping iron. He stared with mock surprise at his watch and said to Roberts, "Seven o'clock in the morning! I hope you haven't been up all night."

In his office Parcells talked about why this week had been so frustrating. Some twenty-five hours from now the NFL's 1987 draft would begin. The Giants, the NFL champions, would pick twenty-eighth and last. "And we got no way of knowing, after the first pick by Tampa, who anyone else will pick," Parcells told people. "I can't even find who Indianapolis will pick on the second round."

Parcells told visitors that the Giants would pick at least twelve players, but their eyes were set on four that they hoped would "fall through." Picking near the bottom on each round, Parcells said, "We have to wait until someone falls through a round and then pick him."

The Giants wanted what Parcells had yearned for in 1986: a big-play receiver, the one who could go for six from anywhere on the field. "We have been getting by with wide receivers who can't run," said Giant receiver coach Pat Hodgson. "They did a heckuva job in the Super Bowl. But now a lot of teams have been going for receivers who can run. Everybody wants a streaky one-play guy like the Jets' Al Toon."

"Of the receivers we have drafted for in the past," Bill Parcells told his assistants, "I have to be pleased with Lionel Manuel and I'm beginning to be pleased with Stacy Robinson. I hope to get guys like those or a little better. I'm going to keep the best guys. You've got to compete for your job every year, and when you don't want to, it's time to quit the game."

After a speedy wideout, the Giants hoped to land a safety. Parcells's eyes showed his anxiety when he talked about the surgery during the off-season on the knee of Terry Kinard, the starting free safety. The other safety, Kenny Hill, was coming back from surgery on both ankles. And Parcells knew that his starting cornerback, Elvis Patterson, had become known around the league as Toast after being burned twice in the playoff games against San Francisco and Washington. So a safety, after a wide receiver, was the second position that the Giants wanted to fill in the draft.

Parcells and Young said they also hoped to fish out a guard or tackle who could eventually replace Brad Benson at left tackle. Even though he pumped iron at seven in the morning, William Roberts still had to prove he could step into Brad's shoes.

And finally, in that gang of four the Giants sought in the draft—four who might one day become starters—the Giants hoped to land a big running back. George Adams, who was supposed to be Joe Morris's stablemate in the Giants' backfield, still limped, his chipped pelvis hurting, doctors still not sure he would play again. And Maurice Carthon, who had replaced George, played only one role in Bill Parcells's mind: as a blocking back.

The Giants had fixed on two players they hoped to be in that gang of four. Number one was Mark Ingram, a 5-11, 179-pound wide receiver from Michigan State who moved down sidelines like something shot from a gun. "Explosive—the big play kind of pass-catcher," scouts said of Mark. The number-two player the Giants hoped would fall through at least one round of picking was Adrian White, a six-foot, 200-pound safety from Florida. "He doesn't have much experience in man-to-man coverage," Giant scouts told Parcells, "but he is a killer of a hitter." The Giants like their safeties and corners to play zone defenses and force teams to run, which means they need backs in the secondary who can blow down ball-carriers.

But while the Giants hoped for Ingram and White, they also knew that when you draft twenty-eighth, as one scout said, "you're like a prisoner waiting to hear his fate. In that situation, everything is totally unpredictable."

At a little after eight o'clock in the morning of April 28, in a huge room at the Marriott Marquis hotel, Tampa Bay began the draft by announcing the choice of Miami quarterback Vinny Testaverde, whom they had already signed. Next came Indianapolis, who chose Alabama linebacker Cornelius Bennett.

Finally, after Denver, picking twenty-seventh, chose wide receiver Ricky Nattiel from Florida, it was the Giants' turn to pick. The Giants had eyed Ricky but decided he might be too small at 5-9. The Giants took more than nine minutes conferring at their table. Then a Giant representative called out the Giants' first-round choice—Mark Ingram of Michigan State. Mark became the first wide receiver in Giant history to be a first-round choice.

And in his office George Young had to smile and think: Bingo! His first choice had fallen through the first-round picking and landed in the Giant nets.

In the living room of his home in Flint, Michigan, the wide-shouldered, mustached Mark stared at a TV screen. He saw the Giant official call his name. He leaped from a chair and pumped his left fist into the air. "I'm ecstatic," he said later. "I'm overjoyed, overwhelmed. There was no team I wanted more. I can't wait to get there and contribute."

In four years he had caught 92 passes for Michigan State, 12 for touchdowns. He averaged 20 yards a catch. He'd also seen his share of troubles. A year earlier he had gone to jail for twenty-four days after a breaking-and-entering incident on the Michigan State campus. He was alleged to have stolen only five dollars, but he'd been on probation after another incident in Flint. "I'm not glad it happened," Mark told New York writers. "But if there's a silver lining, it's that I learned a lesson."

"We investigated it," Bill Parcells said. "Don't worry about it. We picked him, so obviously we didn't feel it was that detrimental."

The second round began. George Young fidgeted. He began to think he had what he calls "a frother." A frother, says George, is a player who makes you froth at the mouth because you can't believe, as your turn comes closer to pick, that the frother still hasn't been drafted. Unbelievably, as George saw it, no one had picked Adrian White, the hard-hitting Florida safety. Denver picked—and let White go. Bingo! The Giants called out the name Adrian White—and two of the four players whom George and Bill had wanted had fallen through the netting and landed in their laps.

"The guy is a big-time hitter," Parcells said of White. "He will help us eventually, and certainly on special teams right away." Adrian's hero, he said, is Jack Tatum, better known as the Assassin. One scout called Adrian the strongest safety ever to come out of college football. Parcells later pointed out that Florida plays a zone defense that is similar to the kind the Giants play.

In rounds three and four the Giants went back to swelling their corps of pass-catchers. The number-three choice was little (5-7, 160) Stephen Baker, a wideout from Fresno State, whose 33 catches averaged out to 24 yards a catch. Number four was slim (6-3, 200) Odessa Turner from Northwest Louisiana, Gary Reasons's school. Odessa ran the 40 in 4.55 (Mark Ingram is a 4.41). But despite his relative slowness, Odessa had impressed the Giants in a workout.

By now the other two players in their gang of four (the Giants didn't identify the two) were gone. With an eye on replacing Brad Benson, Parcells and Young selected guard Paul O'Connor of Miami on the fifth round. Six-foot-three and 284 pounds—thirty gained during a recent muscle-building program—Paul is experienced. He is twenty-four and played five years for Miami, missing most of 1983 because of an injury.

Parcells and Young continued hot on the scent of a big bear of a running back in the sixth round. At six-foot and 215 pounds, Pacific's Tim Richardson seems to have the size. At 4.77 he also may have the speed to flank Joe Morris. He ran out of the wishbone for a 4-7 team in 1986, gaining 5.4 yards a rush.

In round seven the Giants chose another candidate for the offensive line—6-7, 265-pound tackle Doug Riesenberg from California, who switched to offense after three years on the defensive line. Round eight brought tight end Rod Jones, whose career at Washington was interrupted by injuries. On round nine the Giants went for another possibility for the offensive line—Nebraska guard Stan Parker, who needs to develop after starting only part of the time during his senior year. Then, as a second choice on round nine, came another big-back hopeful, Findlay's Dan Wright, who was rated the top small-college running back in the 1987 draft. He had a career average close to 7 yards.

In the tenth round the Giants picked a player they had thought would go earlier—linebacker Chuck Faucette from Maryland, the defensive MVP for the South in the annual Blue-Gray game. And finally, the twelfth choice: a quarterback, Dave Walter, an engineering graduate out of Michigan Tech. "Big and strong," Parcells said of the 6-3, 225-pound passer. "A monster with a cannon for an arm. He can throw the hell out of a football." He would challenge Jeff Rutledge for the job of backing up Phil Simms.

The Giants had picked for defense in 1986. In 1987 they had picked for offense, ten of the twelve draftees looking for jobs as a pass-catcher (four), running back (three), lineman (two) and quarterback (one).

A tired Parcells looked over the list and showed the worry that seldom leaves his face when he talks football. "I have some concerns," he said. "I would have liked to do more in the defensive secondary, but you can't manufacture cornerbacks. We looked at a lot of them, but they were all runts, mostly 5-8 and 5-9 and 170 pounds. For our zone defenses, we need size."

A week later the Giants held a two-day minicamp at Giants Stadium for free agents not picked in the draft. They signed more than a dozen.

On an August morning in Pleasantville, New York, a hot sun beaming down on a green practice field, the toughest of all the Giants, nose tackle Jim Burt, talked to someone who wanted to know if the 1987 Giants would go the way of the 1987 Mets. That championship team had come apart, at least during the first half of the 1987 baseball season, torn by internal bickering.

"This team is a different team than the Mets," Burt was saying. Why?

"Attitude. Coach Parcells won't let us get any bigger than the team. We go by a team concept...and the big thing is winning. Who gets the touchdowns, that's not as important as who wins the game at the end."

And so the Giants marched toward the 1987 season and Super Bowl XXII infused with the same singular sensation that had been foremost in their minds when Super Bowl XXI began:

One...*one*...ONE!

The Giant Record Book

		TD	PAT	FG	POINTS
1932	Ray Flaherty	5	0	0	30
1933	Ken Strong	6	13	5	64
1934	Ken Strong	6	8	4	56
1935	Dale Burnett	6	0	0	36
1936	Tillie Manton	1	15	0	21
1937	Ward Cuff	4	0	2	30
1938	Ward Cuff	2	18	5	45
1939	Ward Cuff	2	6	7	39
1940	Ward Cuff	2	9	5	36
1941	Ward Cuff	2	19	5	46
1942	Ward Cuff	2	18	3	39
1943	Bill Paschal	12	0	0	72
1944	Bill Paschal	9	0	0	54
1945	Frank Liebel	10	0	0	60
1946	Ken Strong	0	32	4	44
1947	Ken Strong	0	24	2	30
1948	Bill Swiacki	10	0	0	60
1949	Gene Roberts	17	0	0	102
1950	Ray Poole	0	30	5	45
1951	Ray Poole	0	30	12	66
1952	Ray Poole	0	26	10	56
1953	Frank Gifford	7	2	1	47
1954	Ben Agajanian	0	35	13	74
1955	Ben Agajanian	0	32	10	62
1956	Frank Gifford	9	8	1	65
1957	Ben Agajanian	0	32	10	62
1958	Pat Summerall	0	28	12	64
1959	Pat Summerall	0	30	20	90
1960	Pat Summerall	0	32	13	71

		TD	PAT	FG	POINTS
1961	Pat Summerall	0	46	14	88
1962	Don Chandler	0	47	19	104
1963	Don Chandler	0	52	18	106
1964	Don Chandler	0	27	9	54
1965	Tucker Frederickson	6	0	0	36
	Homer Jones	6	0	0	36
1966	Pete Gogolak	0	29	16	77
1967	Homer Jones	14	0	0	84
1968	Pete Gogolak	0	36	14	78
1969	Pete Gogolak	0	33	11	66
	Joe Morrison	11	0	0	66
1970	Pete Gogolak	0	32	25	107
1971	Pete Gogolak	0	30	6	48
1972	Pete Gogolak	0	34	21	97
1973	Pete Gogolak	0	25	17	76
1974	Pete Gogolak	0	21	10	51
1975	George Hunt	0	24	6	42
1976	Joe Danelo	0	20	8	44
1977	Joe Danelo	0	19	14	61
1978	Joe Danelo	0	27	21	90
1979	Billy Taylor	11	0	0	66
1980	Joe Danelo	0	27	16	75
1981	Joe Danelo	0	31	24	103
1982	Joe Danelo	0	18	12	54
1983	Ali Haji-Sheikh	0	22	*35	127
1984	Ali Haji-Sheikh	0	32	17	83
1985	Joe Morris	21	0	0	126
1986	Joe Morris	15	0	0	90

*NFL record

— RUSHING —

		YDS	ATT	TD
1932	John McBride	302	84	1
1933	Harry Newman	437	130	3
1934	Harry Newman	483	141	3
1935	Elvin Richards	449	153	4
1936	Tuffy Leemans	830	206	2
1937	Hank Soar	442	120	2
1938	Tuffy Leemans	463	121	4
1939	Tuffy Leemans	429	128	3
1940	Tuffy Leemans	474	132	1

		YDS	ATT	TD
1941	Tuffy Leemans	332	100	4
1942	Merle Hapes	363	95	3
1943	Bill Paschal	572	147	10
1944	Bill Paschal	737	196	9
1945	Bill Paschal	247	59	2
1946	Frank Filchock	371	98	2
1947	Gene Roberts	296	86	1
1948	Gene Roberts	491	145	0
1949	Gene Roberts	634	152	9
1950	Eddie Price	703	126	4
1951	Eddie Price	971	271	7
1952	Eddie Price	748	183	5
1953	Sonny Grandelius	278	108	1
1954	Eddie Price	555	135	2
1955	Alex Webster	634	128	5
1956	Frank Gifford	819	159	5
1957	Frank Gifford	528	136	5
1958	Frank Gifford	468	115	8
1959	Frank Gifford	540	106	3
1960	Mel Triplett	573	124	4
1961	Alex Webster	928	196	2
1962	Alex Webster	743	207	5
1963	Phil King	613	161	3
1964	Ernie Wheelwright	402	100	0
1965	Tucker Frederickson	659	195	5
1966	Chuck Mercein	327	94	0
1967	Ernie Koy	704	146	4
1968	Tucker Frederickson	486	142	1
1969	Joe Morrison	387	107	4
1970	Ron Johnson	1,027	263	8
1971	Bobby Duhon	344	93	1
1972	Ron Johnson	1,182	298	9
1973	Ron Johnson	902	260	6
1974	Joe Dawkins	561	156	2
1975	Joe Dawkins	438	129	2
1976	Doug Kotar	731	185	3
1977	Bob Hammond	577	154	3
1978	Doug Kotar	625	149	1
1979	Billy Taylor	700	198	7
1980	Billy Taylor	580	147	4
1981	Rob Carpenter	748	190	5

1982	Butch Woolfolk	439	112	2
1983	Butch Woolfolk	857	246	2
1984	Rob Carpenter	795	250	7
1985	Joe Morris	1,336	294	*21
1986	Joe Morris	* 1,516	341	14

*All-time one-season club record

— PASSING —

		ATT	COMP	YDS	TD	INT
1932	John McBride	74	36	363	6	9
1933	Harry Newman	136	53	973	11	17
1934	Harry Newman	93	35	391	1	12
1935	Ed Danowski	113	57	794	10	9
1936	Ed Danowski	104	47	515	5	10
1937	Ed Danowski	134	66	814	8	5
1938	Ed Danowski	129	70	848	7	8
1939	Ed Danowski	101	42	437	3	6
1940	Ed Miller	73	35	505	4	7
1941	Tuffy Leemans	66	31	475	4	5
1942	Tuffy Leemans	69	35	555	7	4
1943	Tuffy Leemans	87	37	360	5	5
1944	Arnie Herber	86	36	651	6	8
1945	Arnie Herber	80	35	641	9	8
1946	Frank Filchock	169	87	1,262	12	25
1947	Paul Governali	197	85	1,461	14	16
1948	Charlie Conerly	299	162	2,175	22	13
1949	Charlie Conerly	305	152	2,138	17	20
1950	Charlie Conerly	132	56	1,000	8	7
1951	Charlie Conerly	189	93	1,277	10	22
1952	Charlie Conerly	169	82	1,090	13	10
1953	Charlie Conerly	303	143	1,711	13	25
1954	Charlie Conerly	210	103	1,439	17	11
1955	Charlie Conerly	202	98	1,310	13	13
1956	Charlie Conerly	174	90	1,143	10	7
1957	Charlie Conerly	232	128	1,712	11	11
1958	Charlie Conerly	184	88	1,199	10	9
1959	Charlie Conerly	194	113	1,706	14	4
1960	George Shaw	155	76	1,263	11	13
1961	Y.A. Tittle	285	163	2,272	17	12
1962	Y.A. Tittle	375	200	3,224	33	20
1963	Y.A. Tittle	367	221	3,145	36	14
1964	Y.A. Tittle	281	147	1,798	10	22

— Passing —

1965	Earl Morrall	302	155	2,446	22	12
1966	Gary Wood	170	81	1,142	6	13
1967	Fran Tarkenton	377	204	3,088	29	19
1968	Fran Tarkenton	337	182	2,555	21	12
1969	Fran Tarkenton	409	220	2,918	23	8
1970	Fran Tarkenton	389	219	2,777	19	12
1971	Fran Tarkenton	386	226	2,567	11	21
1972	Norm Snead	325	196	2,307	17	12
1973	Norm Snead	235	131	1,483	7	8
1974	Craig Morton	237	122	1,510	9	13
1975	Craig Morton	363	186	2,359	11	16
1976	Craig Morton	284	153	1,865	9	20
1977	Joe Pisarcik	241	103	1,346	4	14
1978	Joe Pisarcik	301	143	2,096	12	23
1979	Phil Simms	265	134	1,743	13	14
1980	Phil Simms	402	193	2,321	15	19
1981	Phil Simms	316	172	2,031	11	9
1982	Scott Brunner	298	161	2,017	10	9
1983	Scott Brunner	386	190	2,516	9	22
1984	Phil Simms	*533	*296	*4,044	22	18
1985	Phil Simms	495	275	3,829	22	20
1986	Phil Simms	468	259	3,487	21	22

*All-time one-season club record

— PASS RECEIVING —

		NO	YDS	TD
1932	Ray Flaherty	21	350	5
1933	Dale Burnett	12	212	3
1934	Morris Badgro	16	206	1
1935	Tod Goodwin	26	432	4
1936	Dale Burnett	16	246	3
1937	Tuffy Leemans	11	157	1
1938	Hank Soar	13	164	2
	Dale Burnett	13	145	1
1939	Hank Soar	12	134	0
1940	Leland Shaffer	15	121	2
1941	Ward Cuff	19	317	2
1942	Ward Cuff	16	267	2
1943	Bill Walls	14	231	2
1944	O'Neal Adams	14	342	1
1945	Frank Liebel	22	593	10
1946	Ray Poole	24	307	3

1947	Ray Poole	23	395	4
1948	Bill Swiacki	39	550	10
1949	Bill Swiacki	47	652	4
1950	Bill Swiacki	20	280	3
1951	Joe Scott	23	356	2
1952	Bill Stribling	26	399	5
1953	Kyle Rote	26	440	5
	Eddie Price	26	233	1
1954	Bob Schnelker	30	550	8
1955	Frank Gifford	33	437	4
1956	Frank Gifford	51	603	4
1957	Frank Gifford	41	588	4
1958	Frank Gifford	29	330	2
1959	Frank Gifford	42	768	4
1960	Kyle Rote	42	750	10
1961	Del Shofner	68	1,125	11
1962	Del Shofner	53	1,133	12
1963	Del Shofner	64	1,181	9
1964	Aaron Thomas	43	624	6
1965	Joe Morrison	41	574	4
1966	Homer Jones	48	1,044	8
1967	Aaron Thomas	51	877	9
1968	Homer Jones	45	1,057	7
1969	Joe Morrison	44	647	7
1970	Clifton McNeil	50	764	4
1971	Bob Tucker	59	791	4
1972	Bob Tucker	55	769	4
1973	Bob Tucker	50	681	5
1974	Joe Dawkins	46	332	3
1975	Walker Gillette	43	600	2
1976	Bob Tucker	42	498	1
1977	Jim Robinson	22	422	1
1978	Jim Robinson	32	620	2
	Johnny Perkins	32	514	3
1979	Gary Shirk	31	471	2
1980	Earnest Gray	52	777	10
1981	Johnny Perkins	51	858	6
1982	Tom Mullady	27	287	0
1983	Earnest Gray	78	1,139	5
1984	Zeke Mowatt	48	698	7
	Bob Johnson	48	795	6
1985	Lionel Manuel	49	859	6
1986	Mark Bavaro	66	1,001	4

GIANTS' TOP DRAFT PICKS 1936-87

1936   Art Lewis, Tackle, Ohio University
1937   Ed Widseth, Tackle, Minnesota
1938   George Karamatic, Halfback, Gonzaga
1939   Walt Nielson, Fullback, Arizona
1940   Grenny Lansdell, Halfback, Southern California
1941   George Franck, Halfback, Minnesota
1942   Merle Hapes, Halfback, Mississippi
1943   Steve Filipowicz, Fullback, Fordham
1944   Billy Hillenbrand, Halfback, Indiana
1945   Wesley Barbour, Halfback, Wake Forest
1946   George Connor, Tackle, Notre Dame
1947   Vic Schwall, Halfback, Northwestern
1948   Tony Minisi, Halfback, Pennsylvania
1949   Paul Page, Halfback, SMU
1950   Travis Tidwell, Quarterback, Auburn
1951   Kyle Rote, Halfback, SMU
1952   Frank Gifford, Halfback, Southern California
1953   Bobby Marlow, Halfback, Alabama
1954   Ken Buck (2nd Round), End, Pacific
1955   Joe Heap, Halfback, Notre Dame
1956   Henry Moore, Fullback, Arkansas
1957   Sam DeLuca (2nd Round), Tackle, South Carolina
1958   Phil King, Fullback, Vanderbilt
1959   Lee Grosscup, Quarterback, Utah
1960   Lou Cordileone, Guard, Clemson
1961   Bruce Tarbox (2nd Round), Guard, Syracuse
1962   Jerry Hillebrand, Linebacker, Colorado
1963   Frank Lasky (2nd Round, future), Tackle, Florida
1964   Joe Don Looney, Running Back, Oklahoma
1965   Tucker Frederickson, Running Back, Auburn
1966   Francis Peay, Tackle, Missouri
1967   Louis Thompson (4th Round), Defensive Tackle, Alabama
1968   Dick Buzin (2nd Round), Tackle, Penn State
1969   Fred Dryer, Defensive End, San Diego State
1970   Jim Files, Linebacker, Oklahoma
1971   Rocky Thompson, Running Back, West Texas State
1972   Eldridge Small, Defensive Back, Texas A & I
1973   Brad Van Pelt (2nd Round), Linebacker, Michigan State
1974   John Hicks, Guard, Ohio State
1975   Al Simpson (2nd Round), Tackle, Colorado State
1976   Troy Archer, Defensive Tackle, Colorado
1977   Gary Jeter, Defensive Tackle, Southern California
1978   Gordon King, Offensive Tackle, Stanford

1979 Phil Simms, Quarterback, Morehead State
1980 Mark Haynes, Defensive Back, Colorado
1981 Lawrence Taylor, Linebacker, North Carolina
1982 Butch Woolfolk, Running Back, Michigan
1983 Terry Kinard, Defensive Back, Clemson
1984 Carl Banks, Linebacker, Michigan State
1985 George Adams, Running Back, Kentucky
1986 Eric Dorsey, Defensive End, Notre Dame
1987 Mark Ingram, Wide Receiver, Michigan State

COACHING RECORDS

1925	Robert Folwell	(8-4-0, .667)
1926	Joseph Alexander	(8-4-1, .667)
1927-28	Earl Potteiger	(15-8-3, .652)
1929-30	LeRoy Andrews	(26-5-1, .839)
1931-53	Steve Owen	(151-100-17, .601)
1954-60	Jim Lee Howell	(53-27-4, .662)
1961-68	Allie Sherman	(57-51-4, .527)
1969-73	Alex Webster	(29-40-1, .420)
1974-76	Bill Arnsparger	(7-28-0, .200)
1976-78	John McVay	(14-23-0, .378)
1979-82	Ray Perkins	(23-30-0, .403)
1983-86	Bill Parcells	(41-29-1, .570)